"The emphasis throughout *Piloting* ...

tion, but the analysis and wisdom go well beyond that now available in the literature [on negotiation]. This volume is a breakthrough in the use of words, thought processes and managing human behavior responsibly."

Oliver Oldman
Learned Hand Professor (Emeritus)
Harvard Law School

"IPOs in China and Japan, inventions in clean energy, decoding Japanese negotiation strategies, incubators for creativity and innovation, the role of beauty in discovery and bringing ideas to market—Julian Gresser is a Renaissance man with an amazing array of achievements and gifts. He has written a truly original and helpful book with his own hard-won understandings about how innovation can be incubated. Read it, it will enlarge your mind and you will discover your own capacity to do such things. It will grow with you and interact with your discoveries as you make them, taking them to a higher level."

John Tarrant
Zen master, author,
Bring Me the Rhinoceros
and other works

"Mark Twain said, 'You can't depend on your eyes if your imagination is out of focus.' In *Piloting Through Chaos*, Julian Gresser helps us to dream a better future and carefully outlines the steps needed to get there. Brilliantly written and meticulously researched, Gresser warns that we cannot achieve justice and abundance as individuals but only through collaboration, innovation, and fearless exploration of our own depths. And always, he reminds us, with kindness. Gresser is an international attorney, but also a 21st Century Renaissance Man, with a lifetime of experience in business, music, martial arts, invention, and meditation. He is not afraid to ask the big questions and to venture new views of how technology might be an ally in our quest for a better world."

Kenneth Cohen
Author of *The Way of Qigong* and
Honoring the Medicine

"We need a cultural revolution as transformative as were the scientific and industrial revolutions. If human culture is to survive without unacceptable impacts on the planetary environment we must live differently as a culture. This means that the arts and humanities are on the front lines of collaborating with scientists and engineers, we need a 'second renaissance.'

... Julian Gresser in the second edition of *Piloting Through Chaos* presents a sharply focused methodology for attacking some of the urgent problems and seizing the new opportunities."

Roger Malina
Editor, Leonardo

"There is widespread agreement that leadership at any level and in any area requires integrity in the person, the practice, and the profession. It is also clear that this is no easy, simple task, nor can it remain at the mercy of luck, sentimental or institutional formation. Julian Gresser—lawyer, scholar, martial artist, and streets-smart practitioner—now makes available the teaching and achievement of integrity in its integral form. As a foundation president, former commissioner, ambassador, and university president, I have had occasion to enlist Julian's remarkable system and energies. He is a godsend for our troubled times and leaders."

Dr. Glen A. Olds
Chair of the World Federalist Association
Co-Chair-Society for Values in Higher Education,
Senior Scholar-Center for Ethics & Leadership;
Adjunct Professor of Philosophy,
Portland State University
Former US Ambassador to UNESCO

"All of Alpine's portfolio CEOs, General Partners and staff, have undergone training—with dramatic and measurable results. One portfolio company had been mired in negotiations with a foreign company for over a year. In one day's training, they put together a new plan and team, and three months later closed an OEM agreement worth millions."

Dr. Chuck K. Chan
General Partner, Alpine Technology Ventures

"Julian Gresser's work shows with insight, style and imagination how integrity, that most fundamental of human virtues, continues to be vital to success, and even survival, in the ongoing negotiation of life in our rapidly changing world. The added value in *Piloting Through Chaos* is the author's suggestions on how integrity can be cultivated by conscious thought and action, and on how core integrity can affect outcomes in a variety of contexts."

Peter L. Murray
Visiting Professor of Law
Harvard Law School

"Julian Gresser's book reminds me of the title of a book by the Danish philosopher Søren Kierkegaard, "Purity of Heart Is to Will One Thing," Our usual state is to will different things with different parts of ourselves-typified by the conflict between "desire" and "conscience." Gresser has made a powerful case for the development of integrated will, of "integrity" as a sense of connectedness, coherence, wholeness and vitality. His familiarity with Oriental culture makes this book an extremely penetrating and valuable tool. It is delightful to read, and full of deep wisdom."

Willis Harman
President, Institute of Noetic Sciences

"We are all trying to survive during this time of uncertainty and instability. *Piloting Through Chaos* elucidates the path. Julian Gresser's brilliant blending of Eastern philosophy and Western intellect, classic stories and personal experiences is masterful! His insightful process enables us to remember who we are, most importantly, but then to determine where we are and what we want. So whether we are negotiating with our teenage son about his curfew or with a multinational about a merger, the basic steps, The Five Rings, will show us the way. The market is flooded with books and tapes about negotiating... but no one, until now, offers insight into the underlying essence of our interpersonal abilities. This fresh approach, if followed, can be transformative for us as individuals, and as a nation."

Claudine Schneider
Former U.S. Congresswoman

"I must say that I'm enjoying reading [Gresser's] original book once again. I participated in the first bilateral trade negotiations between the US and Japan in 1972, and if the US negotiators had had any of the training and discipline [Gresser] are explaining, it would have made a huge difference."

George Lindamood
Author of *The Accidental Peacemaker*
and other works

PILOTING THROUGH CHAOS

THE EXPLORER'S MIND

for Henry,

In highest esteem

&

friendship,

Julian

April 24, 2018

JULIAN GRESSER

 Bridge21 Publications

Los Angeles

Piloting Through Chaos—The Explorer's Mind
Copyright © 2013 Julian Gresser

All rights reserved. Exclusive English language rights are
licensed to Bridge21 Publications, LLC. No part of this book
may be used or reproduced in any matter whatsoever without
written permission from the publisher except in the case of
brief quotations embodied in critical articles and reviews. For
information contact Bridge21 Publications, LLC, 11111 Santa
Monica Blvd, Suite 220, Los Angeles, CA 90025.

Piloting Through Chaos—Wise Leadership • *Effective Negotiation for
the 21st Century*
First Edition published by Five Rings Press.
Copyright © 1995 Julian Gresser

Grateful acknowledgement is made for permission to reprint
from Steven Johnson, *Where Good Ideas Come From, The Natural
History of Innovation*. Penguin Group, USA. Copyright © 2012
Steven Johnson.

Printed in the United States of America

Book Cover by Chi-Wai Li

ISBN 978-1-62643-000-6

Library of Congress Control Number 2013935407

For Angela,
my pilgrim soul

GETTING STARTED— SMART BOOK APPLICATION FOR I-PHONE OR ANDROID

Here is how to get started scanning the Smart Book codes:

- Download the Neo Media QR Reader bar code scanner application which is available for free at the Apple Store (I-Phones) or Google Play Store (Android).
- Once downloaded, click the Neo Media QR Reader icon on your smart phone to launch the application.
- Begin by pointing your phone's camera at the Smart Book code on the back cover of this book and the Neo Media QR Reader application will play the author's greeting.
- You may now scan any of the SmartCodeFX-empowered bar codes or QR codes in the book.
- They will take you to a relevant link or links bringing additional dimensions to the book. We hope you will enjoy exploring these links.
- Together we can continue to expand and refine these Smart Codes, reaching our goal of a true Living Adaptive Multimedia Book (LAMB™).

smart BOOK.

BRING THIS BOOK TO LIFE
Scan here with your SmartPhone
SmartCodeFX.com

Author's Welcome

CONTENTS

ACKNOWLEDGEMENTS FOR THE SECOND EDITION

I am fortunate in my cherished friends who, catching the spirit of my new adventure, provided freely their ideas and good counsel. To them I express my appreciation: to my publisher, Dr. Gregory Kaplan, a true supporter from the outset; his father, Jim Kaplan, and his able executive associates, Anita Eng and Rebecca Lombardi, who skillfully and with patience assumed management of the project between Hong Kong, India, and California; Noelle Oxenhandler, who took up Occam's Pen and expressed her editor's feelings critically, yet kindly; to old friends whose friendship is vital, continuing, and ever new: William Moulton, Kenneth S. Cohen, Dr. John Tarrant, Josh Soske, Dr. Barry Forman, Dr. Jon Trobe, Professor James E. Schrager, Dr. Elspeth McAdam, Professor Peter Murray, Dr. Roger Malina, Anthony Slingsby, Josh Soske, Tod Brannan, Kelly Pounds, Bill Jaaskela, Al Smith, Ric Eittreim, Jackeline Pereira; and George Lindamood, a comrade-in-arms from my State Department days, who reappeared suddenly in my life after many years, like some guardian angel, just before midnight, offering fresh eyes and invaluable copy editing—an act of singular friendship; and yet with deepest gratitude to Angela, my soul's joy, for her abiding love, loyalty, and support. When thinking of Angela I am touched by Goethe's reminiscence of his own youth:

> A pretty girl in Naples, sweet and slim,
> Cared for him when he was without a friend
> And did so many deeds of love for him
> That he could feel it till his blessed end.

Goethe, *Faust* (translated by Walter Kaufmann) Part I New York: Random House Digital, 1961.

AUTHOR'S PREFACE TO PILOTING THROUGH CHAOS: THE EXPLORER'S MIND (SECOND EDITION 2013)

My earliest memories are of wanting to be an explorer. Africa was high on my list and so was the Amazon; jungles were my specialty. My father greatly admired David Livingstone and, dressed in his smoking jacket, would read passages after dinner from Livingstone biographies to inspire fortitude, gumption, and courage in "his little boy." The Australian writer, Alan Moorehead[1], was another mainstay in our home and from his books I learned of Burton, Speke, Stanley, and Baker and their quest for the source of the White and Blue Nile. I was fortunate at thirteen to visit Ujiji on Lake Tanganyika with my parents and to stand on the hallowed ground where Stanley doffed his hat and exclaimed, "Dr. Livingstone, I presume." I have only recently learned from Tim Jeal's brilliant biography of Stanley[2] that this famous greeting was entirely made up by Stanley for effect months after his historical meeting with the legendary doctor. In my college interview, I recall regaling the man with lurid descriptions of Amazon headhunting rituals and being nonplussed when he blandly inquired, "Do you do this often?" My childhood explorer's fancies always involved hot and dangerous climes full of wild people who leapt out unpredictably from mosquito-infested swamps. Ice, cold, and the moon rarely figured in my early adventures.

Over the years I have been susceptible to intuitive flashes and synchronicities which seem partial to late winter or early spring, for they arrive in this season like migratory birds in flocks. It is as though the greening of the vine and the awakening of ideas in the mind have an affinity, the one ripening the other. One distinctive quality of these flashes and synchronicities is they arise unbidden from some other place, which I call, "The Explorer's Mind." It may be useful if I introduce very briefly these flashes of intuition as their themes will enter and continue to play in my story, and for the most part they have proven true.

Environmental Activist

It was 1972 and the UN community was gathering in Stockholm for the first Conference on the Human Environment. As a young public interest lawyer, I conceived the idea of a global network of environmental centers, starting in Japan, which would press their governments and powerful companies to take enlightened action to protect the environment. I was thrilled when I received a reply to my cold-call letter from the presidents of two of Japan's leading universities, Tokyo University and Hitotsubashi University, inviting me to Japan. I visited Japan and with their support negotiated the establishment of the Center for Human Environmental Problems, which continued to operate for forty years.

Predicting "Strategic" Technologies and Industries

While serving as an advisor to Richard Holbrooke in the State Department during the Carter Administration, I was tasked to devise an effective U.S. response to the Japanese government's promotion of its "strategic" semiconductor industry. In those days the concept of "economic security" was not well understood, especially the notion that certain technologies and industries could become engines of economic growth. To top policy makers in the State Department, national security meant military security ("high policy"), not economic vitality ("low policy"). Working with a maverick foreign service officer who understood how the inside game was played, we organized the Japan Industrial Policy Group, a task force with the State Department as the lead agency, and we gave it the mission of engineering a national industrial plan for the electronics industry. Every major government agency and eight Congressional committees sent representatives. Bob Noyce, the founder of Intel and "father" of the semiconductor industry, and also the president of Texas Instruments both lent their support. Our findings and proposals were published by the House Ways and Means Committee. The report presented a coherent and intelligent strategy for a major U.S. industry.

Drawing on my experience in the State Department I invented a technique called "The Trigger Method" (named after Japan's "trigger" industries) that enables analysts to determine which specific technologies will exert "strategic leverage" on economic growth at any point in time. Although the intuitive insight of the connections between strategic technologies, innovation, economic growth, and job creation may seem self-evident today, it was not in those days. The essential idea of strategic leverage became the basis for a two-year course which I taught at the Harvard Law School and MIT, a subsequent book, *Partners in Prosperity—Strategic Industries for the U.S. and Japan,* and various subsequent governmental initiatives by the U.S. and other countries.

Discovery Engineering and Collaborative Innovation

After establishing a law firm in Japan in the mid-1980s, I practiced Zen during the weekends with a great teacher Yamada Koun in Kamakura. In those days I imagined myself as the knight in Ingmar Bergman's movie, *The Seventh Seal,* seeking a winning move to outwit Death in the chess game of life. As I sat in mediation in the *dojo,* I became interested in what was happening in my body and mind as I was struck with epiphanies and insights. After I returned to the U.S., I read Dr. Elmer Green's pioneering work, *Beyond Biofeedback,* which described his experiences with yogis in India and Native American shamans. I called Dr. Green, visited him and his colleagues at the Menninger Institute in Topeka, Kansas, and familiarized myself with his experiments with the electroencephalogram (EEG) and "creative reverie." I learned that creative reverie is the bridge between the ordinary conscious mind and the treasure trove of the imaginative potential mind. My experience with this technology has led me to learn more about a wide variety of other inventive techniques, methods, and technologies. I assembled this knowledge into a "Discovery Engine," and established a company called Discovery Engineering International (DEI). With financial assistance from a Japanese entrepreneur, I trained various business executives, venture capitalists, government scientists, and engineers in our methods.

During the last ten years, I have extended this work into a new discipline of "Collaborative Innovation" which is now being used in diverse fields from pharmaceuticals to distributed energy. The ability of teams of explorers to harvest the imaginative resources of the mind in solving complex problems will, I believe, become one of the essential tools in the repertoire of twenty-first century researchers.

Wisdom Expert Systems

My explorations of mind and body through Zen, martial arts, and biofeedback inspired a number of other insights and inventions, which have been introduced in the first edition of *Piloting Through Chaos*. The core discovery is the *principle of integrity*, which describes how systems maintain their coherence, wholeness, and adaptive vitality. As explained in detail in Book I, integrity is a state of dynamic balance where the head (intelligence), hand (action), and heart (compassion) work in harmony. As used here, integrity is the embodiment and dynamic expression of wisdom.

The first edition illustrates these ideas in a domain I know well—complex business negotiations, with particular attention to the "shadow" negotiation systems of Japan and China. In the spring of 1984 a series of insights ensued. First, it is possible to measure the degree of the integrity of a system. Second, individuals or organizations which embody integrity will make wiser decisions; in other words, integrity is the enabling condition. Third, wisdom is therefore a skill which can be acquired, *i.e.,* we can learn to be wise. Fourth, it is possible to accelerate the development of this skill by a software program—The Artful Navigator. My invention enables the user to encode the "wisdom genome" of the great figures of history and literature, and also of the wise persons whom we encounter in our daily lives, thus transforming them into our mentors. During the 1980s and 1990s I conducted many programs based on these ideas and was able to demonstrate that wisdom is not only a personal virtue, but also an organizational asset. In other words, companies that learn to make wiser decisions gain competitive advantage. Wisdom remains, for me, the most precious of all attributes. No matter how brilliant our technological virtuosity in the coming decades, I do not believe we will be able to meet the challenges we face nor deliver the abundance these technologies promise if we do not learn to use our new tools wisely.

A Global Network of Explorer's Wheels

Some months ago, these wide-ranging ideas converged in the image of an Explorer's Wheel—a great spiral encompassing eight realms. This was an intuitive insight. My selection of realms is subjective and based on my own life experience. The realms are:

- The Past
- Wisdom
- Beauty

- Life Force
- Discovery/Invention/Innovation
- Philanthropy
- The Networked Brain
- The Future

At the center is a "gate" into any or all of these realms. This gate is the Explorer's Mind, and its core attribute is what I call "Trust the Connection." At this point, Trust the Connection may appear, to many readers, a somewhat vague and abstract notion. I aim to show by specific examples and exercises, as well as live commentary and insights from recognized "masters," that it is actually the opposite. The more I practice, the more tangible and palpable is my experience. In those times when I feel connected, I can journey freely in these realms. My experience is subtle and beautiful, alive and continuously reborn. I suggest to my readers that you and I will be able to enter into a "wormhole of the psyche," a powerful energy vortex that will take us to another place in space and time. This Explorer's Mind offers a fresh mode of looking at the world, multi-dimensionally, where you can discover new patterns and relationships. I have found the Explorer's Mind to be an infinitely unfolding treasure hunt.

The Explorer's Mind dwells in the intertidal zone of "what if?" But for explorers the possible is so vivid and palpable that many cannot distinguish the boundary between what is and what might be. For them, the Future has arrived! The Explorer's Wheel invites us to step out of our consensus reality into the realm of the implausible where magic, wonder, and beauty abound. Here is a sampling of possibilities:

- What if the Explorer's Mind is a state of natural benevolence and abundance?
- What if the Past is not a dead thing, but alive, and we have within our power the capacity to bring the shades of what has been back to life?
- What if imaginative inquiry turns out to be a key to longevity, and we can grow younger even as we age in years?
- What if small and generous acts in one part of the world set in motion eddies of kindness in remote places and in surprising ways? Scientists call this the Butterfly Effect. What if there is a way to track and reinforce it?
- What if the Future is enveloped within the Present? How might we use our prescience wisely and on behalf of humanity?

- What might happen if our technological genius is at long last aligned with our enlightened consciousness so that exponential technologies can be devoted to their highest and best uses for humanity?

- What if our brains, which can change themselves and societies, start to act collectively and on their own accords, aided by revolutionary advances in information/communication technologies? Inspired by the creative energies of a thousand spinning Explorer's Wheels, what dreams will we begin to dream that we have never dared to dream before?

I will discuss all of these possibilities in the ensuing chapters.

Once again it is spring time. I am revising my last chapter about the quest for a more abundant life. I read Dr. Peter Diamandis' and Steven Kotler's recently published book, *Abundance*.[3] Perfect timing—I cannot find a better discussion of the leverage of exponential technologies. With an appendix of over forty pages of data, the authors support their basic claim: the widespread perception that the world is coming apart and hurtling downward is an illusion, a species of "consensus trance." Their central thesis is that we live in a world of abundance, not scarcity. What limits us is our inability to harvest the available resources efficiently. However, the good news is that this limit is now diminishing—exponentially. The driving force here is the continuous, ineluctable progression of information/communication technologies (ICT). This progression follows Moore's Law, which states that circuit (microchip) integration will double every two years with corresponding increases in computing power and reductions in cost. The authors contend that these powerful "exponential" forces can be harnessed to deliver a hitherto unimagined abundance to everyone on the planet. The combination of ICT with vast infusions of capital from a new generation of "techno-philanthropists" (Bill Gates, Richard Branson, Jeff Skoll, etc.), powered by armies of Do-It-Yourself (DIY) entrepreneurs, and targeting billions of new Third World customers, constitutes the unstoppable engine of a coming "Age of Abundance."

Please scan

Peter Diamandis and Steven Kotler effectively make the case for the beneficial forces generated by ICT. However, their book enables me to focus my analysis of the Explorer's Mind on five areas where their core argument, in my view, can be strengthened. In the fundamentals and their essential optimism, we have the same stance.

First, in their book the authors make only one passing reference to wisdom.[4] It is treated as beside the point. But wisdom does matter. It is the laser beam that must guide the powerful technologies that Dr. Diamandis and Ray Kurzweil are advocating. I believe the heart gentles intelligence and allows head and hand to work in deeper harmony. There is something cold and mechanistic in a future which marches in rigid lockstep of "smooth" statistical curves, even if they point to increasing abundance.

Second, "the shadow," as Carl Jung called it—the largely unconscious side of the human psyche—is not addressed. The dark side of genetically modified foods, nuclear power, and a ubiquitous hard-driving ICT (including cyberwarfare) is scarcely considered. But the shadow matters very much. *Abundance* brilliantly attends to the launching of rockets but there is virtually no analysis of what to do when the rockets misfire and come down. I am, like the authors, an admirer of technology, but I believe we ignore the shadow at our peril. An understanding of the shadow will make our delivery systems even stronger.

Third, oddly, there is no mention in *Abundance* of major advances in brain science—in particular the discoveries relating to neuroplasticity, or the connection between brain, mind, and consciousness. The new discoveries of the human brain, however, are arguably the most exciting new frontier—particularly when combined with the very trends the authors have so ably outlined. The Human Connectome Project, a nationally-funded quest to map the circuitry of the human brain, is the logical sequella of the Human Genome Project. We stand at the frontier of a brave new world where our brains and the genes that inhabit them can, and will, change by themselves.

Fourth, Asia has become the world's crucible of manufacturing. For example, there are over one billion installed smart phones in China alone. Contrary to the stereotypes fostered by the mass media, China may be shifting to a more globally collaborative stance toward innovation. My work is very much engaged with Asia, and I believe that the transformations now underway will only hasten the technological marvels the authors of *Abundance* envision.

Finally, the authors arouse our appetites to join the Global Abundance Game. They may be correct. This could be the most exciting game in town. But how can the average person, who may not be at the level of their genius, join the party? What about the millions and millions of others who may also want to play? In my book, I am especially interested in addressing how any imaginative person can engage in this new world of abundance. Book I provides some essential tools of artful negotiation; the new edition, Book II, introduces the meta-skills of the Explorer's Mind, supported by a few recent inventions.

The first invention is a four-dimensional book. By simply pointing your smart phone at the smart link to Peter Diamandis, he will step out of the page and greet you. Not only that. If your interest is piqued by his TED lecture and you thirst for more, our universal smart bar-code platform—supported by an intelligent server—will learn with you, ferreting out other lectures by Dr. Diamandis and also those of his mentor, Ray Kurzweil, and other thought leaders in the New Abundance Movement.

This second edition of *Piloting Through Chaos* is conceived as a LAMB™—a living, adaptive, multimedia book. A LAMB™ is living in that it engages interesting people around the world who may want to jump in and join the conversation. They will paint their personal vision and tell their stories. My hope is that this conversation will become the chronicle of our times.

Here I must offer an important caveat: the reader may feel that parts of the revised edition are quite rough or incomplete, while others are better worked out. This is intentional. I want the reader to sense the power of the rough-hewn material, alive and quickening, before it is fully formed. Some parts condense whole fields of research. They are meant to serve as beginning threads in the conversation. A LAMB™ is adaptive; it will be constantly updated, following the leads of the members of Explorers' Network, some of whom become collaborators in the process. In short, the book adapts to the palates and preferences of its participants. The issues described are too current and alive to be captured in a static format. A new agile model of publishing is required. Thus, the LAMB™ is designed as a bridge between the paper and online worlds.

Because the revised edition is more multi-dimensional than an ordinary book, I want to say a word about how I conceive its voice. First, let me explain that I am a musician. I play a number of wind instruments and I constantly listen to music. Some weeks ago I was driving home from Los Angeles, listening to two Bach cantatas, and an idea came to me: I shall write the revised section as a choral fugue—with first one voice, one theme, then another, then many, all blending together. I shall call my cantata, "Toward a More Abundant Life." My idea is simply a metaphor, and the intended form is freer: let a myriad of voices combine, riffing off the basic structure. In this sense the composition is closer to jazz, written on a larger scale.[5]

The third invention, supported by our intelligent servers, is a Network of Explorer's Wheels™[6], which will enable you to probe deeply into domains of greatest interest to you. You will learn to experience the world "intertidally". You can design your own personal Explorer's Wheel™ or create Explorer's Wheels for your group, organization, or special cause. The intelligent resources of the Network are readily available. You can enter the Network through any gate or learn about everything from any one principle, idea, or situation. The system is holographic—at its core, every part contains and reflects the whole.[7] The Network offers a new vehicle for continuous, life-long learning on your own time, at your own pace, according to your fancy. I conceive a day when hundreds, even thousands, of these Explorer's Wheels will spin and gain a powerful creative velocity, helping all of us toward a common purpose—the realization of a more abundant life.

My hope is that this second edition can build five bridges. The first bridge will connect youth and age. My generation has been exposed to the ancient wisdom traditions by studying the classics, starting with Homer, Shakespeare, and the King James Bible. We have experienced for ourselves how rapidly our lives are being transformed and how connected or disconnected we are becoming by the new technologies. Although we grasp the potential of the smart phone and the coming ICT revolution, we don't quite get what all the fuss is about. On the other hand, young people today understand connectivity well, as theirs *is* the world of social media. Yet as fewer and fewer schools teach the classics, many young people today cannot see how the wisdom of the past has any meaningful relationship with their daily lives or concerns. The Explorer's Wheels can hold this conversation.

The second bridge spans East and West. Here, I am both rapporteur and protagonist. I am professionally engaged in establishing a Global Innovation Center in Beijing with a Chinese company in the field of packaging and logistics. We are planning a program for the one hundred top innovative CEOs of China who already are, or aspire to become, the next generation of innovation champions. The opportunities for our new company, Global Innovation Integrators (GII) are significant. Contrary to the massive negative images in the mass media about China, GII China's establishment may signal a new openness among Chinese business leaders to reach out to the world and to collaborate in designing a twenty-first century global innovation infrastructure.

The third bridge explores the relationship of brain science and ICT to the mind and consciousness. In 2012, the *Wall Street Journal* announced Paul Allen's gift of $ 300 million to the Allen Institute for Brain Science. The Institute already has produced a "brain atlas" which combines various imaging techniques to document brain structure, biochemistry, and genetics with new computational tools to analyze the data. A recent discovery notes that 80 percent of all known human genes are actively at work in the brain. What will be the impact if computing power increases seventy fold? This is possible today by replacing current switching networks with optoelectronic computing. Optoelectronic computing is the technological interface between the brain, mind, and human consciousness. There is a reason that kaleidoscopes produce beautiful images and multi-dimensional thinking constellates synchronicities. It is because the Explorer's Mind is primed to receive them. Imagine what new frontiers will open if a Network of Explorers' Minds can extend the power of connectivity—infinitely— supported by a next generation of tools which run essentially on light.

The fourth bridge extends to women explorers, whose contributions historically (with only a few exceptions) have not been recognized. We may know about Madame Curie, Beryl Markham, Amelia Earhart, Isak Dinesen, or Jane Goodall. But how many of us have heard of Gertrude Bell, Alexandra David-Neel, Florence Von Sass Baker, Isabella Bird Bishop, Annie Peck, or the Society of Women Explorers founded in 1925?[8] The founders (Marguerite Harrison, Blair Niles, Gertrude Shelby, and Gertrude Emersen Sen) are all forgotten. I hope my book opens opportunities for legions of enterprising women explorers who know the thrill of the quest.

The fifth bridge connects science with the arts in a vision of a twenty-first century Humanism and a Second Renaissance. During the Italian Renaissance, masters and their students glided easily from science to the arts, viewing the world through the eyes of classical Greece and Rome. Today we have become confined in professional silos, imprisoned in our narrow specialties. It is hard enough to keep abreast of new knowledge in our own specialties. Who has the time to cross over disciplines? Yet it is precisely in this intertidal zone, the nexus between fields, where the giant breakthroughs will be found. An especially rich candidate for exploration is the convergence between science and the arts. There are today thousands of scientists around the world who are also accomplished musicians and artists.[9] When Europe emerged in the fourteenth century from centuries of want and deprivation, a new economic prosperity provided the conditions—the soil—of the Italian Renaissance. In the same way, the coming Age of Abundance of Peter Diamandis, Steven Kotler, and Ray Kurzweil may well inspire a distinctly twenty-first century global Renaissance.

It may be useful for the reader to understand why, after so many years I decided to write a second edition of *Piloting Through Chaos*. In part it was simply artistic exuberance. As Mark Twain once remarked, "What is it that confers the noblest delight? What is that which swells a man's breast with pride above that which any other experience can bring to him? Discovery!" I have found some lovely pebbles by the seashore, and I take much joy in showing them to you.

There is also a more serious intention. It does not take much insight to look at the world and see and feel how much suffering there is, how much of that suffering might be prevented, and how often calamity falls crazily and unfairly on those who have had the least part in causing it. Nor does one have to be a genius to see how vulnerable we are and unprepared to deal with the fall-out from natural disasters like Fukushima in Japan or the mayhem of a biological or nuclear terrorist attack. Many of the tools presented in *Piloting Through Chaos*, including the methodologies for anticipating catastrophe and dealing with risk and contingency, have direct and practical applications for these existential challenges of our times. My samurai spirit and my instincts as a public advocate are aroused for action.

I have no desire or intention to become a guru, nor do I approach my subject with any religious or spiritual agenda. I appreciate kindness and wish there were more of it in the world, and I believe that the exploration of spirit is closely allied with an expanding appreciation of beauty. I keep a special look out for beauty when it suddenly appears in daily life. It is my sanctuary. The wonder of it is you need not do anything to find beauty in the world; it is everywhere. You simply let your eyes be dazzled.

It is a rare and special opportunity for an author to have a chance to pick up an early thread of childhood and to follow it through each stage of his life; to gather the work of his middle age, and as he approaches the next bend in the journey, to weave the strands together into new patterns. I am grateful for this chance. As I approach seventy years, I am still experimenting and exploring. I am still learning how to be steady and resourceful in chaos.

It is an ancient custom among explorers before embarking on a voyage[10] to offer a gift to the gods. I thought it might be entertaining in this case to reverse the process, and so I offer to you a gift of my constant companion these days, Daikoku. He is the Japanese god of good fortune and the harvest. May he accompany your galleons and ensure a merry journey as we explore these realms together.

AUTHOR'S PREFACE TO PILOTING THROUGH CHAOS (FIRST EDITION 1995)

If you were flying the friendly skies on #101 bound from New York to Los Angeles, conceivably it might matter to you that:

- The pilot is not insane.
- The plane has a specific direction so that you don't change course every 15 minutes.
- #101 is well-built and won't fall apart over the Rockies.
- Reliable instruments are on board in case you hit rough weather.

Suppose you could have the same sturdy navigational system in your business or personal life? At any time under all conditions you could instantly assess:

- Where you are
- Where you want to be
- How to get there
- How to adjust to change
- How to correct errors
- How to repeat successes
- What moves to make next

That's my purpose in writing this book: to give you the **Pilot's Compass.**

I came upon this "navigation system" in a curious way. In the early 1980s I moved to Tokyo and opened a law firm. In my business dealings there I faced some of the world's most financially powerful, resourceful and cunning negotiators. I began to ask myself these questions: How is it that some of the smartest, most effective American and European managers behave in their Japanese dealings like deer caught in a car's headlight? Why is it that virtually every European and American company operating in Japan is hostage to its Japanese management? As the months passed, I made two interesting discoveries.

First, I discovered that a large number of Japanese corporate teams and the Japanese government itself were deploying a largely hidden (even from themselves!), culturally embedded system of navigation. This system comprises at least a hundred moves which cause havoc within the decision-making process of their opponents, foreign as well as Japanese, by attacking its core "integrity."

Second, I concluded that the antidote lay not in casting blame or finding fault, but rather in helping my clients focus on what they could actually manage—specifically, redeeming and rebuilding their compromised "integrity." I began to counsel my American and European clients in this way, and even some Japanese clients in their negotiations with other Japanese, and I soon found that once they understood and could predict the moves under the "code," they managed very well.

As I say, the key to my discoveries was integrity. It is such an old-fashioned word—even schoolmarmish or boy scoutish—who would suspect what revolutionary possibilities it conceals? But the more I have looked inside and around this word, the more it began to reveal a mysterious and dynamic power.

What is this **power?**

Integrity is the capacity of every human being, indeed of any living system, to remain connected, coherent, whole, and adaptively alive. It can be understood on several levels:

- **First,** it is a state of being. **You know** when you are in the state, and you know when it has been compromised.

- **Second**, integrity is a principle of ethical and conscious action. Ethics flows from consciousness. When a person has integrity his or her actions will naturally be ethical ones.

- **Third**, integrity is a principle for corporate and societal organization. Companies and enterprises of every kind that build integrity will be those that are profitable, well run, and happy.

- **Fourth,** integrity is a standard for policy making. In the area of environmental law, for example, integrity analysis offers a new way to reconcile conflicts and discrepancies among air, water, land use, endangered species and a host of other protective laws and regulations.

- **Fifth,** integrity is a force of nature. If entropy is the power in the physical realm that pulls things apart and wears them down, integrity is the countervailing force that valiantly stands up to entropy and keeps us whole, joyous and alive.

In integrity, I found the cornerstone of a new theoretical and practical approach to navigation in the world. I should explain how my concept of "navigation" based on integrity differs from conventional notions of negotiation. Navigation is broader and includes intelligent and wise decision making, character and effective action. This distinction has critical and practical implications, particularly for the popular so-called "win-win" school of negotiation.

- **First,** as a way of bypassing positional bargaining and resolving some kinds of disputes, the "win-win" model has made important contributions. But as a system of navigation I have found it overly concerned with the result, too in need of resolution (agreement), and not willing enough to accept, indeed to enjoy, the process. And this flaw, I have found, is very dangerous, because it entirely misses the fact, so evident to me in my own Japanese dealings, that the negotiation—the navigation process—is continuing and unending. In Japanese negotiations there is always another river to ford or a new mountain to climb, and one is never out of the game.

- **Second,** the prevailing "win-win" school places far too much emphasis on strategies and tactics and too little on the development of character from which all sound tactics I believe must spring. And this unwillingness to address the basic and hard issues of changing habits and behaviors is also a critical failing. In my work in the United States, Japan, and other countries the model did not prepare me adequately to deal with the shadow—the duplicity, treachery, stupidity, and cruelty swirling around the world. Only character, I have come to see, can hold the ship together in the face of these.

- **Third,** because the "win-win" model is not rooted enough in the ooze of life, because it steps back from and will not come to grips with darkness and turbulence, it also fails to see the light. Too sheltered and cloistered, it does not understand that the process of navigation itself creates countless opportunities each step of the way to develop and to transform ourselves.

Toward the end of the 1980s I began to test and put my new system into practice. I scored a number of successes during this period, including helping a San Francisco-based trading company transform its $8 million Japanese branch into a Japanese company listed on the Tokyo Over-the-Counter Exchange with a capitalized value of over $1 billion. What was most curious and paradoxical about this case was that everyone benefited: the owners, the investing public, the managers, the employees, the underwriters, even both governments, each of which claimed credit for the success. One of the great commercial "win-win" victories in the history of U.S.-Japanese commercial relations was achieved without any of the parties giving a thought to "win-win" at all! I have seen the same result in many other cases in which I have since been involved.

As my docket of cases expanded and my experience continued to develop, I soon found I had more than enough material to prepare a program of instruction featuring Japan, and based on my method of cultivating integrity, which I now call, The Five Rings. In 1991 I began to conduct training and coaching programs for teams of negotiators at leading companies in the United States, Japan and Europe, as well as at the European Commission. These programs provided me with the opportunity to refine my methodology and my ideas were very well-received. The model was still not complete, however. On a personal front I continued to struggle with the desire to embody more deeply in my own life the principles of effective action that I had worked so hard to give my clients. In this struggle I made an important discovery. I naturally assumed that integrity was the means of becoming a more effective navigator. Then suddenly one day I realized that the converse proposition was equally true: the daily negotiations I was in—even casual encounters—provided the means to fortify integrity. In other words, the process of navigation—precisely because it is so focused, practical and engaged—is itself the vehicle of transformation.

This discovery made the threads in the pattern come together and enabled me to see with fresh eyes. "Winning" and "losing" became less important. Creating value and meaning in life, becoming productive and useful to others became the focus. To work on the quality of integrity—to polish and refine it like a jewel—was in itself a great joy. No special magic was required, no special effects in the form of external stimuli or mental fantasies. For the first time in my life I found more than enough magic in the mundanity of daily transactions, meetings, confrontations, and accords.

This is not to suggest that I have become stuck, however happily, within my office walls. Quite the contrary. Like a plant putting forth tendrils, my practice of integrity has led me to see new connections among things I never saw connected before. The first connection or reconnection has been with nature. Now as I take walks in the Marin Headlands near my home, everywhere I look I can see how nature expresses and celebrates its integrity in every leaf, every stone, and in the humblest creatures.

At the same time the practice is enabling me to tap the richness of human culture in a way that seems to me radically new. Now when I encounter great works of art, literature, and music, they are far more than exalted forms of entertainment. Through my practice I have begun to detect a common, underlying structure in the masterpieces of Shakespeare, Mozart, and Leonardo da Vinci, and in the works of other masters, and to see that it is their perfect integrity that endows them with such force and power.

Perhaps the most interesting discovery for me is how the skill of integrity can be refined and perfected by using the latest breakthroughs in information technology. During the past two years in collaboration with Tod Brannan, an expert software designer and engineer, I have come upon a series of inventions that can be best summarized under the code name, "E-Mail from Shakespeare." Together we have developed a way to reanimate not only Shakespeare but all the great figures of history, living and dead, and not only masters of literature but also musicians, artists, and creators of all kinds, and, by the computer, to invite them all to become personal advisors, friends, and coaches on our most practical and pressing issues and concerns. We call our new software program, The Artful Navigator.

In sum, the cultivation of integrity has provided for me an answer to the ancient question of what it means to lead "a good life." Tested in the fire of the most practical human interactions, the practice is anchored in the deepest waters of human experience and fueled by our highest aspirations. For ultimately, the implications are global.

It does not take a prophet to see we are heading into an electric storm without a compass. Around the world each year more people go hungry, more Bosnias crop up, the living environment dies a little more, and the criers of bigotry and violence go about the streets. In the United States a new cynicism and nastiness has crept into our political life and the faith of the electorate in truthfulness and decency is breaking. At the basic level where most people live their lives, they look for assurance that things will eventually be okay. But there are no assurances in the 1990s and they feel powerless and afraid.

There is a natural tendency in this century of extraordinary technical accomplishment to believe we can solve any problem solely by our wits without our hearts also. But the tools themselves—the computer and telecommunications, for example—are not making us any wiser, and there is a fair concern among a broad section of sober-minded people that they are only breeding new forms of vulgarity and brutality, and in the end, will leave us feeling more truncated, fragmented, and alone.

I see a way out that offers hope. Let us make integrity the magnetic pole of our navigation system—a common language and method of operation linking all peoples—and let us use our new tools—multimedia, the Internet, perhaps someday a Wisdom Super Highway—to help us discover new and better ways to think and learn and get on together. It is to this special goal that this book is dedicated.

Julian Gresser
Sausalito, California
Fall, 1985

The Reader's Compass

In writing this book I have in mind two large groups of readers. The first are people in business who seek to become more effective, but who will understand that one key is learning how to find greater joy, meaning, and satisfaction in the work itself. This broad group includes senior and middle managers, lawyers, physicians, architects, designers, teachers and other professionals, and tradespeople of all kinds. It includes environmentalists, political and social activists and other reformers who are looking for a more practical means to move their cause robustly forward; and also new leaders at the national and local levels who today are searching for a fresh outlook, a new vocabulary, and a better way to solve the country's problems.

The second group encompasses other persons not in business who have chosen a spiritual path or an artistic one, who have in some sense removed themselves from the world of affairs, but who still want to make a useful contribution and don't quite know how; and also those who lack a practical method to maneuver when their feet are in the fire.

In its organization, the book is straightforward and practical and is designed to help you quickly grasp the elements of the method and then to serve as a reference. Chapter I introduces the book's concept of integrity through an initial case study. Chapter II begins with the importance of clarity of vision and a mission of service and then goes on to develop the basics of The Five Rings. Chapter III is concerned with more advanced skills and powers that come through the steady cultivation of integrity. Chapter IV offers a simple program of practice. Chapter V explores how The Five Rings can provide a common language and system of navigation for large numbers of players around the world interlinked by the Internet and other new networks of communication.

Whenever possible I have illustrated the key principles and moves by cases and stories which will enable you to learn vicariously and by example. Many of these cases are drawn from my own professional experience, but some are ancient stories and there are many classical references. This also is part of the method, because I want to show the richness and interconnection of things that are at once timely and timeless.

For this reason also the book is written in the form of an imaginary dialogue with Tod Brannan and his wife and colleague, Paula Fox. In Greek the original meaning of "dialogue" was "through" (dia) "logos" or reason. A dialogue was a discourse on the theme of sanity and good judgment. My purpose is to open a dialogue with you, my reader, and to extend the first threads which you can then weave closely and usefully into the patterns of your own life.

SOCRATES' PRAYER

Beloved Pan, and all ye other gods who haunt this place,
Grant me the beauty of the inward spirit
And may the outer and inner man be as one.
—Phaedrus

Book I

PILOTING
THROUGH CHAOS

I

INTEGRITY IN ACTION

*"The dragon fly
perches on the stick
raised to strike him."*
—Basho

*"In combat if you know where to move you are
already too late! The opportunity is lost. You must
feel it and act before you have knowledge of it."*
—A martial artist

"All things are ready, if our minds be so."
—Shakespeare—Henry V

"Those who can change are free."
—The Artful Navigator

I met him for the first time in his office on Route 128 near Boston.
Let's call him Flanagan. He was the president of a small, struggling
electronics company. Although he was a brilliant physicist and an
engineer, he found himself over his head in a negotiation with one
of the giant Japanese conglomerates. For months he had gotten
nowhere, and he had this awful sense that his company's precious
know-how—its only asset of real value—through unwitting disclo-
sures by him and his staff, was leaking from his company like a
sieve.

Soon after, Flanagan joined a "pool" of executives who were training with me over months to become more effective in their Japanese negotiations. He approached the training with the same dedication—the same curiosity of mind—with which he approached the design and engineering of a new integrated circuit. But then I lost touch with him for about a year after the program ended.

"How is Flanagan doing?" I asked an acquaintance one day who knew him well. "Haven't you heard?" he responded. "He's had a sensational success.

The Japanese have invested over ten million dollars in his company, and the venture capitalists on his board can't believe it. "How did he do it?" I asked. "The last I heard he was floundering."

"You should call him and find out yourself," my friend replied.

So I did. Flanagan and I met for dinner at a Japanese restaurant in Boston. He looked years younger. He had a hard, life-tested quality that was very pleasing. This is the story Flanagan told me with a twinkle in his eye.

Flanagan's Story

I arrived in Tokyo foolishly unaccompanied by my chief lieutenant or even a reliable translator. I don't think I'll do that again. Anyway, on the way to our meeting—I had come for the signing ceremony for our "technology joint venture"—my host, who was sitting in the taxi beside me, passed me an envelope. "It's the final draft," he said, smiling, and then returned to looking blankly out the window at the coffee shops, sushi bars, pachinko parlors, and crowds that were already bustling to their jobs at 8:30 on this Monday morning. I scarcely bothered to look at what was inside the envelope, as I and my lawyers had already reviewed every word and every nuance in the text of this agreement a hundred times. "Enough," I said. "If I can't trust these people now, I never will."

But then I got this feeling—call it intuition—that I ought at least to have a look. I opened the envelope and began to scan the text. What a surprise! A different deal. I couldn't believe my eyes. "What is this?" I began to stammer to my Japanese host. But by this time we had arrived at our meeting place, somewhere on the thirteenth floor of a large grey building in the Marunouchi area of Tokyo. We got off at the twenty-first floor and I was escorted past lines of pretty bowing girls and attendants to a waiting room with immaculate white doilies on the arm rests of leather chairs, and from there into a large conference room, where thirteen Japanese executives rose in unison exactly in attention as I entered the room. My ordeal had begun.

"What did you do?" I asked.
"What could I do?" he continued.

The first thing I did was panic. What does one say or do in such a situation? I felt like bounding right out of the room shrieking. Now that might have been an interesting tactic! But instead I got a grip and remembered our training, settled down, and decided to have some fun.

I needed time to regain my bearings, so I resolved not to understand anything. Even if I did understand, not to let on, and to let them do all the talking, all the explaining, while I struggled to grasp their meaning. I wanted them to expend some of their time and effort, and get involved in trying to help me understand, while I figured out what to do. Actually, having no translator along helped my strategy.

So that's how we spent the whole day, the thirteen executives earnestly explaining, I earnestly trying to understand and never quite catching on. Then we adjourned. Everyone was tired, but they were more exhausted than I. I was beginning to find my second wind.

The next morning we reconvened. I was greeted with a slight nod and a grunt or two—a glimmer of recognition by some of the thirteen executives, who sat exactly in the same positions as they had the day before. An attendant brought in some black coffee. Otherwise no one moved. There was only silence.

Flanagan poured himself a cup of sake and watched for my reaction.
"Silence?" I repeated. (I have seen such situations before, and they usually take odd turns.)
"Utter silence."
"For how long."
"First five minutes, then ten, fifteen maybe. No one said a word." Flanagan's eyes were sparkling in delight. "I got up, poured myself some coffee, because I'd be damned if I would be the first to speak. I just planted my feet and held on.

"About twenty minutes later, they couldn't stand it any longer. 'Dr. Flanagan, what did you think of our proposal?' their spokesperson blurted out. 'We spent all day yesterday discussing it with you. Surely you must have an opinion.'"

"Frankly, I'm very disappointed," I said. "I appreciate very much all the time you have spent in explaining your ideas to me, but actually this is not why I came to Tokyo. This is not the deal we have been discussing for months, on which we agreed three weeks ago in Boston. I'm going home. Please call a taxi."

"Dr. Flanagan," the lead man rose from his seat, "This is a great mistake, a cultural misunderstanding."

"I must," I said. "Please ask your assistant to call me a taxi. I have checked and there is a United Airlines flight leaving Narita at 5:30 p.m. I don't want to be late."

"You can't go! There's a misunderstanding!"

"Kindly call me a taxi. I'm going home," I said in a level voice.

"So that's what I did." He took a long swig of sake and smiled at me.

"Very good, very good," I exclaimed, sensing the momentum building in his story. But what did you do next?

"Nothing. I did absolutely nothing. They sent me a stream of faxes that week and the next, but I did not respond to them. I waited to think things over, get my bearings, and sort out what I really wanted from them."

"What happened then?"

"Finally, I replied to their faxes and told them I was prepared to discuss the original transaction, but no more games. Do you know, they canceled their vacations and came to visit us, and then things got back on track. There were a few other ups and downs, right up to the end. They tried to squeeze a few additional concessions by telling me that the president of their parent company, a multibillion dollar conglomerate, had committed to come to the signing ceremony, and unless I signed on the terms they wanted, the meeting would have to be canceled. This would be embarrassing since everything had been arranged. But I saw no reason to give in, and I told them so. And then they dropped these last conditions."

"How have things worked out?"

"Marvelously. They gave us everything we asked for and more. Under our arrangement we have committed to train several of their people and we have honored every promise we made. I have taken a personal interest in seeing that the engineers and their families are well cared for. They have learned from us and we are learning from them. And now we are discussing the next phase of the project. Somehow our silent confrontation in Tokyo put things back on track. It's as if we gave them a sense of who we are—of boundaries—which actually was comforting to them. We both gained room to breathe and to respect each other a little better."

Brannan:	In a nutshell, Julian, what is the central lesson of this case?
Gresser:	Trainability—the ability to adjust instantly and creatively, especially in unpredictable and surprising situations. In this sense the different attitudes and peculiar practices of business in Japan (at least from Western eyes) present wonderful opportunities to develop this skill. Flanagan could have let his fear and panic overwhelm him. But he possessed that intangible quality of character—I call it *gravitas* or weightedness—to hold on. And from this place of self-containment came a sense of play. The game was serious but he had a taste for the hunt.
Brannan:	What is the relationship of trainability to chaos—the central theme of this discourse?
Gresser:	We have been taught to believe we have no control over the chaos in our lives. Like the fates, chaos is simply here and we are stuck. In our need for certainty and order, we see chaos as an aberration and are surprised when it suddenly appears. But chaos is always with us. Flanagan's story introduces the idea that there is also almost always negotiating room, a path. Trainability is the ability to discover the path.
Brannan:	You say that trainability is a quality of character. What then is the relationship of character to chaos?
Gresser:	The Greek philosopher Herakleitos wrote over two thousand years ago, "Character is destiny." This idea is even encrypted in the original meaning of the Greek word for character, *charattein*, "to engrave." Thus by our own hand we imprint our unique story on the tablets of our life. The same idea is contained in the *I Ching* and in most of the other great books of wisdom. We have far more leverage over the "external" fates than we

even dreamed possible, and the beginning of this realization is when we gain dominion over ourselves.

Please scan

CHAOS AND CHARACTER

Flanagan's story makes this point: Strategy and tactics are useful but they are insufficient. To deal effectively with the upheavals, the great issues in life, as they step out of the void called "chaos," tactics must be built upon a foundation of character. In this respect it seems to me much of the contemporary writing on negotiation is deficient. There is too much stress on strategic "moves" and too little emphasis on the deeper character work which is so essential in the difficult times of the 1990s. That is why the original narrative was subtitled, *Wise Leadership* • *Effective Negotiation,* because these two are inseparably entwined, especially if we include within the definition of "leadership" the most basic of all abilities, which is the ability to lead oneself.

Our great epic heroes confirm this point. Odysseus was not only a master strategist he was also a superior man (the Greek word is *aristos*). Tactics were important, but in the end it was force of character and a keen intelligence that brought him safely home to Ithaca.

Please scan

Brannan: What is the essential quality that enabled Flanagan to adjust so adroitly? Is there an algorithm to the method that anyone, not only kings and epic heroes, can grasp easily?

Gresser: There is. I call it "integrity." By integrity, I mean a sense of connectedness, coherence, wholeness and vitality. Integrity is the capacity of every living thing to maintain its hold in the face of entropy, disorder and uncertainty, its link to the living world, its ability to carry on its life, however humble. Take the smallest, simplest creature—a paramecium, for example—and you will see integrity in action! Surround this little fellow with a toxic substance, and he will fight to hold integrity, the right—if one can use this word about so humble a creature—to be whole and to continue his existence. The paramecium understands integrity very well.

INTEGRITY AS
A PRINCIPLE
OF NATURE

THE PHYSICAL
EXPRESSION
OF INTEGRITY

Tod, integrity is a physical experience, not only a theoretical principle. You **know** when you have integrity. You can feel it in your joints. You feel it as you breathe, you can feel it in your heart. If I attach a thermistor to your finger, you will have an objective way to gauge the degree of your body's integrity. If you become suddenly frightened—in other words, disconnected from the source of your own vitality—the temperature in your finger will fall and there will be many other changes in key indicators—for example, staggered breathing, rapid heart rate, hormonal changes, changes in brain waves and so forth. Your integrity will be momentarily compromised. If the fear persists, gradually you will lose the connection to your power source. (This is precisely what happens in a state of **panic** which contains the root meaning of "everywhere." In panic your consciousness is widely dispersed and without a center.) On the other hand, when you are at ease and have a sense of time to spare, when you feel, as I am sure you often have, abundant and vital, the temperature will rise in your fingers, perhaps to 96°. At such times you have a sense of just being in the flow, especially in action, and of a brighter, happier world growing within you.

Although Deepak Chopra in his book, *Ageless Body, Timeless Mind,* Bernie Siegel in *Love, Miracles and Medicine,* and other authors do not explicitly identify integrity as the key to the healing processes they are writing about, the body's ability to understand how to restore healthy balance—its integrity—is at the core of the new science of mind/body energy medicine. We have not invented integrity. Rather we are pointing out that this force of nature which is so important in the new healing sciences also has powerful applications in the realm of action.

I can make this abstraction of integrity more concrete through a single image.

THE CHINESE CONCEPT OF "TE"

In ancient China when the dikes gave way and the floods came and the barbarian hordes poured over the mountains from the west—signifying to the Ruler and his (her) people that the Mandate of Heaven had been lost—only human virtue (*te*) or integrity, the Chinese sages believed, could reverse the challenges of nature. What is the *te?*

It is written with a complex character, so beautiful it could be a poem. On the left is the character for "action." Integrity always demands action. On the top right is the character for the number "10," which can also be read "whole" or "balance." Underneath is the character for the number "4," but if this "4" is repositioned and read vertically, the meaning transforms into "eye." Thus there are four "eyes"—the external "eyes" of logic, intelligence, and common sense—and then there is the inner eye of direct-knowing or intuition. Four eyes that can see singly as one. Underneath is the character for "heart." Integrity is the state wherein the eye of discovery, logic and intelligence is in balance with the heart in action. See Illustration I, Integrity.

Take any person, any situation, and if you examine closely you can tell in an instant the degree of its integrity. Is this person grasping or cunning? Perhaps there is too little heart. Even if by his actions he has become immensely wealthy, there is a flaw (in integrity) that will devour him. Is that a person of great heart and intellect? Perhaps. But can she translate her vision into action? If not there may also be a problem with integrity. Then there are those who despise logic and navigate through life only by heart. They too are off balance, out of integrity.

Brannan: You seem to be using "integrity" in a very special sense, different from the conventional meaning, which is associated with ethics and morality.

Gresser: Yes, this is true. They are related, of course, but in my view ethics and morality naturally flow from integrity. The truly ethical person is a person whose mind and heart is in balance with action.

INTEGRITY

KEY:

1. 彳 = Action

2. 十 = Ten, Whole Balance

3. 四 = Four, Eye

4. 心 = Heart

Illustration I

Brannan: Once someone understands the algorithm, "integrity," how can this be helpful, at least a source of comfort, when we are frightened or feeling that control over our life is slipping from us?

Gresser: Conceptual understanding is the first step, but it is not enough. To know your integrity, you must embody it. You don't possess integrity like some physical object or a piece of information. You must live it. This is its great challenge and its lasting worth.

INTEGRITY AS
A SKILL

After hundreds of hours of training people all over the world, I have found that integrity is a **skill** which can be learned, developed, and passed on to others. In a way, the practice resembles the inner Chinese martial arts such as *tai chi* or *qigong*. Many of the "moves" by which we cultivate integrity are not seen by others. They take place underneath the surface. Only the results are seen and the changes in our behavior and action.

In the earlier example, it is easy to see how Flanagan outmaneuvered his opponents, his outward moves and tactics. Less obvious are the gradual changes in his character that took place only after months of training, the development of his integrity that stabilized the foundation and which enabled him to respond with agility in that difficult situation.

Brannan: How does a player begin to develop the skill of integrity?

Gresser In my experience, the development of integrity is hastened by the steady cultivation of five core values.

THE FIVE
CORE VALUES
EARN WHAT
YOU WANT:

The first is **"Earn What You Want."** If you would have something you must pay for it, as Emerson says, "line for line, deed for deed, cent for cent." It is in the buyer's interest to pay a just price. It is in the seller's interest to charge it. This is the natural law of compensation. There are no free rides in nature.

Brannan: This requires a bit more explanation. I belie[ve] many people feel very good when they purchase or sell something at a real "steal." What's wrong with that? It seems to me they're just getting what the market will bear.

Gresser: We are not trying to introduce some new, even more dour form of Calvinism. If you negotiate effectively, and come away with a bargain from a used car salesman or at a flea market, you've earned what you want. I'm really focusing on the issue of gouging from either the buyer's or the seller's position. What I'm saying is you'll pay a price. Perhaps the price will be in the form of buyer's or seller's remorse, perhaps in a more subtle, indirect way. But there will be repercussions, because things are interconnected. There is an underlying "integrity" in the fabric of human—indeed all natural—interactions and processes. The point is less whether the price is "good" or "bad," "fair" or "unjust." It is hard to find a correct answer to such abstract questions. The critical issue, it seems to me, is whether we are willing to take a "hit" for our actions. If we are a seller and gouge our clients, are we willing to accept that our clients may leave and go elsewhere? If we are in the market to purchase a house and we hoodwink an old lady, are we willing to deal with her executor or her outraged children? If we are willing to take on these things (the "hit"), to pay the price, we will **earn** what we want in the sense I am using it here.

Where and how to take the "hit" is a fundamental question which goes right to the essence of any undertaking. If our purpose is simply to feed our desires, we will tend to see the "costs" of our enterprise as detriments. However, if our mission is one of service to others and based on integrity, and if the actions we take truly serve the mission, it is very much in our interest to pay the full price of its attainment. Although this may appear a bit of a paradox at this point, the principle should become clearer when we get into the discussion of mission and purpose in the next chapter.

Brannan: What is the second core value?

Gresser:

NO
ASSUMPTIONS,
NO
EXPECTATIONS

"No Assumptions, No Expectations." We live in a world that assumes, presumes, and consumes everything, and therefore to have no expectations seems an implausible virtue. People are encouraged to have expectations. The law protects them. And yet they entangle us and deplete our energies. In giving them up lies the source of true freedom.

Brannan: Yes, but do you really believe for a practical person in business faced with making thousands of quick decisions that this principle is really workable? It seems to me if we make no assumptions we are starting at ground zero every time we begin a negotiation. We always must make decisions based on limited information. Assumptions are useful in filling in the gaps. My view is we must make assumptions and that is okay so long as we make clear in our planning what items are "assumptions" and what are "facts." Then intelligence is gathered to validate or reject the assumptions.

Gresser: Your point is well taken. What I'm trying to do at this stage, illustrated in the cases to follow, is to show: 1) how we limit our possibilities and thereby impoverish ourselves by not testing our basic assumptions; and 2) how dangerous this habit of making assumptions can be in the practical world of negotiations. Flanagan would have been a dead duck if he hadn't been quick enough to spot his own invalid assumption (intentionally planted by his opponents) that a deal had been reached in Boston.

Brannan: What is the third core value?

Gresser: The next value is **"Few Needs."** We must be clear about what we mean by "need." What do we truly need in this life, Tod? Air, water, food, shelter, and a little sleep, but not much more.

FEW NEEDS

We don't need success. We don't need strokes—people telling us how wonderful we are. We don't need money, except to provide for our own and our families' welfare and well-being. We don't need fame or security. We don't need approval from the outside world. Therefore we urge people to equip themselves to pass through the chaos of the 1990s by paring down their needs and by taking joy from little triumphs and small, but not insignificant, things. The fourth core value is **"Embrace the 'No.'"**

EMBRACE
THE 'NO'

Brannan: Hey! Hold on. A little too swift. I happen to like my new BMW and I believe most other people enjoy their creature comforts as well. I also don't think you can dismiss so easily the basic human desires—I'd even call them "needs"—for success, praise and love!

Gresser: Okay, okay! Tod, I'm not urging people to buy a sackcloth and ashes and turn themselves into yogis sitting in caves. Here again the critical issue is to become **conscious** of how we have been "programmed" and how we program ourselves. Look at the language we use. How many times a day do we sloppily say, "I need to have this" ... or "I need to do that" ... or **"I really** need, because otherwise"...? Do we really **need** all these things? All these "needs" are really the voice of the subconscious whispering endlessly to us, "Look, my friend, if you don't feed yourself a little more you'll surely die." That subconscious "need"-voice, Tod, is not your friend. For most, if not all, of these so-called "needs" are delusions! We will not die—that's a fact—if we don't satisfy them.

We've just focused a moment ago on **No Assumptions/No Expectations.** How many of these do you think might vanish in an instant if we could let go of our delusory needs? Why, they'd fly right out the window! Letting go of needs is about reaching for freedom.

I realize this practice is not easy. But again, I have observed in the realm of practical action time after time, the negotiator who doesn't need the deal and who can put aside assumptions and expectations is the one who, like Flanagan, will be able to adjust in any contingency and will hold the edge. We must remember also that we are speaking here of skills that cannot be mastered in a day, but take diligence and dedication over weeks and months. Yet these are also skills that in the end will be worth the effort, because they will have lasting value.

The fourth core value, as I say, is **"Embrace The 'No.'"**

Since early childhood we have been pro-grammed to believe that we are wrong (bad) when we receive a **'no.'** Many children are rebuked by their parents: "Johnny, how many times have I told you, 'No'!" So naturally we feel a need to get to 'yes.' Not achieving an agreement ('yes') is perceived as a failure, a sign of our inadequacy. Yet in my experience a **'no'** is a very rich source of wisdom, wonderful conditioning, and often an excellent indication of how and where to move next.

'No' raises another more basic point. In my view every individual has an inalienable **right** to exercise a veto, to say, "I will not submit. I will stand upon my integrity." I am not saying the exercise of this right is costless. You may have to pay a price. But respect for another's right to **'no'** and respect for our own right to veto seems to me fundamental.

Therefore we train people not to fear the **'no,'** to give the other person space to breathe, to make the tough decisions, which often are the ones that involve a **'no.'**

Brannan: The way you present this fourth principle sounds good in theory, but I should think it is very hard to implement in practice, especially if you believe, as most people do, that a **'no'** is final. When there is a lot of money and effort at stake, the idea of embracing a **'no'** may be hard to swallow.

Gresser: Things do not always turn out as they first seem. In my experience the process of negotiation is rich and unfolding. A **'no'** may appear absolute and final at one stage, but then something happens, circumstances change, and the other party discovers a new need we can fulfill, and things click when they didn't before. Then too, a final **'no'** may not be such a bad thing because it almost always opens a new door. I will explain the dynamics of **'no'** in action in the discussion of The Five Rings.

Brannan: Four core values so far. What is the last?

Gresser: The fifth and last value has two parts. The first is **"Presence is All."** Just as the point of our entire method is integrity, so really there is only one tactic—one tactic that subsumes all others— and it is presence. When we are fully present, we build a foundation, a platform from which springs our creativity, our life force, our ability to discover, to stretch, and to realize our true human potential.

PRESENCE
IS ALL

Brannan: Julian, would you say Flanagan was being present or simply "playing dead"? If this is a form of presence, I think you should explain how.

Gresser: Flanagan got a grip. He could have let his needs—his panic—get the better of him, and then he would have become completely unpresent. To put the point more precisely, because he was trained like a fighter pilot, Flanagan knew how in an instant to become present to his panic and to find there his power. It is a very sophisticated concept that I will develop with care and detail later. Panic, as I have said, is one of the ways chaos presents itself. If we can train ourselves to remain present in chaos, we will find, as Flanagan did, the path of opportunity.

The corollary of presence is **"Each Moment has Equal Dignity."** Ours is a world where everything, it seems, has unequal dignity, and most people are treated with no dignity.

EACH
MOMENT
HAS EQUAL
DIGNITY

When we train ourselves to allow each moment its special dignity, then everything has value. When each moment has equal dignity, we live in the eternal present.

II

THE FIVE RINGS

"If we could first know where we are and whither we are tending, we could better judge what to do and how to do it."
—Abraham Lincoln

"Integrity is its own mission and purpose."
—The Artful Navigator

"In his recent concession speech, President de Klerk of South Africa praised his rival, Nelson Mandela, as follows: 'Mr. Mandela has walked a long road and now stands at the top of the hill. A traveler would sit down and admire the view, but a man of destiny knows that beyond this hill lies another and another. The journey is never complete.'"
—The Artful Navigator

Brannan: Julian, there is a strong sense in your examples and explanation that you believe in the richness of "inner" and "outer" processes and the importance of self-knowledge. But, you know, I'm not sure how many people really think the way you do or will easily accept what you are saying. Just last week I had a curious experience in a plane on my way back from New York that makes this exact point.

I was sitting next to this businessman and we started talking. He asked me what I did for a living, so I told him a bit about our work together. He was a project manager and said he was constantly involved in negotiations all over the world. When I began to get into the substance of the method, he said something that startled me. He said: "Look, I've got a budget. I write the terms. I'm fair, but if the other person is uninterested, that's okay, I just go on to the next one. You see, **I'm in control!** I've been negotiating in this way all over the world for the last 25 years and I have never once needed to know a thing about myself! So why is self-knowledge so important?"

I had some difficulty answering him because it seemed to me the answer was so obvious. Perhaps there are some assumptions about the benefits of self-knowledge that you and I are making that ought to be challenged right at the outset. How would you have responded to that man's question?

Gresser: Suppose that man loses his precious budget? What will he do? Or what will happen when he grows old or is laid off? Does he assume such things cannot happen? Worse, what if one day he looks in the mirror and discovers a suspicious growth on his neck? He will panic and because he will not know himself he will have no anchor. We live our lives infused with the conceit that we are invincible and immortal, as if our flesh were brass impregnable. But what will happen to this good easy man when, with a little pin, Life bores through his castle walls? Good-bye, project manager!

This is what happened to so many stockbrokers at the time of the Great Crash. Not knowing themselves, they **identified** with the stock market, and when it crashed, they crashed also. They literally jumped out of buildings. They didn't realize they were the players, not the pieces.

We must know ourselves first so that we can take back control—adapt and change—at the times when our lives begins to shake beneath our feet. And this is perhaps the most important reason a method—a disciplined process—may be of some help.

Brannan: Very well. What is the first step—the first decision—a person must make?

Gresser: To see what he or she truly wants.

Brannan: To see?

Gresser: Yes. Vision drives action. If we cannot see our way through something, it is much harder to do it. Otherwise, we must see our way feelingly. It is a separate art which we can discuss later.

I would like to illustrate how vision enables action by an old story.

There were once two tribes that made their living by fishing. A great escarpment of mountains divided the two communities, so that no intercourse of any kind was possible.

VISION DRIVES ACTION

The dilemma of the first tribe was this. Although the schools of fish were plentiful, one could never know when the sea gods might withdraw their favors and the fish would swim away. If only there were a way to enter the pools beyond the reef, where it is said the great fish come to play and mate and raise their young. But the elders of the tribe had also said that it was quite impossible to venture that far out, that there had been many attempts and some had perished. And so the village resigned itself.

One day a rumor entered the village that a miracle had occurred among the people beyond the mountains. It seems that someone had come up with an extraordinary invention called a "canoe." By means of this "canoe," people—even the elderly and children—could now journey out beyond the reefs and were feasting on the rich schools of fish.

No knowledge of canoe-making of any sort passed across the mountain, only that it was possible to gain access to the pools, and this by means of a "canoe." A few months later, with no other "knowledge" than it was possible, a wood-carver in the second village independently discovered the art of canoe building.

Tod, do you see the point of this story? Simply to acknowledge possibility will change the probabilities. We must allow ourselves the freedom to see the kind of life we want—professionally, personally, physically, spiritually—to brush aside all the beliefs we have become so comfortable in telling ourselves—the beliefs about what is **not** possible. This is the first decision, the first act.

Brannan: And what is the second?

Gresser: To prepare a mission and purpose. If you are a pilot and find yourself in an electric storm, how will you feel if your compass fails and your instruments malfunction? Today we are in an electric storm and how many people have the compass intact? The mission and purpose is the pilot's compass.

Brannan: I'm not sure I follow you ....

Gresser: How many people can instantly tell in any situation: where they are, where they want to be, or how to get there? Very few. The first, most basic step in knowing how to do these things is to prepare the mission and purpose. That is the reference point. It tells us instantly where we have come from, where we are heading, when we fall off, and how to get ourselves back on course.

MISSION AND
PURPOSE—
THE COMPASS

Brannan: How does one go about preparing a mission?

Gresser: The first decision, the first step I recommend is for the listener to set aside some afternoon or evening, a few hours, and in this space of time to reflect deeply on the following two questions, in each of the four quadrants in life: professional, personal, physical, spiritual.

- **What is it I really want?**

This really is the key, because, as I have suggested and will explain in more detail later, it is essential at this stage to stretch, to brush aside all the baggage about what is **not** possible. We want to get in touch with what truly matters.

And the second question is:

- **How can I best earn what I want with the gifts I now have (*i.e.*, my resources, my contacts, my station in life, and so forth)?**

We **earn** what we want by connecting our gifts to the concerns of others. In this sense, the mission is a **path of service,** for nothing in this life comes free except the air.

After my students have reflected upon these two questions, I ask them to compose a single statement of mission. It does not have to be lengthy. The key is to capture in a few powerful strokes what they want and how, by using their gifts and resources, they propose to get there.

Brannan: Can you give some examples?

Gresser: All right. Here is a **physical** mission statement: "To build health and vitality so that I can live an abundant and vibrant life that will permit me to realize my true gifts and make whatever contribution I am here to make." Note even here the element of service. We seek vitality, not for ourselves alone, but also because it helps us realize why we are here.

People may have widely different objectives in their physical lives and the means of achieving these missions may also differ greatly. The means are incorporated within the mission statement. A person might write: "I will accomplish this mission through vigorous exercise in my favorite sports of tennis, golf, and windsurfing, and by long hikes in the mountains, where I return to the wellspring of my true nature."

Brannan: What about a professional mission, for example, the mission of our own enterprise, Lōgōs Networks Corporation.

Gresser: Our mission is clear. It states in part: "To put in the hands of dedicated persons a proven means by which to build integrity, which will enhance their ability to discover, to take greater delight in their work and their pastimes, and to navigate effectively through the chaos of the 1990s and whatever may come after."

The statement of means would then identify those areas of our experience and expertise that will help us accomplish this mission—for example, my knowledge and experience in Japan and other parts of Asia, your many years in building computer systems and networks that are easy to operate and fun to use.

Brannan: How does this exercise in mission building relate to integrity?

Gresser: A good question. Most people live fragmented and scattered lives; for example, their professional lives are divorced from their personal life. They are so driven they scarcely have time to recreate themselves physically or spiritually. The process of building a life mission and with it a sense of life purpose will itself begin to restore coherence, wholeness, and sense of connection and vitality, which is how we define integrity.

AM I HERE BY
INTEGRITY?

Whenever we are lost or confused, there is only one question that needs be asked: "How does this next decision or action reinforce my overall mission?" If the next decision fails to do this, or if the situation you are in will undermine your mission, instantly you know you must adjust. On the other hand, if your next decision or action advances your mission, you can know with certainty you are on the right track. You will know you are here by integrity.

Brannan: Could you elaborate a bit on the concept of coherence of missions?

Gresser: This is an important point. I have found it useful to think of missions as building both "horizontal" and "vertical" coherence. For example, few people recognize any direct relationship between their physical exercise and their professional work. But when the underlying objective is to cultivate integrity, then the interplay of these two life quadrants becomes clear (horizontal coherence).

COHERENCE OF MISSIONS

Do you remember, Tod, when I asked you what was one of the great challenges in your life as a tennis player?

Brannan: I remember well.

Gresser: And you reported, 'To beat my chief opponent. I always lose to X. What I really want is to win."

Brannan: Yes, that's what I said.

Gresser: And what then happened?

Brannan: You suggested I was so focused on the result, on winning, that I was losing focus on the present. So I resolved to forget about winning altogether and just to concentrate on the ball, and my game has improved.

Gresser: That's it. Just concentrate on the ball! By improving your tennis skills—learning to stay present or to maintain focus, for example—you improve your negotiation skills, because they are essentially the same skill set. Thus perfecting your tennis game can strongly advance your professional mission! The process of developing integrity is what encourages these "overlaps" in our professional, personal, physical and spiritual lives, and we begin to discover interconnections among the parts we never thought possible before.

By "vertical" coherence, I refer to the hierarchy of missions. You and I have overall professional missions in which our work with Lōgōs Networks Corporation (LNC) is a part; and under LNC we may have several main projects, each of which will have its own subordinate

THE HIERARCHY OF MISSIONS

mission. And within each of these projects we may have hundreds of matters or cases, again each containing its own ancillary mission.

Most people are unaware of the interplay of these various activities. No one stops to ask, how does this matter advance my "higher" project mission, or how does this project really enhance my overall professional mission?

By taking the time to ask such questions—and there always is time if we truly want to make the time—by learning to adjust, align, and when necessary, to stretch, we build stability and solidity in our life, which leads to a deeper sense of meaning, vitality and promise.

Brannan: A mission implies an allocation of resources.

Gresser: Yes, that is true. It is one thing to know what we want, and where to aim *i.e.,* the mission; quite another to make a commitment—and the commitment is key—to allocate our scarce resources in that direction. The question is what are our available resources? This brings me to the subject of the budget.

There are four elements in what we call **"budget."** They are **time**, to which we assign a value of 1; **effort** with a value of 2; **financial reserves** with a value of 3; and **creative emotion** or **vitality** with a value of 4. By "value," I refer to the relative importance in a negotiation of each of these four elements. In other words, creative emotion or vitality is four times as valuable as time; financial reserves are worth three times time; and effort twice as much.

BUDGET =
TIME X EFFORT
X FINANCIAL
RESERVES X
CREATIVE
VITALITY

These ratios are not precise nor based on extensive academic research. Rather they derive from my personal experience of thousands of hours of negotiations.

At the outset, we urge people beginning to work with us to make a conscious allocation of these critical elements of **budget** in the four quadrants of their lives.

We refer to these elements in the aggregate as **"integrity budget units"** (**IBUs**) because, as we will see, integrity can be enhanced or disturbed by how wisely we expend these resources. The first task is to come up with an overall budget in terms of **IBUs** covering how we propose to expend these four critical elements in our professional, personal, physical and spiritual lives in a 24-hour day.

People's allocations differ greatly and no one formula is correct. One person may allocate **IBUs** in his life equally, *i.e.,* 25 percent professional, 25 percent physical, 25 percent personal, 25 percent spiritual. Another person might allocate 50 percent to her professional matters and subdivide the remainder equally. Others may shift allocations over time. In my case, for example, launching our enterprise has consumed enormous amounts of **IBUs** and there has been a price—a great price—I and my family have had to pay. There has also been a great cost charged against all the things I enjoy and like to do in other quadrants of my life. Soon I will make some adjustments. Such allocations and sacrifices are largely personal, and there is no one correct solution. The mission statements and your own integrity are your best guides. The essential point—which cannot be emphasized enough—is to become conscious, for when we become aware of how we are expending our precious reserves, what we will sacrifice and for what purpose, we can begin to make intelligent decisions, to adjust, and to apply these resources to their best possible uses.

Brannan: You know, Julian, it occurs to me that we have become so comfortable with setting **IBUs** it almost seems second nature. But this practice may seem quite alien, especially to people who are not involved as we are in business.

Gresser: Your comment raises an important point for both business and non-business persons. For some people engaged in business who like measuring things, the value of tracking **IBUs** may be immediately obvious. But others may dismiss the technique on the grounds that it is not really possible to aggregate in any meaningful way the different elements of budget, *i.e.,* time, effort, financial reserves and creative vitality. Possibly non-business persons will wave their hands in dismay, believing the technique to be simply too remote from the way they think.

And yet, when we look a bit more deeply into the practices of many artists and other creative people, I believe you will find, as I have, that they do in fact have an accounting system—perhaps not as formal as ours—but nonetheless a systematic way to husband their time and creative energies. For example, I know many writers, and almost all of them have a special time of day in which they write. They are very disciplined about guarding this window of creativity from intruders, be they children, spouses, friends, or clients. It is very clear to them that their creativity is not a "free good" and that unless they develop some intelligent way to conserve their precious resource, they will squander it.

For me, the bottom line for both business and non-business readers is this: We make no claim to scientific precision. We have developed an accounting procedure that we have found to be easy to use and helpful in achieving the objectives of the method. Many persons involved in business and outside of business will, I believe, also find this technique helpful. Some persons may simply not find it their cup of tea. The key point, however, is that our readers develop for themselves some practical way to account for expenditures of their scarce resources of time, effort, financial reserves, and creativity, for to do otherwise is unconsciously to assign a value— indeed a value probably inconsistent with their true feelings—and that value will be zero.

Brannan: Let us return to the main concourse and review where we are. We have moved from the theory of integrity and the five core values to the beginning of the discussion of the "method." You suggested that the first step is to get in touch with what we truly want and then to build a mission in the four quadrants of life. At that point a person is in a position to begin to decide how he or she wishes to divide up the available time, effort, financial reserves, and creative vitality that comprise the "life pie."

Suppose someone is willing to invest the time you say is required to do this—and I believe you noted that it would take only a few hours—how can he or she immediately begin to enter the fray?

Gresser: I call our method **"The Five Rings."** It provides a way to analyze the structure and flow of our decisions and those of others, and to negotiate effectively in any situation. Each ring presents an opportunity to develop integrity in a focused way through the cultivation of the five core values.

Brannan: Before you explain The Five Rings, Julian, it is important to define "negotiation," because you appear to be using the term in a very special and uncustomary way.

Gresser: Thank you for making this point. In the method I adopt the third definition of negotiation in *Webster's New International Dictionary*, "To move forward successfully, to get across or through an obstacle," as "to negotiate a river or to negotiate the mountains." Negotiation is the process of moving any cause forward. To give you a sense of how important this definition can be, when do you suppose, Tod, Flanagan's negotiation with his Japanese colleagues ended?

Brannan: I would imagine when they reached a final agreement to invest in the technology joint venture.

Gresser: That is what most people in business might suppose: The negotiations end when we reach agreement, when we obtain a 'yes.' Actually, that is when Flanagan's real negotiation was just beginning. "Real" in the sense that he was at great risk if he believed the play had ended, at exactly the time his opponents were marshalling their forces for the next attack. Because Flanagan was "trainable" he caught on quickly to the danger he was in. He did not assume a negotiation was over simply because an agreement had been reached. In playing the "game" of integrity the negotiation with ourself and others also never ends. The method, **The Five Rings,** is a means to keep us alert. In an instant, it allows you to determine:

THE FIVE RINGS

- Where you are
- Where you want to be
- How to get there
- How to adjust to change
- How to correct error
- What is the best next move

  (See Illustration 2, **The Five Rings.**)

Brannan: What is the **First Ring**?

Gresser: The **First Ring** is called, **"Know Yourself."** Its purpose is to help you set your course and to build a plan of action. **Ring 1** contains several basic moves. They are:

RING 1— KNOW YOURSELF

- Get clear about what you really want in any negotiation or encounter.
- Build a mission or path of action.
- Set your budget in terms of IBUs.
- Devise a simple plan.
- Initiate the first action.

The **mission**, the **budget**, the **plan**, and the initiating action are all specific to the engagement.

There is something now you should notice about each of the "moves" in **Ring 1**, and it holds true of the entire method. I want you to focus on this question: What can we manage?

Brannan: Time and money ... I'm not sure. Many people believe they are "managing" when in fact they are completely out of control.

THE FIVE RINGS

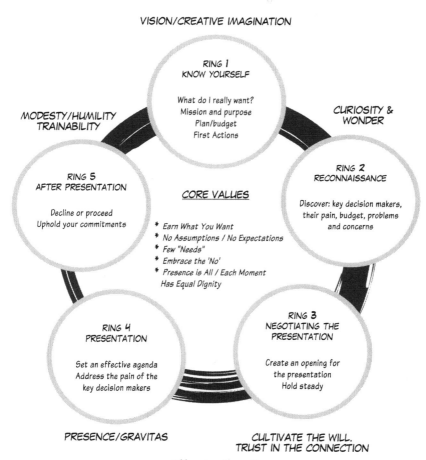

VISION/CREATIVE IMAGINATION

RING 1
KNOW YOURSELF

What do I really want?
Mission and purpose
Plan/budget
First Actions

MODESTY/HUMILITY
TRAINABILITY

CURIOSITY &
WONDER

RING 5
AFTER PRESENTATION

Decline or proceed
Uphold your commitments

CORE VALUES

* Earn What You Want
* No Assumptions / No Expectations
* Few "Needs"
* Embrace the 'No'
* Presence is All / Each Moment
  Has Equal Dignity

RING 2
RECONNAISSANCE

Discover: key decision makers,
their pain, budget, problems
and concerns

RING 4
PRESENTATION

Set an effective agenda
Address the pain of the
key decision makers

RING 3
NEGOTIATING THE
PRESENTATION

Create an opening for
the presentation
Hold steady

PRESENCE/GRAVITAS

CULTIVATE THE WILL.
TRUST IN THE CONNECTION

Illustration 2

Gresser:	Precisely. Can we manage numerical results?
Brannan:	Hardly.
Gresser:	I agree. We can never manage numerical results, and yet how many businesses distribute benefits or impose penalties or make their fundamental policy decisions based on numerical results? The best way to put an athlete, an employee, or a sales person in a slump is to tell them they must hit ten home runs, bill X thousands of dollars,

or sell Y units by the end of such-and-such a quarter. Numerical results can be a useful guideline, but determining success and failure by a single numerical index simply invites frantic and unproductive performance.

Next. Can we manage other people's actions and behavior?

Brannan: I doubt it

Gresser: Throughout history all sorts of people, particularly despots, have tried and always they have failed. A wonderful book on this subject is Victor Frankl's *Man's Search for Meaning*, which recounts how he survived the Nazi death camps at Auschwitz. In an especially poignant passage he describes how, under the most egregious conditions, the prisoners struggled to retain their last power to choose—to choose to see and appreciate beauty.

From the window of a boxcar being transported to another work detail he writes:

> If someone had seen our faces on the journey from Auschwitz to a Bavarian camp as we beheld the mountains of Salzburg with their summits glowing in the sunset, through the little barred windows of the prison carriage, he would never have believed that those were the faces of men who had given up all hope of life and liberty. Despite that factor—or maybe because of it—we were carried away by nature's beauty, which we had missed for so long.

If even the Nazis could not completely stamp out in the minds of their prisoners the instinct toward choice, why do we presume we can manage how other people will think, believe, or act?

One last point, Tod. Can we manage time?

Brannan: I believe so. There are many time management courses around ....

Gresser: I know about the courses. But can we ever manage the flow of time? No. Time flows on and on, and we fools of nature are carried away like small craft on the great current, no matter how we tell ourselves otherwise.

Here is the critical point. In negotiations we will get ourselves in terrible difficulty if we allow ourselves to believe we can ever manage or control numerical results, other people's actions, or the flow of time. Because we cannot manage these things, in our frustration and despair we will fall into need, lose hope and our integrity will be impaired. For this reason the moves in Ring 1 and throughout **The Five Rings** focus us on our own actions and behavior over which we have some large measure of control. By asserting ourselves here we gain some incremental margin of influence over the uncertain and destabilizing forces of life.

Brannan: On this same theme of reclaiming an edge, what about situations where someone is really out at sea? Are there any default moves?

Gresser: Ring 1, as all the other rings, has its "default" moves, so that if at any moment you cannot see what to do, the method will help you. Suppose a player jumps over the first few steps right into the thick of action; for example, she makes a phone call or has a meeting without a clue as to what she really wants and without a mission. Then suppose this player begins to observe that things are not going quite as well as she hoped, that there is some kind of "problem." The method provides an instant "diagnosis": no mission, I am not clear about what I want. The default move is equally explicit: regroup, clarify, prepare a simple mission. If you do these things with full awareness and presence, you will instantly feel your powers collecting and your integrity building.

The **Five Core Values** apply to each ring and to every part of it. Each ring provides a practical context and an opportunity to practice.

Each ring also offers a unique opportunity to develop special powers. For example, **Ring 1** presents an opportunity to develop vision and to harness the power of creative imagination to intentionality.

Brannan: You have mentioned the story of the fishing villages and how by dropping the "delusion" of impossibility the second village began to discover a solution to its dilemma. How might the same principle apply in business?

Gresser: I will tell you. In the mid-1980s when I was working in Japan, I conceived the idea of taking foreign companies public on the Tokyo Over-The-Counter Market. I wrote a letter to a friend at Arthur Andersen setting out how my strategy might be practically accomplished. I didn't hear anything for six months. One day I received a phone call from my friend saying he had found a candidate. The candidate was Getz Brothers, a San Francisco-based trading company that had established a respectable market share in Japan importing pacemakers, heart valves, catheters, and other cardiovascular products. Getz had $8 million in net income based upon approximately $70 million in general revenues.

No one was interested in the project. Getz was virtually unknown outside its industry. It had no products of its own and its business was highly vulnerable because it was based on short-term distribution contracts of other companies' products. The leading American underwriters, Goldman Sachs and Morgan Stanley, would not even return our phone calls after the first hour. (By now we were a team of two, the acting president and I.) The Japanese government immediately told us that our plan was not possible. We were not public in any other market, and there was a "rule" stipulating that no foreign company could go public on the Tokyo Over-The-Counter market unless it was publicly registered in another country. We were operating through a branch, and there was another rule, we were told, prohibiting branches from going public.

In short, everything was impossible! But we could see possibility through other people's impossibility, and so we began. We did some research and found that Japanese companies could in fact go public under the U.S. NASDAQ rules. The restriction on non-public companies appeared to violate the principle of reciprocity in liberalizing the Japanese capital markets which the Japanese government had only months before recognized. We negotiated and obtained a concession on this point. Next we set up a wholly-owned subsidiary and transferred the assets of Getz's branch into this new company. This solved the objection relating to the branch. In the subsequent months we negotiated hard on a hundred other objections.

It is a long story with many curves and reverses. In the end we prevailed. Three years later Getz went public with a capitalized market value of $450 million. Two years later its value had climbed to over $1 billion, and several years after that the owners sold the company for $1.2 billion—and this despite the fact that the Japanese economic bubble had burst and many foreign and Japanese companies were suffering drastic deteriorations in their stock values.

We paid little heed to what people told us was "impossible," we knew what we wanted, we had a clear mission, and negotiated with determination based on integrity.

Brannan: Tell us something about **Ring 2**.

Gresser: **Ring 2** is called "**Reconnaissance.**" Its purpose is to identify the "decision makers" who can make what we want happen. We are after answers to these essential questions:

- What is their pain?

RING 2
RECONNAIS-
SANCE

- What is their available budget (in the sense we have already discussed)?

- What problems, concerns, or reservations do they have that might impede taking effective action?

..nnan: It is important that you elaborate on the concept of "pain" because, really, it seems fundamental to the entire method.

Gresser Yes, that's true. Most of the world's great spiritual traditions take suffering as their point of departure. Pain is also the crucible of discovery. In *Agamemnon*, Aeschylus writes in the voice of the Chorus, "He leads us on the way of wisdom's everlasting law that truth is only learned by suffering it."

PAIN: By "pain," we refer not only to calamity. A joy that is unrealized or frustrated can also be painful because there is a gap between our hopes, aspirations, and present reality. This gap can be very painful. In **Ring 2** we seek to understand the pain of others, and then to decide what is the best way to help them see their pain. If they fail to see their pain—and many people try to bury unpleasant things or to escape from them—they will not be able to discover the path that will lead them out of pain. That is our task—our basic mission—to link what we want to the pain of those who are in a position to make what we want happen, to help them see their pain, and then to help them discover the path to take it away.

You know, Tod, behind this discussion of pain there are also some important insights into the behavioral dynamics of decision making. Shall I outline these?

Brannan: Yes, please do.

Gresser: How would you answer this question: Are decisions made rationally or emotionally, and in what proportion?

Brannan: I'm not sure. I suppose it depends.

Gresser: I have observed that decisions are almost invariably made emotionally, 100 percent, and rationalized thereafter. The decision makers will first reach an emotional decision ('yes' or 'no') to embrace our cause, and later they will rationalize it. And the principal source of this

EMOTIONS AND DECISION MAKING

emotion is pain. If you can understand the emotional source, you will understand the direction in which those persons will move, and you will be better able to guide them to an effective decision.

Gresser: Take Supreme Court Justice Steven Breyer, for example. During the Senate Judiciary Committee Hearings Senator Paul Simon asked Justice Breyer, "Will there be someone who will speak for those who are least fortunate in our society?" And Justice Breyer answered, "I hope so," noting, however, that most of his written opinions expressed what is in his head rather than in his heart. He continued, "Judge Wisdom (the esteemed Court of Appeals Judge John Minor Wisdom) gave me some good advice. He said if you feel you want to write a purple passage because you feel so strongly, write it and don't use it, because people want your result and are not necessarily interested in your feelings .... What I'll try to do is set out the facts as dispassionately as possible, for the facts will speak for themselves, and that can have an impact, too. That's how I've approached it."

In my experience there is a continuing dialogue between emotions and the intellect, but the emotions drive the chariot and the intellect holds on as best it can to the reins.

Brannan: What else happens in **Ring 2**?

Gresser: In **Ring 2** we must stay close to the earth, testing our principal assumptions and continuously reminding ourselves, "What is this? ... let me explore a bit more ... perhaps I really don't know." In **Ring 2** all the senses are engaged, especially the eyes which are curious and seeking and full of wonder.

CURIOSITY
AND WONDER

Brannan: To unveil the key decision makers, to understand their pain, to assess their budget, and to explore their problems and reservations may be easy in some circumstances but very hard in others.

Gresser: True enough. There are many barriers that frustrate reconnaissance, particularly so in transacting business in foreign countries. Take Japan, for example. The Japanese are past masters in deploying blockers, agents, and scouts. The key decision makers, referred to poetically as "the dragon in the clouds" (*kumo no ryu*) or "the black curtain" (*kuromaku*), are often never seen. At the same time the Japanese government's intelligence network is superb. The purpose of an agent or scout is to plant or draw out information, usually with the adversary utterly unaware of what is happening.

Brannan: Can you give an example?

Gresser: Yes. During the past 25 years in which I have studied the Japanese system of negotiation, I have come upon a hidden code consisting of over a hundred basic moves and tactics, some of which are so sophisticated and culturally embedded that they are hidden even from the Japanese themselves. The subject of the code is really a separate and fascinating discussion. But here is a case that captures the flavor.

Some years ago a West Coast architectural firm had encountered difficulty in obtaining payment for the services it had rendered a Japanese designer. After months of excuses and delay the president approached me and asked for my help. I prepared a "pain" letter which contained this key clause. "After all the years it has taken to develop a reputation in Japan as a lead designer—particularly all the hurdles and frustrations you have had to surmount, as a professional woman in Japanese society, why would you want to have your reputation tarnished and become known as someone who walks away from her commitments?"

The letter containing this sentence was approved and, I assumed, duly sent out.

Weeks passed. I did not hear from the president. About two months later I got a call from him asking me to attend a strategy meeting. The bill remained unpaid.

During the meeting the actual letter which had been sent to the designer was being passed around the table. I glanced at it casually. To my surprise the key section, **"particularly all the hurdles and frustrations you have had to surmount, as a professional woman in Japanese society,"** had been deleted! The sentence was crucial because it focused the spotlight clearly on the price she had paid to reach her level of professional accomplishment in Japan and the price she must now pay in losing her good name.

"What's going on?" I asked the president. "What happened to the sentence we worked on together, the one pointing out the risks to her reputation as a professional woman in Japan?"

"Sachiko didn't think it was a good idea," the president told me definitively.

"Who's Sachiko?" I asked, puzzled.

"Oh, Sachiko is our new cultural coordinator. She said that your sentence was very offensive, and that under no circumstances must we ever offend if we want to do business in Japan."

Sachiko was a recent 23-year-old graduate student in psychology. She was sincere, dedicated, and generally wanted to be of service to the architectural firm. She was also an unwitting spy. Her actions were culturally programmed, hard-wired. She was completely unaware of the damage she was causing.

The president corrected the error, sent out a second letter, and was back in the game in a few weeks.

Several months later, in response to increasing pressure, the designer came to San Francisco and a satisfactory accommodation was worked out. But the most basic first step was getting around the agent/scout and dealing with the designer directly.

Brannan: What about default moves in **Ring 2**?

Gresser: If in the midst of **Reconnaissance**, a player starts to feel out of control, as with **Ring 1**, there are always safe harbors.

Negotiation is rarely about telling and almost always about asking and discovery. If you have not obtained even initial answers to the basic questions in **Ring 2**, you are well advised to default to **Ring 1**, because you may have more work to do on your intention, your mission, or plan of action.

If you are still dissatisfied with the answers you have received, you may wish to refine your questions in the next round and to nurture the other players' discovery process more carefully.

It is very important not to negotiate a presentation (**Ring 3**) until you are reasonably certain to whom you should present (*i.e.,* the key decision makers). If you are still unclear, you have more work to do in **Ring 2**.

The core values of **Earning What You Want, No Assumptions, No Expectations, Embrace The 'No,' Presence,** and **Each Moment has Equal Dignity,** all directly apply in **Ring 2**. They are always the safest harbors.

Brannan: What is **Ring 3** about?

Gresser In formal terms, the purpose of **Ring 3** is to position yourself optimally for your presentation. To do this you must:

RING 3 NEGOTIATING THE PRESENTATION:

1. Help the key decision makers begin vividly to see their pain. It is an act of compassion.

2. Navigate effectively, like Magellan, around all the external obstacles, the blockers, spies, agents, and scouts, and also through the internal impediments we ourselves set up to obstruct our own progress.

In **Ring 3** you must become even clearer about who is really making the decisions, what is their pain, their budget, and any problems or concerns that will impede their reaching an effective decision.

There will be tests. Your challenge is to hold steady, to manage your resources wisely, and to keep advancing the mission.

One of the key tests in **Ring 3** is what I call "no dumping, no spilling." "No dumping" refers to letting your emotions bleed out. "No spilling" refers to the spilling of information, in both cases, to blockers, agents, spies, false decision makers, or to people who may not have your good interests at heart. To spill or dump under circumstances where you have not laid a proper foundation for presenting this information is almost always risky.

No one is immune. Spilling happens to ordinary persons and to presidents. For example, some years ago President George Bush visited Japan, ostensibly to urge the Japanese to open their domestic automobile market. I don't know whom he thought he was negotiating with, but at a formal state dinner he spilled his case (literally) all over Prime Minister Miyazawa who most certainly wasn't the real decision maker. With even a modicum of preparatory work in **Ring 2**, the President's mission to Japan might have been far more successful. A Japanese friend who observed this spectacle remarked to me at the time in disgust, "President Bush is a dragon without clouds," by which he meant a decision maker who makes himself available and doesn't have the sense to remain in the shadows.

Ring 3 involves not only tactical maneuvers around blockers, scouts and agents, it also provides a wonderful opportunity to develop character. **Ring 3** is the space in which often the darkness envelops us—for example, we are betrayed, we lose hope, we get nowhere; doubts, fears, and obsessions all rise to the surface and whisper to us, "Give up, you cannot do this, why even try?" I call these the Voices of the Trolls, who seek to shipwreck us on the rocks of our emotions, insecurity and vanity

Brannan: What can be done?

Gresser: We must remain steady—to see the darkness as an opening and a challenge to our Will to carry on, no matter what the consequences and in spite of all reverses.

Do you remember Churchill's famous speech which aroused the fighting spirit of England during one of the darkest and most perilous periods of World War II?

Please scan

We shall not flag or fail. We shall go on to the end. We shall fight in France, we shall fight on the seas and oceans, we shall fight with growing confidence and growing strength in the air, we shall defend our island, whatever the cost may be. We shall fight on the beaches, we shall fight on the landing grounds, we shall fight in the fields and in the streets, we shall fight in the hills; we shall never surrender.

His was a giant **Will.**

Gresser: You know, Tod, every man and woman, and even small children, can cultivate this spirit of fearlessness, to move through the darkest times into the light. I have a client, a Swedish builder of prefab houses, who has been inveigled by five companies belonging to one of the giant Japanese conglomerates. With the encouragement of the Swedish and Japanese governments, he entered into a joint venture partnership to build and sell Swedish houses throughout Japan, including the construction of an entire Swedish village in Hokkaido. He dedicated his factory to supply the venture, he hired architects and designers, and worked for over four years without pay to prepare a unique system of construction. But as soon as his partners obtained his know-how, they defaulted on the deal, violated his copyrights, refused to purchase materials and parts from his factory, which caused him great financial hardship, and then seized the factory forcing it into bankruptcy.

When we met three years ago, he was despairing. The first thing we did was to build a mission of service. I told him, "If you focus only upon your personal grievances, your sense of outrage, few people will rally to your cause. You must link your grievances to the concerns of others. Therein lies your power."

And that is what he did. He resolved to spend his time, his honor, and his money in helping other Swedish business people and the Swedish government (if it would listen) to learn from his personal misfortune and to become more adept in their Japanese negotiations.

He has spent the last few years mostly in **Ring 3**. It has been a productive time, and he has rebuilt his damaged integrity. He has learned to take joy from little victories and to profit from his many errors, frustrations, and defeats. And still he carries on with humor, dignity, and balance, steadfastly working on his mission to obtain fair compensation and to help other Swedes deal more vigilantly with Japanese companies and the Japanese government.

He has made much progress. Gradually many Swedes are waking up to the real game that is being played by the Japanese Embassy, the Japanese government, and by the big Japanese companies in Sweden. As of this writing, he has secured two court decisions confirming that his company is the rightful owner of the copyrights, and that his adversaries have infringed, and continue to infringe, these copyrights. A member of the Swedish royal family has written to the Japanese Vice Foreign Minister requesting that the dispute be amicably resolved. The Swedish police have become involved. A member of the Japanese Diet (Parliament) has questioned officials of the Japanese Ministry of

Construction and has learned that, despite the recent earthquakes in Kobe, Osaka and Sakhalin Island, in which over 7,000 people have died, the Japanese Ministry of Construction never bothered to test houses that were imported by the conglomerate from a rival supplier after three of the companies repudiated their agreement with my client.

We have discovered that 600 families, including many children, are now living in these houses which have not been tested for earthquakes, and no one has cared to warn them.

The battle continues and I believe in the end the Swedish builder will win—if "winning" means he will receive fair compensation. But in another sense he has already won. He has moved far along toward accomplishing his public mission and his experience has deepened him greatly. He is a much wiser and, for this, a richer man.

Brannan: What are the default moves in **Ring 3**?

Gresser: The most basic rule of **Ring 3** is: be careful about spilling information or dumping emotions prematurely to non-decision makers. We are "programmed" to spill, and therefore much of this behavior may be unconscious. However, if you spill prematurely, you may find that you are falling into "need" and your later presentation may be less effective.

Brannan: How are we programmed to spill?

Gresser: In our universities, for example, most professors lecture rather than listen or really seek to learn from their students. The students are rewarded more on what they write or publish than by how much they truly understand and can embody their understanding in action.

Brannan: What can you do if you have spilled prematurely by making a presentation to a non-decision maker, for example, to a blocker?

Gresser: You should seriously consider withdrawing the presentation, as I will explain in a moment, and returning to the basic task of helping the key decision makers see their pain more clearly. Moreover, if you still do not have a good understanding of the key questions—who makes the decisions, by what process, what is their pain, what is their negotiating budget, or what are their problems or reservations (their **agenda**), you have a clear signal that you should not proceed to **Ring 4**, and that substantial work remains in **Rings 2** and **3**.

Brannan: What are the elements of **Ring 4**?

Gresser: **Ring 4**, **Presentation**, creates an opening. Our task is simply to attend. To remain present and steady in action—when we fall or when we ascend—is perhaps the critical survival skill of this or any other age. So if you stumble—lose your sense of connectedness, presence, or *gravitas*—take note of the error. You may learn something valuable in **Ring 4** that will serve you well in any situation.

RING 4
PRESENTATION

Ring 4 has a few useful rules that can be summarized in five questions.

First, **what** is the decision you seek? The more precisely you can define this decision, the more on point will be your presentation.

Second, to **whom** should you present? The basic rule is to focus on **who** is in a position to make the **decision** you want. We are not interested in the theoretical decision makers. For example, do not assume that the key person is necessarily the head of a division. The real decision maker may be the president or the chief executive officer. But the top dog may not be the key person. Often underlings run the show. It takes discipline and patience to ferret out who are the real decision makers.

The third question is **when** to present? The presentation step in **Ring 4** demands that we contain ourselves—in other words, to "hold" integrity. Before we present our case, our proposal, our product or service, we must determine the other person's pain and budget.

As I indicated earlier, the art of negotiation is to help others come to terms with their deepest joys and sorrows, *i.e.,* the pain, and then to help them discover the path to take it away. If we do not know the pain, or if the decision makers cannot see their pain, what use will be our presentation?

The same principle holds true of **budget**. Why present to someone who does not possess a budget, or who will not make available time and effort, financial reserves, or creativity? Enterprises without an adequate budget are usually ill-starred.

Brannan: What about the agenda for a presentation?

Gresser: I'm coming to that. Establishing a valid agenda is another precondition of an effective presentation. As with **budget**, you will run into trouble if you present your case prematurely without first establishing a context or a foundation. I call the foundation, the "**agenda.**"

A valid agenda has five elements. They are:

1. "Real" or objective problems.
2. The other party's issues, reservations, or concerns which may erupt into serious difficulties or problems at a later date.
3. Our concerns and reservations.
4. What we want.
5. What happens next.

We must endeavor to address all these issues **before presenting,** because otherwise they can rise up and haunt us. Again, this tendency is particularly vexing in transacting business in countries like Japan, where reticence is highly valued. Many American negotiators conclude what they believe to be a final agreement, hold a victory celebration, and then are flabbergasted when the Japanese negotiators raise new concerns or objections. Such cases vividly point out the clash of cultures at the "agenda" step— the need of Americans to reach for clarity and certainty, the appreciation of the Japanese, Chinese, and other East Asian societies, of uncertainty and ambiguity.

Brannan: What is the fourth question?

Gresser: **Where**—the issue of venue. Here we must balance the desirability of making the decision as easy as possible for the other party against the cost to us of our doing so (see **budget**). Should we drive to their office or place of business? Again the best way to answer such questions is to determine first how significant this person's decision is to our mission. You must ask yourself, will the potential benefits of this decision exceed their actual costs to me in time, effort, financial reserves, and creative vitality?

Brannan: What is the last question?

Gresser: **How.** After we determine to whom and when to present, the final critical question is: **how**? As I have said, the key is full presence. We take the pain of our opponents and their concerns, one by one, in the order of their importance to **them**, and we help them see how each of these issues can be effectively addressed. We do so simply and clearly, without wobbling, exaggeration, or adornment. Remember, the goal is to stir their emotions and to help them see—by their hearts and stomachs—the possibility of hope for a solution.

The principles of formal presentation are straightforward. When we attend fully—embodying the **Five Core Values**—we will provide just enough information and in the time available. Many people incorrectly believe that they must cover "everything." But "everything" is a bottomless pit. Your presentation will exactly fit the requirements of the setting if you will let your integrity be your guide. People judge not only by contents of the message. The superior person will look underneath the data for the intangible, subtle clues and signals in which you reveal who you really are.

Brannan: Have you covered all the elements?

Gresser: There is one more thing.

Brannan: What is that?

Gresser: After you present in the manner I have described, you must allow the other party space to reject your presentation. You must acknowledge their right to say 'no.'

Brannan: It will be hard for many people to digest this.

Gresser: I agree. But the principle fits squarely with the core values. Most people associate a **'no'** with failure, a loss, a mistake, or simply with being wrong. In point of fact a **'no'** is none of these. It is simply a decision, like any other decision.

'NO'

Do you understand why a **'no'** can place an untrained person in a predicament, for example, when he/she rejects a valid proposal because of price or some other condition? The rejecting party is in pain, and we, the presenter, hold the solution. If we graciously acknowledge the **'no,'** bonding may actually take place, particularly if the pain is unresolved. I have seen many cases where **'no'** is first given and graciously received, and then weeks pass and more resources are invested in finding a solution to the original problem, and then in the end the 'no'-giver relents and in exasperation pays a far higher price for the original services that were offered.

A **'no'** can be of great benefit to us in other ways. A **'no'** helps us rationalize the uses of our own scarce resources. A **'no'** says, "invest here, not there." Also a **'no'** is wonderful conditioning—a hit—like a cold bracing shower. In time, as the pain of receiving a **'no'** recedes, so will our need, and the more we allow **'nos'** to strip away illusory needs and allow us to live simply, the freer we become. It is also axiomatic that those who can receive a **'no'** in good humor are also better able to exercise the veto, which is a critical skill of leadership.

Brannan: If one runs into trouble in **Ring 4**, what are some of the default moves?

Gresser: The most common difficulty involves multiple decision makers. In most large organizations it is commonplace for many people to be involved in an important decision. In such cases you must negotiate hard to make your own presentation, to stand or to fall upon your own sword. It can be a serious error to allow another party, who is untrained or may have a different agenda or be under different pressures, to plead your case. Even if that person is well-disposed toward you, he (or she) may unwittingly sabotage your presentation.

In these situations an intelligent course is to present to **all** the key decision makers simultaneously. If this is not feasible, you must negotiate an agreement from one of the key players that, if your presentation is convincing, he/she will facilitate a meeting with all the others. In this negotiation you must help that person see the potential for embarrassment, of attempting to sell you or your product, service or cause, with inadequate information. If the party remains adamant, the default move may be to return to **Ring 3**, lay a new foundation and devise a new strategy for a later presentation.

If your presentation becomes confused and you sense you are losing your bearings, just relax, be friendly, and return to the other party's dreams, concerns and frustrations.

If you sense your presentation is premature or incomplete, you may decide to table or even to withdraw it. You might apologize: "You know, I have more work to do in understanding how I can be of real service to you. With what you have told us, I would like to revise our proposal and see if it will not address even more clearly the issues you are struggling with."

If your integrity tells you that you are pressing too hard and the other side begins to move away, give yourself and your opponent room to breathe and to say 'no.' On such occasions usually there is far more time and space than your impulsiveness and needs would have you believe.

Brannan: Let us turn now to the last ring, the **Fifth Circle**.

Gresser: **Ring 5** is called "**After Presentation**," and it presents a great challenge to a player's integrity. If you commit to another person, **Ring 5** requires that you work diligently in carrying out

RING 5 AFTER
PRESENTATION

your commitments. If you receive a **'no'** in **Ring 4**, you must decide in **Ring 5** whether you will accept the **'no'** and abandon your negotiation, or whether to continue in spite of it. Even if the other side accepts your presentation, you may still conclude that you do not wish to proceed.

Most players incorrectly assume that simply because a proposal or a presentation has been accepted or an agreement has been reached (*i.e.*, a 'yes'), that the game has ended. In fact often the real play, the hidden negotiation, is about to begin.

There are four basic questions to ask yourself in **Ring 5**:

- Do I wish to proceed or shall I exercise my own right (*i.e.*, a **'no'**) to discontinue the play?
- If I decide to begin, what actions can I immediately undertake to help the other party?
- If I have received a **'no,'** what actions are now open to me?
- If I decide to proceed in spite of a **'no,'** how will this advance my mission?

MODESTY AND
HUMILITY

The key qualities you can cultivate in **Ring 5** are modesty and humility, which lead to trainability, which we have already discussed. The word "humility" comes from the Latin, *humus* meaning "earth." When we stay close to the earth we can adjust with remarkable agility.

There is a sequence in many negotiations which resembles combat: I move (action), you respond, I counter. If you can hold steady in the face of your opponent's responsive move, you will control the game and keep the initiative. The determining factor will be your ability to remain loose, light, and free. **Ring 5** is a marvelous training of this skill.

In **Ring 5** the spotlight is upon the circularity of a negotiation, indeed, of the life process itself. If you view a "negotiation" as an unfolding opportunity to practice and to refine your integrity, the negotiation never ends. There is always a new mountain to climb, a new stream to ford, always more work to be done. This is why the last hexagram in the *I Ching*, the Chinese *Book of Changes*, is entitled "Before Completion."

The default moves in **Ring 5** are straightforward.

If the response to your presentation in **Ring 4** is a 'no,' you must now decide what to do—whether to continue to play or not. The first step is to return to **Ring 1**, examine your original **mission** and **budget**, and assess the amount of **budget** you have expended up to this point. Again, the key is to be conscious about your decision, so that it is based on what you want, your **mission** and your **budget**. If you decide to continue to play, you may wish to begin in **Rings 3 and 4**, laying an even stronger foundation for your next presentation.

If the response in **Ring 4** is affirmative, you must decide if you wish to continue the game, in other words, to give the other players what they want. Remember, you always have a right to say 'no'—to decide, upon reflection, not to continue.

If you decide to proceed, your task is to work as diligently as you can. By entering your opponents' world and focusing upon what pains them, you will greatly strengthen your own integrity.

In every case, **Ring 5** ultimately redirects you back to **Ring 1** and requires you to refine your original mission in the light of experience, to become even clearer about what you truly want, how you will arrive there, and the price you must pay.

Brannan: Julian, in a nutshell can you summarize **The Five Rings?**

Gresser: **The Five Rings** offers a disciplined, orderly process for analyzing the flow of decisions. Each circle creates an opening to develop integrity through the practice of **The Five Core Values.** Instantly we can know where we are, how we got there, and where to go next. We are always in the game even when we fall out of it. We practice with little things, the incremental steps by which character is built, so when challenges suddenly appear, we are ready. We want the taste of them.

III

LIGHT AND SHADOW

"I have no parents. I make heaven and earth my parents.
I have no home. I make awareness my home.
I have no life or death. I make breath tides my life and death.
I have no divine power. I make integrity my divine power.
I have no means. I make understanding my means.
I have no body. I make endurance my body.
I have no eyes. I make the lightning flash my eyes.
I have no ears. I make sensibility my ears.
I have no limbs. I make promptness my limbs.
I have no strategy. I make unshadowed-by-thought my strategy.
I have no designs. I make opportunity my design.
I have no miracles. I make right action my miracles.
I have no principles. I make adaptability my principle.
I have no tactics. I make emptiness/fullness my tactics.
I have no friends. I make you, mind, my friend(s).
I have no enemy. I make carelessness my enemy.
I have no armor. I make compassion my armor.
I have no castle. I make heaven/earth my castle.
I have no sword. I make absence of self my sword."
—14th century samurai

Brannan: Julian, you have outlined a structure of decision
making and effective negotiation, which you call
The Five Rings. I think the time has come to link

the method to the principal theme of piloting through chaos, and this brings us to the core skills.

Gresser: If our entire enterprise has one purpose, that purpose can be condensed into one principle. All technique is contained in one core skill—one noble tactic—and that is Presence. **Presence is All.** I call this practice "**building the container.**"

But first an introductory comment on chaos itself. Most people associate "chaos" with randomness, discord or turbulence. This is its modern meaning in physics. But if one returns to the original meaning, one doesn't find these elements in the definition. Chaos derives from the Greek word of the same name, which meant "gape" or space; in other words, the void. Now these terms, over time, have incorporated value judgments that connote trouble or danger. For example, in the Christian literature chaos is seen as the instinctive enemy of order, as Pandemonium, the City of Lucifer, or as the abyss, the frightful domain of witches and trolls. Because of such awful associations we have come to believe that the abyss must be filled up, the gap spanned, and the primordial forces of nature controlled. None of this, as I say, was part of the original meaning. Really, it was value-neutral, simply the void—absolute emptiness.

THE ORIGINAL MEANING OF CHAOS:

The original meaning leads us to a rather interesting insight, which the ancient Chinese sages also understood well: the abyss, in its emptiness, contains all things. It contains danger, but it also contains opportunity. The Chinese character for "crisis" (*weiji*) is written by combining in a single character the ideographs for danger and opportunity, suggesting that these two coexist and are coequal in every moment. Shakespeare also understood this principle when he wrote, "Sweet are the uses of adversity." But Shakespeare never tells us why adversity is sweet or how to turn it into opportunity. Shall I demonstrate how, through the **practice of presence**, adversity can become sweet, right now?

Brannan:	Yes, please do.
Gresser:	Okay. Let's begin with our friend and colleague, Paula Fox, who is here with us today. Paula, you're a businesswoman, can you describe a situation that is causing you great uneasiness or concern—one in which you can see chaos beginning to lap at your feet?
MS. FOX: BUILDING THE CONTAINER	Yes, unfortunately it's only too easy. Tomorrow I'm going on a business trip to the East Coast where I will meet two colleagues. One of the men is very easygoing, no problem. But the other is a bear. What particularly gripes me is how pushy he is, how he always wants things his way, talks incessantly, and then insists on going out to dinner together. I'm really torn. The project is very important. A lot is riding on it. I don't want to offend him or have a scene. I don't want to make an enemy. But at the same time I really don't want to spend my dinners with this person. Actually I like sitting in my hotel room after a ten-hour day, watching television, relaxing, and ordering room service. I am worried about this situation. I am apprehensive about the meeting and, quite frankly, I'm really not looking forward to the trip.
Gresser:	Very good. Now, Paula, what I'd like you to do is simply to bring your attention into your body. Okay? Then sketch in your mind an awful but likely scenario that might occur in—where was it?
Ms. Fox:	Boston.
Gresser:	Okay. Boston. Really allow your imagination to run wild. Terrify yourself and once you really are feeling ghastly, if you would, give us a report of what starts to happen inside of you. Just close your eyes. Shall we begin?
Ms. Fox:	(Speaking with her eyes closed) Okay. I arrive. We spend the day together and I feel exhausted and suffocated. Joe suggests we have dinner. I decline. He insists. I say I don't want to. He makes some snide comment. I feel bad. He

presses me. There's a blowup. We're not on speaking terms. Then a real mistake occurs—somebody didn't pay attention. The contract is lost and I'm blamed.

Gresser: Perfect! How do you feel in your body about this scenario?

Ms. Fox: Awful.

Gresser: Splendid! Can you be a bit more descriptive?

Ms. Fox: My heart is fluttering—I feel angry—this is so unnecessary! I have a constricted feeling around my throat as though I can't breathe. My chest and neck and stomach are tight, and I have indigestion.

Gresser: Marvelous! Now just relax. What I would like you to do is to bring your awareness into your body and simply report to us how you're feeling. For example, if you start to feel frightened, just report the feeling or the emotion and then how it materializes in your body. If you feel angry, just note your anger and the accompanying physical sensations.

You don't have to change or suppress anything. Just attend. You are the witness, the observer of the movie that's beginning. How do you feel about proceeding in this way?

Ms. Fox: I feel fine. It seems interesting.

Gresser: Okay. Continue attending and watch what is happening.

Ms. Fox: (A minute or so elapses. She quietly watches her movie.)

Gresser: Anything special going on?

Ms. Fox: No.

Gresser: Good. Just keep your consciousness in your body. Just relax, let go, and attend.

(A few minutes later)

Ms. Fox: Well, my breathing is settling down a bit now, and my heart is not racing so much.

Gresser: Fine ... anything else?

Ms. Fox: Let's see ... my stomach feels better ... more settled. The tightness around my neck and chest is relieving some and my hands are starting to warm up.

Gresser: Paula, you're doing very well. Just hold steady and keep attending to your body and relax.

(A little later)

In this practice it is necessary to open some space and be patient for the changes.

Ms. Fox: The tension is **really** beginning to break up! I feel freer and lighter. I have the sense of collecting power and energy. I'm not quite sure why the situation got me so down. All I really have to do is just tell Joe in a nice way that I'm exhausted. I see how to handle this situation now. It all seems quite simple.

Gresser: Very good, but before you move back into the Thought Tower in your head, just shuttle back into your body and keep checking out what's happening. Do you notice anything else?

Ms. Fox: I have a lot more energy—I mean, **a lot more.** I feel great! Tingling. (She laughs) This is great!

Gresser: (Turning to Tod Brannan) It may be helpful to summarize what has happened here in just a few minutes. First, Paula was very apprehensive and fearful, and her anxieties were beginning to breed even more exaggerated pictures and images. A true runaway catastrophe was in the making. All of this, of course, is in her head. Simply by becoming the observer, by watching how her fears were surfacing in her body (and by watching herself watching herself!) Paula began to get a grip and to restore integrity. And the more she attended to the **physical expression** of her emotions in her body, the more—and this is the beginning of the miracle—the physical sensations and the emotions themselves began to transform. And then later her snapshot of this sliver of reality, which is colored by her emotions and the images created by the emotions, also began to change, and she seemed lighter, younger, and more alive.

Is that not so, Paula?

Ms. Fox: Yes, that's true. That's what happened.

Gresser: This in essence is our practice. We attend fully to each moment—to each moment with its special dignity. And suddenly things begin to change and we begin to change and there is an opening—a little opening in the darkness, a little glimmer of light. Churchill once remarked, "We create the interior, then it creates us."

Brannan: Very interesting, Julian. Help us understand some of the practical ways to use this technique of "**building the container.**"

Gresser: When we are frightened and helpless, Fear decouples us from our body. By becoming present in our body, we restore the connection.

Fear, like jealousy, is green-eyed and mocks the meat upon which it feeds. Thus Fear makes little and private things, as in Paula's case, great and momentous. And when Panic occupies the stage, no other player has a chance. The **practice of presence** holds the line and reminds us who we really are. It is very hard for our grandiose fears to take over when we are truly present.

The practice applies not only in the troughs but also at the crests of life. When things are going really well and we are jubilant, that can be a point of particular vulnerability, because now we have expectations and grow inflated and arrogant. At the crest we are in peril because we are unconscious. The practice of working with the darkness is enormously useful because it helps us hold integrity when we begin to come into the light. It reminds us of the importance of *gravitas*, of steadiness, focus and follow-through. In some sense it requires greater character to continue modestly at the height of success than under the spur of necessity.

But there is another subtlety to the practice, which I can introduce by way of an old Chinese story, probably from the late 5th and early 6th century A.D.

Brannan: Yes, please do.

Gresser Two sages were once together. "Where are you going?" asks the elder.

"I am wandering the world at random," replies the younger man.

"And what do you think of wandering?" the patriarch inquires.

"I do not know," responds the younger.

"Not knowing is most intimate," the elder man observes.

Most intimate—This is the great secret. When Fear comes up, as in Paula's case, the fear of what an uncertain situation might hold, we can settle down to find peace and intimacy with ourselves in the mists of not-knowing. For it is in the mists that we make our discoveries, as she has done.

This ability to be at ease in not-knowing is also one of the links to true creativity. Keats once wrote:

NEGATIVE CAPABILITY:

"It struck me what quality went to form a Man of Achievement, especially in literature, and which Shakespeare possessed so enormously—I mean, **negative capability,** that is, when a man is capable of being in uncertainties, mysteries, and doubts, without any irritable reaching after fact and reason."

This **no irritable reaching** after fact and reason holds a clue not only to creative expression in the arts; it is also the mark of the martial artist and of the great negotiators. For when you are loose and light, your heart open and your body peaceful and happy, the openings—especially in the darkness—come to you in legions when you least expect them, and then resistance gives way.

Brannan: The concept of **negative capability** seems very important as a literary skill. But what is its greatest test in the field of negotiation? Where does the rubber really meet the road?

Gresser: I would say around issues of time. Perhaps the greatest point of vulnerability in any Ring is when we lose our sense of connection, believing that we're out of time. The dynamic is clear: we feel a sense of urgency, this produces **need; need** churns and upsets the emotions, consciousness is dispersed, we begin to panic, we act impulsively, which usually produces an untoward result and only aggravates our sense of crisis. Do you remember Flanagan? He could have panicked, seeing all the months of preparation fly out the window. But he held. He did not reach for a closing or even certainty. Actually he turned the time-need dynamic around on his Japanese hosts by using the Sword of Silence. It was they who couldn't stand the slowdown in the pace; it was they who needed to reach irritably, both on the second day and in the weeks following, after fact, reason, and certainty.

I have seen this time-need issue in many international and domestic negotiations. Right now I have a client, a semiconductor company in Los Angeles, which is negotiating a technology-development agreement with a huge German conglomerate. Every time the president of this company jumps the gun out of need (ignoring what he has learned) and impulsively asks for confirmation or spills information, the Germans pull away. Every time he holds together around time issues, resists the impulse to make a phone call or to send a fax, the Germans call or approach him in a welcoming way. It's a fascinating demonstration of the "dance" of integrity in full-motion video.

Brannan: Are there other tests?

Gresser: As your skill advances, the tests get harder. The more conscious you become, the more painful it is to be unconscious. But then you must have compassion when you fail. The next step is to be generous to oneself, and to know that often,

	when we are most perplexed, it is at that moment that the angels of our better nature walk through the door. It is then that the miracle happens.
Brannan:	How can we prepare for such things?
Gresser:	By *gravitas*. Someone once asked Coleridge, "How can angels fly?" And he answered him, "Because they take themselves lightly." The more present and rooted we are, the less encumbered by vanity, the easier for our spirits to soar. The practice is straightforward. Track five times this week when you have felt overwhelmed, shuttled into your body and attended to what was happening. Then track five times this week when you allowed your fears to overwhelm you. Then a third case: When your fears appeared and you started to succumb, note five times you exercised your Will, entered into your body, and like Odysseus and the Sirens, held onto the mast of being present, and observed what magic happened then.

We are dealing with deeply-rooted, early pathways of behavior, and of these the programming of Fear from childhood seems the most entrenched. We must be patient with ourselves. Steadiness and practice are everything.

Zuigan, a great master, used to remind himself to be present throughout each day.

"Master, Master," he would say.

"Yes, yes," would be his reply.

'Thoroughly awake?" he would inquire.

"Yes, yes," would be his response.

"Don't be deceived by others," he would warn himself.

"No, no," he would respond.

This "Don't be deceived by others," refers not only to the external world. It refers also to the inner—to our fears, conceits, and dilemmas, to our sense of helplessness that wastes our powers, that pulls us from our true connection, our line to the way things really are, which is our integrity.

Brannan:	The story of Zuigan suggests that staying awake may be the key.

Gresser: Yes, staying awake. And what things we can discover when we are awake! How beautiful and plentiful and filled with hope this world really is.

I would like to focus now upon the techniques of discovery, because it is fair to say that every step in a negotiation creates an opening for ourselves and other players upon the stage which is the world. The great negotiators are all explorers and discoverers.

Brannan: Okay.

Gresser: The first principle of discovery is **No Assumptions, No Expectations**, which perhaps you remember is also the second core value. Assumptions and expectations, and the hunger that drives them, impair our ability to see things as they truly are. The stronger the hunger, the greater the distortion. Thus we are interested in what Leonardo da Vinci called *saper vedere*, how to see.

NO ASSUMP-
TIONS/
NO EXPECTA-
TIONS

Brannan: Are you suggesting that even seeing is a skill and that most people do not know how to see?

Gresser: I am. Virtually all of us live in a semi-trance and our society enforces a consensus on reality. I say, "Accept **my** version of reality, and I'll go along with **yours**." And so we become deadened and succumb.

One of the most dramatic examples of consensus trance is the first entry of Captain Cook's ship, the *Endeavor*, into Botany Bay, Australia. "There she was," writes Alan Moorehead in his wonderful book, *The Fatal Impact*,

CONSENSUS
TRANCE

> with her high masts and her great sails, and then she passed within a quarter of a mile of some fisherman in four canoes. They did not even bother to look up. Then when she had anchored close to the shore, a naked woman carrying wood appeared with three children. She often looked at the ship, but expressed neither surprise nor concern. Soon after this she lighted a fire, and the

four canoes came in from the fishing. The people landed, hauled up their boats and began to dress for dinner, to all appearance totally unmoved by us ...

But later when small boats were put to shore, the natives raised a great alarm, recognizing the sailors as human, although a palpable evil with their odd clothes and pale faces. The first sight of the *Endeavor* had apparently meant nothing to these people, because it was too strange, too monstrous to be comprehended. It appeared out of nowhere like some menacing phenomenon of nature, a water spout or a roll of thunder, and by ignoring it or pretending to ignore it, no doubt the natives hoped it would go away.

Psychologists call it a negative hallucination. We become so inured, so clubbed down, that the mind no longer trusts and refuses to process what the senses report, and the only thing that is real is what is tried and familiar.

You might think it implausible that consensus trance occurs every day in business.

Brannan: It would seem implausible but let's have an example.

Gresser: I will give you a modern example of consensus trance.

I was once training a group of executives in their Japanese negotiations. "What is it you want?" I asked one of them.

"I want our Japanese joint venture partner to invest more money in the venture," he instantly replied.

"Fine. Now, what is it you **really** want?" I pressed him.

"I just told you." He was somewhat nonplussed.

"What do you **really** want?" I repeated... "if you were to drop all your assumptions about what is not possible."

"I can't think of anything else," he replied.

"It's okay, take your time," I said. You have to be gentle with people when they go into the discovery mode.

"Nothing else is coming up," he said, a little impatiently.

Five minutes passed, then ten minutes. Some people in the workshop were becoming uneasy. Remember Flanagan? Unlike Flanagan, these people were not trained. They were unused to silence. Finally the executive blurted out, "All right, you've pushed me hard. What I really want is to take over my joint venture partner. That's what I want. But you know it's **impossible!** No foreigner can ever take over a Japanese company, **you know** that."

"I've been involved in several takeovers."

"What! You can do that?!! Well, if that were **really** possible—and I'm very skeptical—that's what **I really** want."

And so on. Somehow he seemed to have physically grown larger in his chair, become brighter and more alive. And all that had really changed was that he had put aside the crutch, the belief which had served him too well and too long, that what he really wanted was quite impossible.

I will give you another example, a French case that grounds the move of "no assumptions" in an even more real-life business setting.

The president of a major American electronics manufacturer faced a dilemma over his company's joint venture. On one hand, he felt duty-bound to uphold an oral promise to invest $5 million in the French joint venture company. On the other, he had a vague, uneasy feeling—not so much about the investment itself, but about his French partner's real intentions. A $5 million investment would not be an excessive burden if it would help the venture grow and prosper. But the joint venture company had never been profitable since beginning operations in the mid-1980s, and the American president was not even sure how important profitability was to his French partner. Then too, increasingly, his French partner was pressuring him to transfer core manufacturing and other know-how to France.

If the French partner simply intended to use the joint venture as a vehicle to acquire critical technology, the American president was clear that he would not be interested in transferring manufacturing operations to France, nor would he want to go through with the $5 million investment, nor even to encourage in any way the joint venture's further development. The problem was how to discover his French partner's real agenda?

Being a man of the world, the first thing the American president did was to take stock of instances in which his own integrity and that of his core team had been upheld or compromised. He observed that he and his colleagues had developed a vested interest (a **need**) **not** to see. They had become so imbued by their own desires and hopes for the joint venture, with what it would do for **them,** that it never really occurred to him to look deeply into the concerns or motivations of the French partner. Embedded in his own needs and desires were a number of critical assumptions about the nature of the venture itself. Basically, the American president had been assuming all along that his French partner naturally shared his hope that the joint venture would flourish. The American president also assumed that his company had actually entered into a "partnership" in the American sense of the term (*e.g.,* a fiduciary relationship), and that the joint venture itself naturally was the owner, not the French parent, of all technology transferred to it under a license.

This was not how his French counterparts perceived the venture. They did not view themselves as "partners" in any way, except when they made use of the delusion of the

Americans to serve their own interests. The senior executives in the French parent company felt entitled to all the technology in the venture. Although the license clearly specified that all technology transferred was solely the property of the joint venture, the key French managers believed it only "fair" that the parent company should be able to use the technology because of its substantial equity investment and loan guarantees to the venture.

While engaging in this process of self-reflection, the American president began to scrutinize significant lapses or mismatches between the behavior of his French partner and the stated purpose of both parties to the joint venture. The first thing he noted was a curious lack of interest on the French side in making the joint venture profitable. For example, despite protests by the Americans, no plans of any sort had been prepared to realize the goal of profitability. The American president began to pay more careful attention than he had in the past to the kinds of questions the French parties were asking at all levels of this company—questions about patents, about technical problems, about bottlenecks in their solutions—many questions quite outside the ordinary ambit of concerns of the joint venture. He began to receive strange reports, which he had hitherto largely ignored: for example, the discovery late one evening of a French engineer faxing sensitive information back to the French parent company. This engineer had been recruited from the U.S. company's chief competitor by the French Chairman of the Board of the joint venture, and then seconded to work at the U.S. company in California.

A clear picture began to emerge of the incompatibility of the French mission with the expectations and hopes of the Americans. The pattern became so clear it seemed a face peering out across the many months in which the two companies had operated together.

Using the yardstick of integrity, the American president asked himself, "Why should we invest $5 million in a joint venture in which our French partner appears to be operating on an entirely different mission, one which is incompatible with our own?" Without accusation or recrimination the American president quietly resolved not to invest further in the joint venture and looked for other more exciting opportunities in Europe.

The key to "winning" this negotiation was the American president's determination to reclaim his integrity, the "inner negotiation." This occurred when he began to distance himself from his "needs" and at last truly to listen. At this point he started to uncover all sorts of unnoticed "facts" directly pertinent to the critical issues before him. He began to challenge his own assumptions and to look with fresh eyes at what was really going on. He paid particular attention to instances where integrity in his company was being violated and when it was upheld. And as he probed deeply, he discovered his French partner's true agenda, which had been "obvious" all along in the flux of events, conditions, and circumstances. Without engaging in "mind-reading" he reached an **effective decision** that ultimately saved his company millions of dollars and years of wasted effort.

When we allow ourselves to come in touch, to see what might be possible just underneath the surface, what a transformation occurs! Until he became willing to challenge his assumptions, the American president in the French joint venture was content to move blithely towards a disastrous investment; the student in the seminar could not imagine taking over a Japanese company; the villagers could not conceive that it was possible to cross the reefs by means of a canoe. Simply to allow ourselves **the chance to see** will affect the probabilities that what we see happens.

HOW TO SEE

The method of how to see is straightforward. Anyone can learn it with only a little practice.

The first step is to identify and to write down succinctly what you **believe** you want. Next, identify any assumptions you are making about what is impossible. Look for assumptions that crib your ability to see. Drop these assumptions. Put them aside, even when they pull at you. Then rephrase what you want. Look for a fresh way to express it. We want our emotions and our creative imagination, which are always curious about novelty, to express themselves.

Finally, see if you can stretch a little more. This "little more" is where often real discovery begins. When we were children we played in a sea of wishes, for in the mind's eye of a child everything is possible. We want to recapture this original innocence.

I have found in my life, Tod, that when we drop our assumptions and expectations, put them aside like old and tattered clothes, suddenly we are less burdened and more alive. Each moment presents itself, in all its freshness, and we are free.

Brannan: Your example illustrates one of the uses of **No Assumptions** in identifying what we really want. Are there other tactical uses?

Gresser: I will give you a very advanced example which illustrates how Presence and **No Assumptions** work together. I am before a client and we are discussing his dealings with Japan. Suddenly I start to feel fear, a tingling along my forearms, a bristling on the hairs of my neck. My heart is beating faster. "Why am I feeling afraid?" I say to myself, "There is no cause for fear. Yet here is fear! Might I be assuming anything? Let me see." I pause and think for a moment. My client observes none of this internal dialogue.

"Well, look at this! I am assuming this is **my** fear, my anxiety. This **'mine'** is the problem. Let me drop 'mine' and see what I can see. It is not mine at all. It seems it is **his** fears, yes, look at the quiver under his eyes, how he holds himself.

Fear has crept into the room. Even the walls now seem to shudder."

Like a tranquil lake, our body/mind can pick up even the most subtle perturbations of some passing breeze.

When we develop **gravitas**, our mind can discern all sorts of strange things in the field, and the clearer we are, the clearer the mirror becomes. This is one of the tactical uses of equanimity and compassion.

This technique of **No Assumptions, No Expectations**, is celebrated in some of the classic Japanese *chambara* (samurai) movies. I don't know if you have ever seen the movie *The Seven Samurai* by Akira Kurosawa. The story is a simple one. A village is threatened by brigands. A group of seven samurai comes to its aid, but in the ensuing battle all but two are killed. In one of the early scenes, the archer, the elder statesman of the group (who survives) seeks to recruit a masterless warrior (*rōnin*) to the cause. He devises a way to test the degree of skill of the candidate. A young man who aspires to join the band is planted behind the door with a stick. His instructions are to attack anyone who passes through the entry.

Please scan

The street is busy with the traffic of merchants and *geisha*, petty officials, and *tatami* makers. From time to time a *rōnin* passes by. The archer hails him. The *rōnin* approaches, smiles and enters through the doorway. The young man attacks but he is easily repelled. "Very fine!" the archer compliments the *rōnin*. But the *rōnin* is insulted at the impudence of being tested and leaves in a huff. Several other candidates appear, but for financial and other reasons, all refuse.

Finally, just as the archer and his comrades are about to give up, a samurai appears at the threshold. He pauses. Something is amiss. Perhaps a physical sensation or merely a shadow crosses his mind. We do not know. Then he laughs—a great belly laugh. Ha! Ha! Ha! He sees and understands. How amusing! He is the man the archer has been looking for! No assumptions, No expectations, the true martial artist.

The story embodies the true spirit of the samurai: "I have no means, I make understanding my means. I have no eyes, I make the lightning flash my eyes. I have no tactics, I make emptiness/fullness my tactics."

Brannan: This seems a prescription for combat but can it apply equally to a negotiation?

Gresser: The same. I will show you. Let's turn to tactics. In particular, one tactic, the question.

Most people believe that you ask a question to obtain information.

Brannan: Yes, most people believe that.

Gresser: Yet there is another, more interesting use of questions and that is to facilitate discovery. Each step in a negotiation is an opportunity to discover something singular about ourselves and our opponents: "What is this? I don't know. Let me see .... The steady, curious mind is the negotiator's mind. So it follows that telling is rarely negotiating...." "You should know that...." How many people will accept what you tell them? We live in an age of sceptics. Asking rather than telling, letting the eye of discovery open, that is a much better practice.

THE
QUESTION

Brannan: Let's return for a moment to basics. When you speak of discovery questions, what precisely do you mean?

Gresser: There are two kinds of questions. The first is the interrogatory—'who,' 'how,' 'what,' 'why,' 'where,' 'when.' I call the interrogatory the "**brush**" because with a single sweep you can help another person see the entire canvas. The second are verb-led questions—'do,' 'can,' 'should,' 'will,' 'may,' and so forth. I call this form, the "**scalpel**" because it is useful in delicate conceptual surgery. Because verb-led questions invite really only three possible answers—'yes,' 'no,' and 'maybe'—their range of discovery can be quite limited.

Brannan: What are the consequences of using one form of question or another?

Gresser: The important point is to understand the relationship of the **form** of the question to "need." An untrained player will often fall into the trap of beginning an interview with a verb-led question—"Are you pleased with our new product line?" How much discovery does this question invite? "Yes, we are." "No, we're not." Or equivocally, "Yes, we are, but not really, because ...."

An untrained player will see a **'no'** as a rejection or as a sign of failure. A 'maybe' will also be unsettling. As I said before, in the West we have been programmed from when we were very young to feel a need for resolution (agreement) and to fear uncertainty. There is much "irritable reaching," as Keats put it, after fact and reason. Therefore I recommend to beginners, open an encounter with the "**brush**," "What are the great challenges you face in your work? In your highest hopes where do you see your enterprise by the year 2020?" and so forth. I ask of my students no more than I ask of myself, to be wary of the impulse, the lunge for fact and certainty, which is embodied in the verb-led question.

Brannan: What are the uses of the "**scalpel**"?

Gresser: Microsurgery. "Is the dot on the butterfly's wing pale green?" "Will you marry me?"

But again, the "**scalpel**" is not for the faint-of-heart. "Will you marry me?" How many young men have spent years of precious budget, time and effort, financial reserves, and their most creative emotions on the horns of this 'maybe.' And I have seen over the years the same behavior with countless desperate foreign executives seeking a 'yes' from their elusive Japanese opponents.

Brannan: "Can you give an example of how to use the two kinds of questions in opening the discovery process in a business situation?"

Gresser: Selling is a common situation. In selling, your task is to help the prospective purchaser discover how the benefits incorporated into your mission can solve his (or her) pain. (The reader may want to review at this point the discussion of **mission and purpose**.) The first step I recommend is to take a "snapshot" in your mind of the discovery you want the other player to make. Here is how to do this:

- First find the pain.
- Next connect the pain to the benefits you bring.
- Finally wrap the benefits into an interrogatory question.

For example, suppose I am planning a workshop with some colleagues in London. Our target is the legal counsel of large European companies. We want to feature the applications of **The Five Rings** process in international negotiations and alternative dispute settlements. My associates in London tell me that European lawyers, like their American counterparts, are under terrific pressure to save money for their companies and to handle their overwhelming case load more effectively. Also, they are continuously harassed by senior managers, who generally are not lawyers, don't care about the subtleties of the law, and want "results."

Once we begin to understand the "**pain**" of the general counsel, the next step is to connect the pain to the greatest benefits we convey, either by our cause, our product, our service, our person, organization, and so forth.

In this case it occurs to me that these general counsel do not possess a skill-based system that will enable them to conserve budget and help them deal more effectively with their own senior management. By "system," I refer to a measurable way of instantly correcting errors or repeating successes and a process that helps us do this with ever-increasing skill.

If I were before one of these general counsel (the same text might also be adapted to advertising copy), I might begin as follows. Here is what the dialogue with the general counsel could look like:

Gresser:	"What are some of the toughest issues you are facing today in your job?"
Counsel:	"Tight budgets and pressure from senior management."
Gresser:	"What kind of headway are you making in settling cases more efficiently?"
Counsel:	"So-so. We do well with some, not so well with others."
Gresser:	"And with your top management."
Counsel:	"That's a continuing headache."
Gresser:	"A continuing headache ... how?" (Once a player expresses some pain, you need to follow up with a second interrogatory—in this case, **how.**)
Counsel:	"They don't understand. They expect everything yesterday."
Gresser:	"How much cost saving does your top management want over the next year?"
Counsel:	"At least 10 percent."
Gresser:	"Did I hear you say 10 percent?"
Counsel:	"Yes."
Gresser:	"What about 20 percent or 30 percent?"

Counsel: "They would be ecstatic, but it's impossible."

Gresser: "When you speak of cost saving, what are you specifically referring to?"

Counsel: "Pounds saved."

Gresser: "But what about time and creativity? How do you go about conserving these elements?"

Counsel: "We really don't pay much attention to them."

Gresser: "I see. In addition to saving money, how important might it be for you also to conserve time, so that you can focus your creativity on what is most important to you?"

Counsel: "It would be great, but how would you go about it?"

Gresser: "There is a way. We can come to that in a moment if you like. But let me ask you, if I may, what system do you have today to achieve significant additional levels of cost saving?"

Counsel: "I beg your pardon?"

Gresser: "What **system** do you possess today to achieve not only 10 percent, but possibly even 20 percent or 30 percent, in the areas we are discussing?"

         (NOTE: It is general good practice to stay close to the original question, without changing the language. If you change the language of the question, you will alter slightly the discovery. Just relax, hold integrity and observe.)

Counsel: "I guess we don't have a system" (the basic discovery).

Gresser: "We may be able to help you on this one.... When was the last 'win' you had with your senior management?"

Counsel: "What do you mean by 'win'?"

Gresser: "A time when you felt you negotiated effectively and came away having achieved your mission and feeling good and clean about yourself—a time you knew for sure you were doing a good job and being of service to your company and the world."

Counsel:	"I don't know. I don't remember."
Gresser:	"We have a way to help you if you are interested ...."
Counsel:	"I am interested. Show me." And so forth.
Gresser:	Now this is just an overview, but I wanted to give you the flavor.

Can you see? There is little telling, much asking, mainly using the "**brush**," trying to explore and to understand that general counsel's world, always asking oneself as we proceed: "How can I help? Where is his or her dilemma? Can I really fix it?"

Brannan:	Isn't **how** one asks a question as important as the substance of the question itself?
Gresser:	You are quite right. And that brings me to the subject of "**nurturing**." The greater our integrity, the more we are able to nourish ourselves and others. Generosity of spirit comes naturally to us. We feel abundant and our cup overflows. And yet, when dealing with others, sometimes it is necessary to have a touch of the coyote.

NURTURING

Brannan:	What do you mean?
Gresser:	It may be a perversity of human nature that most people feel better (okay) about themselves when another person is not quite okay, and slightly diminished (not okay) by the good fortune of others.
Brannan:	Oh, come on! That is a pretty cynical view of the world.
Gresser:	No, I don't think so. Someone hears that a friend in the same line of work has just obtained a great reward or benefit. How does that person feel? Wonderful, of course, at his friend's success. But in his voice, if you listen carefully, you can detect a note of sadness, even envy. The voice says, "Why not I? Am I not as good? Why should I not also enjoy such benefits?" Another person hears of her friend's misfortune. Her husband has run off with another woman. She meets her

friend and commiserates. Listen carefully. In her voice of consolation there is a note of glee! "Thank God it is not I," she tells herself. She feels relieved and a little better.

NOT-OKAY-ON-PURPOSE

Here's the point. In the practice of integrity, we generally want to make room for the other person to feel okay by becoming slightly not-quite-okay-on-purpose. This is particularly useful around pain. When a person is struggling with something painful, the process of discovery naturally shuts down. After all, most people have not been trained to "hold" steady, to be open and present to their pain. So your task is to create the container that will hold their pain, and often one element in the process is for you to be **not-okay**. It takes much containment to have the sense of humor to be **not-okay-on-purpose**.

Brannan: Sounds pretty manipulative and tricky to me.

Gresser: It can be. If **nurturing** comes solely out of tactics and is motivated simply to gain advantage, it degenerates into manipulation, and you will pay a heavy price in your integrity for playing the coyote.

But when **nurturing** comes out of abundance and a recognition that we must allow and build an opening for discovery, then it has a solid base and it can be grounded in integrity. I believe there are both Western and Eastern archetypes and stories that reinforce what I am saying. Odysseus, the most crafty and resourceful of all men, was also a man of noble character. Abraham Lincoln, a man of seemingly inexhaustible compassion, was also sly and crafty as a fox. Both Odysseus and Abraham Lincoln deeply understood human frailty.

I should also like to point out the clear relationship between **not-okay-on-purpose** and managing **need**. Most people need to be okay, need to feel better than their fellows, so it is quite a good exercise to practice becoming comfortable with just being wrong, not okay, or looking silly and uninformed. Try it. It is not easy. I am not saying make me your fool, but simply that it often is useful to adopt what the martial arts schools refer to as the "low stance."

For those who feel uncomfortable with the idea of purposely adopting a pose of being not-okay, a little story may be helpful. It suggests the relationship of nurturing to empathy.

> It is said that after the death of the great master Hakuin, a visitor approached a blind man who was sitting before the temple where the master used to teach. 'Tell me about Hakuin," the visitor asked the blind man.
>
> "He was a very special person," the blind man began, adjusting his position on his begging mat. When most people hear about the misfortune of a friend, I can detect in their voice, along with the sorrow, a note of happiness. And when they learn of the good fortune of another, I can hear sadness behind their happiness. It was never so with Hakuin. When he heard of another's misfortune, you could hear in his voice only sadness and when he learned of another's good fortune I can remember only happiness. There was no distance.

As our integrity increases, the "distance" between ourselves and the other closes, until like Hakuin there is no distance at all, and tactics are no longer necessary. In the meantime it is good practice to do what we can to put the other person at ease in order to facilitate discovery.

Brannan: You have been describing situations where we ask the questions. Suppose our opponent starts to ask us questions? How do we respond?

Gresser: The key point to remember is that you can always say 'no.' You don't have to give out a scintilla of information more than you wish to. This brings me to the subject of the "**parry**" and "**reverse**."

PARRY AND REVERSE

Think of the "**parry**" as a **connector**, *i.e.,* "and..." "I'm not sure." "I understand." "Good idea." "Good question." "Hmm..." "Well, let me see." "I want to ... what you are saying." Or sometimes simply pure silence. The **connector** cuts in both directions. It parries your opponent's questions and it also helps draw out a party who is beginning to divulge information.

The **reverse** simply repeats a question with a question. Crudely performed, it will be obvious that you are holding back information. Expertly executed, interposing a **parry** before the **reverse**, and then struggling, which is a form of being **not-okay-on-purpose,** will make the **reverse** become invisible! The more the tactic flows out of a sense of presence and timing, the more powerful it is, and the less you or the other party will sense it as being manipulative.

Brannan: How about an example from your practice?

Gresser: Here is a case, again from my experience in Japanese negotiations. The Japanese team arrives with a long and detailed list of technical questions, obviously prepared with great care and thought. Suppose I run a small company which manufactures electroencephalogram equipment. The scene is in my Topeka, Kansas office. We are in **Ring 3**—positioning and negotiating the presentation. The dialogue might proceed something like this.

Gresser: "Mr. Honda, I want to commend you for the amount of time you and your staff have devoted to preparing these excellent questions."

Mr. Honda: "Thank you very much, Mr. Gresser. It's a pleasure to meet you."

Gresser: "How can I be of service to you?"

Mr. Honda: "Well, we have only a few questions. May I begin?"

Gresser: "Yes, please do."

Mr. Honda: "Let me see. We do not quite understand why you are using analog circuits to detect the alpha beta brain waves."

Gresser:	"Excellent question, Mr. Honda. But frankly I'm really not qualified to be of much help on this one, as I am not an engineer myself. Let me ask Mr. Hartzell, who is here with me." (Mr. Hartzell has gone through extensive training, and will help me in this negotiation as a blocker.)
Mr. Hartzell:	"Yes, this is a very good point, Mr. Honda, but it's a complicated question. Let me see. I'm not sure in what respect you're speaking."
Mr. Honda:	"We're particularly interested in how you track and set amplitudes and frequencies."
Mr. Hartzell:	"Interesting (resisting the impulse to spill). In order for me to be of best use to you, let me understand ... how could this be helpful to you and your company? (Note the interrogatory coupled with **nurturing**.) Perhaps I can be more specific. What problem are your engineers struggling with that we might help you address?"
Mr. Honda:	"Hmm (somewhat puzzled). I'm not sure (a 'maybe')."
Mr. Hartzell:	(Pure silence. Resists the need to fill up the space.)
Mr. Honda:	(Returning to the battle) "Well, we are having some difficulty with lag. During EEG measurements with digital circuits ..."
Mr. Hartzell:	"Lag. How interesting. What seems to be the problem?"
	And so forth.
Gresser:	Who did most of the telling in this negotiation? Who asked most of the questions? Who spilled information? Who held integrity? You will find that the laundry list/fishing expedition style of negotiation can backfire. In fact it is a great liability, because the skillful negotiator who knows how to ask questions and to listen will quickly go upstream to the hidden intention. All you have to do is remain loose, not be afraid to say 'no,' and stay focused on your mission. It's all play once you have the hang of it.

Brannan: Yes, but to develop this sense of fun and play requires, as you say, real steadiness and an ability to stay awake. Are there any moves that build steadiness and alertness right in the thick of things?

Gresser: One useful technique is the "**Pendulum**." See Illustration 3. The question is this: Where should you "position" yourself, emotionally, when another player (your "opponent") starts to discover and become enthusiastic or excited over what you are saying? This is the first question.

THE
PENDULUM

THE PENDULUM

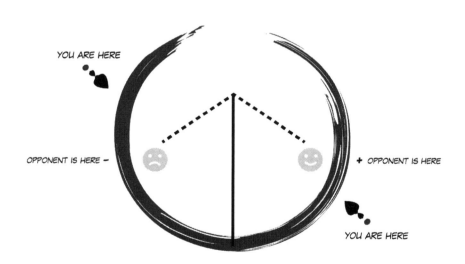

The Pendulum

The chart indicates where, ideally you should position yourself on the pendulum: When your opponents become excited you can also become enthusiastic, but not as excited as they. When your opponents have doubts, hesitate or become negative, you must acknowledge their concerns and point out that what you are proposing may not be suitable for them.

Illustration 3

The second is, where should you optimally be placed when the emotional **Pendulum** swings the other way, and your opponent begins to doubt, objects or becomes outright negative?

Brannan: I don't have a clue.

Gresser: Well, where do you suppose?

Brannan: I imagine you share your opponents' excitement when they are positive and try to persuade them of the merits of your cause when they are unconvinced.

Gresser: That has not been my experience.

There is a natural tendency, when someone starts to assent, particularly if he (or she) becomes enthusiastic about our proposal, for us also to become excited. Their enthusiasm is infectious, the creative imagination gets to work, and a hundred swirling expectations immediately issue forth. If we do not watch out, soon we are stepping ahead of ourselves. But it is an unstable branch, for just when we start to feel giddy, our opponent will back off, sensing that something must be wrong if we are that excited.

It is fine to rejoice along with another's discoveries, but our focus should be upon building the container that will hold their and our emotions. The optimal "place," in my experience, is to be positive and curious when our opponent is positive, but not quite as positive as he or she. This is what I call the "**Positive Pendulum**." Being "neutral," uninterested or detached, however, will only deflate another player unnecessarily.

THE POSITIVE PENDULUM

THE NEGATIVE PENDULUM

The **Negative Pendulum** works in reverse. When things turn dark or negative, our need and impulsiveness will cause us to push back and try to convince other player to change his (her) mind. A sensitive opponent will become even more disaffected and thereby set up a negative spiral: We become needy, our opponent becomes even more rejecting, we begin to panic, and so forth. Your best shot is not to push back at all—simply get out of the way.

"I don't buy what you're saying," says your opponent. "I'm not sure I'd buy it either," you say. Whoosh! No one's at home! Only empty space. What can the other player do? In most cases out of sheer confusion at such a bizarre response, your opponent will move back toward the positive pole.

And you know, this may be the "right" move, the effective move from the perspective of integrity because you will have signaled that you are a person who respects a **'no'** and has a sense of fun, who is patient when things don't go your way, no matter what direction the **Pendulum** swings. That is the kind of person you yourself will want to be associated with.

Brannan: What if the **Pendulum** rests in the doldrums, at dead center?

Gresser: Then you probably must churn the emotions to get the energy moving. Take some contrary and unexpected action. There is nothing like breaking the tedium of convention to stir the pot. As a negotiator I would rather have consciousness in chaos than inertia or unresponsive idleness.

Brannan: Any other tactics you can recommend?

Gresser: Next comes the "**checkpoint**." Up till now we have been discussing techniques that facilitate discovery. The **checkpoint** and taking notes both facilitate and confirm discovery.

CHECKPOINT

Most people have an agenda, some critical bit of information they hold back, either consciously or unconsciously. Japanese culture, and to a lesser extent other countries of East Asia, place a premium on what is unstated, uncertain, concealed, unexpressed, and silent. Whereas each player has a right to volunteer only as much or as little information as he or she wishes, it may be important for us, in the interest of avoiding making invalid assumptions, to test the discoveries we have made. This is the function of the "**checkpoint**." The **checkpoint** simply repeats back in the language of the other player what you have heard—repeats it back at least three times.

Brannan: What's so special about the number **3**?

Gresser: Our system is filled with magical numbers: **The Five Rings**, the **Five Core Values** (5 being a "power" word, *i.e.*, the first five books of the Bible [Pentateuch] the Pentacost, the Pentagon, etc.), the 4 eyes of integrity—3-in-1— which suggests the divine trinity in unity, and the balance of opposites, 2-on-2. There is also a famous line in Goethe's *Faust*, 'The devil knocks thrice!" Less mysteriously, 3 seems sufficient to help get us through the first layers of delusion.

Brannan: Why use the **checkpoint** in the first place?

Gresser: Because you want to verify that what you are hearing is in fact what is being said. If you fail to do this and merrily proceed on your way, you may be greatly surprised when your opponent challenges you later. "That's not what I said. That's not what I meant at all."

Brannan: How about an example.

Gresser: A person agrees to invest in your company on what appear good terms for everyone. "Bill," you say, "I'm delighted at the prospect of your becoming an investor, but I just want to make sure this deal is really for you." (**checkpoint 1**)

"Yes, Julian," he says, "I'm excited about working together." "Great," you say. "We're most happy that you feel comfortable with the terms." (**checkpoint 2**)

"Perfectly," he says. "We had a few differences, but I think this arrangement will work for everyone." "Excellent," you say. "I just wanted to confirm that you felt the way we do." (**checkpoint 3**)

The next day perhaps you check once again, "We're very pleased to be working together. In fact, there are some new opportunities, X, Y and Z, that could be very promising." (**checkpoint 4**)

"That's great," says the investor. "I have some ideas I also wanted to discuss with you."

The untrained and needy player will skip over the **checkpoint**. He will be afraid that the investor will renege and the investor, sensing the need, will begin unconsciously to have buyer's remorse. If you are not afraid of **'no'** and you respect the other player, you will extend the courtesy of the **checkpoint**. My experience suggests that this simple move can bring you closer.

In some cultures, like Japan, you must repeat the **checkpoint** more than three times, sometimes five and six, even ten times, to get to the real feelings and to the real intention. (In Japanese, the unstated, deeper sentiment is translated, *honne*, which means literally "basic sound.")

There are many famous stories illustrating how a failure to use the **checkpoint**, along with poor translation, has created ludicrous misunderstandings in U.S. Japanese relations. One case involved the meeting between President Nixon and Prime Minister Sato during negotiations to open Japan's textile market. After hearing President Nixon's urgent request, Prime Minister Sato concluded the meeting with the promise of *"zensho shimasu."* President Nixon's translator rendered this phrase, "We will do our best," whereupon Nixon returned triumphant. "Japanese concede!" the American headlines puffed. But everyone in Japan understood that *zensho shimasu* means something like, "Well, we'll do our best, but we're very sorry that most likely things won't work. Very sorry that we can't help you out."

A rudimentary use of the **checkpoint** would have fleshed out this basic difference in perspectives.

Brannan: **Note-taking** seems such an innocuous thing. I'm not sure I see why you call it a "tactic."

Gresser: Ah, there is **note-taking**, and then there is **note-taking**! **Note-taking** has several generally underestimated uses. First, it helps us focus. **note-taking** demands that we listen carefully. The manual act of coordinating eye, hand and ear forces concentration.

Second, we create a record. But this is not an ordinary record. It is a record generated from the eyes of system. "Is this player arrogant?" "How quickly does he reveal emotions?" "How 'trainable' is she?" "What curious things are happening in the ecology of this situation?" Questions such as these contain all the clues, and without **note-taking** it is hard to recall the nuances.

Finally, **note-taking** prepares the counter-move. Do you remember? **Action-response-countermove**. Your opponent's reaction to your initiating action will create the opening. Your notes, common sense, and your intuition will guide you to the best next move.

The question now is, in this play and counter-play, where is the mind? Where should the mind be at the point of combat?

Brannan: Combat?

Gresser: Yes, combat. Each point in a negotiation is combat. First and foremost, combat with ourselves—combat with our vanity, our conceits, fears and lethargy, combat **with** routine and mediocrity. To this also add combat with the blindness, ignorance, or viciousness of our opponents.

Tod, where should the mind be?

Brannan: I don't know.

Gresser: Empty mind, open heart (in Japanese and Chinese the character for "mind" and "heart," *shin,* is the same.) A blank slate. Your opponent moves, the move is written down upon the slate. Your opponent speaks, the words are inscribed. An impression, perhaps an idea, comes up, you take note. "What is this?" Nothing else. Quietly you observe, you watch the play.

The Pure Self watches the self. You sense the right moment and you act. When the full conceptual understanding takes form and aligns itself with reason, it is already too late! Here is an example of how far ahead of conceptual understanding is the heart/mind if not obstructed by the ego.

I participated yesterday in a panel in Dallas, Texas, on the theme of negotiating in Asia. We were running late when we began and the head of the conference asked the chairman of our panel to shorten the presentations so that the audience could have time for questions. But the chairman felt he had come a long way and was not about to be restricted, so he spoke for 40-45 minutes, the other two participants went on for about 20-25 minutes each, and when it came time for me to speak, I had barely 15 minutes left. Even then there was no time for questions from the audience.

I saw clearly the challenge before me, *i.e.,* not to fall into need, to stay present and not to rush my presentation, to focus on what was really essential. I knew this in my head, but as I began to speak I could feel myself speeding up. My mouth and mind were racing and my body was left far behind. I woke up fifteen minutes later, after my mouth, out of sheer exhaustion, had come to a standstill. I was completely disgusted with myself, not because of missing equal time to speak, but because I missed a far more interesting opening.

What I should have done was this. I should have strode into the audience and used the limitation of time as a golden opportunity to focus the audience's attention upon this critical issue in a negotiation: how to turn limitations of time to advantage. I should have asked my listeners what **system** they possessed to seize the initiative in their Japanese or Chinese negotiations when they believed—or were meant to believe—they were out of time (a discovery question). I should have asked each person, as I stood before the conference tables, how he or she stays present when the pressure's on. I should have asked why we westerners feel so compelled to fill things up, to tell instead of ask, to preach instead of learn. And by my questions I would have helped them see, each one, how convention and routine deaden our reflexes into mediocrity. (Each person on the panel, I am sad to say, behaved in this same routinized, competitive way, grasping for attention and positioning for advantage.) I could have done all of this in less than five minutes—there was more than time enough! And then, suddenly, I should have sat down and let the silence settle. In so small a time two-hundred legal professionals from all over the world would have had a sense of the lightning flash that words can never convey.

Let us turn now to the last of the discovery tools. I refer to **PIPs, Player Integrity Profiles**.

Brannan: Yes, that's a very interesting subject. Let's deal with that.

Gresser: If character is really the determinant of our destiny, as the Greeks and Chinese have written, what are some of the essential elements by which this source code of action is governed? For if we can uncover the core, we will be able to trace a hundred other qualities that constellate about it. Is there a way to predict how another's foibles will play upon our weaknesses, how another's strengths will enhance our own? How can we use this knowledge for reconnaissance in following the path of **The Five Rings**?

PLAYER
INTEGRITY
PROFILES
(PIPs)

PIPs (Player Integrity Profiles) affords a first glimpse into character by identifying the most essential elements from the perspective of integrity. The great Chinese military strategist, Sun Tzu, wrote twenty-three hundred years ago, "Know yourself and know your enemy, and you cannot be defeated in a hundred battles. Know yourself but fail to know your enemy, and you will win half the time, and lose the other half. Do not know yourself and fail to know your enemy, and you will lose every battle." **PIPs** is a modern adaptation of Sun Tzu's basic precept of military strategy.

Here are the essentials of **PIPs**. See Illustration 4. The first is the element of **matching/ mismatching.** In essence, does the player walk the talk? Does he act as he claims? By observing carefully you will know whether this person is authentic. Is someone behind the mask? Or do we have a priest who takes advantage of his flock, a lawyer who bilks his (her) clients, an expert on fitness who smokes or is obese?

PLAYER INTEGRITY PROFILE (PIPS)

Critical Factors	Low	Moderate	High
Matching (No Mismatching)			
Containment			
Trainability			
No Need, Non-Attachment			
The Pain/Need Ratio			
No Assumptions			
No Expectations			
Embraces "No"			
Controls Arrogance, Vanity & Greed			
Sense of Ease/Time to Spare			
Listens			
Ability to Attend			
Focus			
Nurtures			
Gravitas			
Thoroughly Awake & Present			
Sees the World As It Is			
PIPS Total Score			

Illustration 4

Whenever you find a mismatch, in a deep sense, you find a flaw in integrity. In **PIPs** we assess this factor of matching/mismatching, as we do all other elements—low, moderate or high.

The second element is **containment.** One can think of integrity as a living "container," which is character. By working on character we can build the container. We can learn to "hold integrity" against the assaults of life.

If the container is constricted there is no breath, no life. If the container is too porous, it will hold very little. There can be no integrity. Some people live solitary and shut-up lives, shuttling back and forth like crayfish between dark recesses. Others leak like sieves, pouring out their feelings, needs and opinions to anyone who will listen. Both have serious problems with containment.

Trainability is the third element. Does this person embrace error and failure, reach for challenges, adjust nimbly and intelligently? Can she be like water, adapting willingly to the environment? Or is the fear of failure so strong, the self-sabotaging behaviors so entrenched, the character so brittle, that easy change is rarely possible?

No need/No attachment is the fourth element. There is a saying, "The great way is easy. No picking, no choosing." The superior person, the person of integrity, will have few real needs. You will see little clawing for advantage.

The pain/need ratio is the fifth element. Here is an essential clue. How well can this person hold on to integrity before the Face of Pain, or does a little pain bring on a great panic? Persons of high integrity understand how to hold steady (high pain/need ratio) and will find their power within their pain.

No assumptions/no expectations is the sixth. We have already reviewed this principle at length. Find a penchant toward assumption and expectation and you will find a weakness that will breed ten other flaws.

Embraces the 'no' is the seventh. Is this person terrified of 'no,' needs to be right, or unwilling to appear silly or foolish? These qualities flock together.

The eighth element is **arrogance, vanity, and greed**. There can be little integrity when these qualities dominate, because everything will be inflated, inverted and distorted.

A sense of ease and time to spare is the ninth test. Those who need to grasp or become servants of their desires and expectations have little time to spare. They will never be at peace.

If they are ill at ease and have no time, how well will they listen, how easily will they attend?

The abilities **to listen well** and **to attend** are the tenth and eleventh elements. They do not always align with a sense of ease and time to spare, but usually they do. It is said, "When the universe roars only the heavenly dragon observes with calm delight." The person of high integrity—the dragon—listens and observes when the rest of the world is steaming.

The twelfth test is **focus**. This quality does not always track with others. A player can have a focus of steel and score poorly in all the other qualities. A person of high integrity, however, who is fully present in the moment, can usually bring extraordinary powers of concentration to any issue at hand.

Nurturing is the next test. When you meet this person do you feel enriched and affirmed in her presence, or does she make you feel more lonely?

Gravitas is the fourteenth variable. *Gravitas* refers to a sense of weightedness—the whole person is before you. Here he is! Right here. Half of him is not musing somewhere in the past, the other half not distracted by the future. *Gravitas* transforms a person's creative potential into action. Some people have good ideas but can't embody them because they lack *gravitas*. But when you are grounded and connected, you will have the courage to take risks.

Thoroughly awake and present is the fifteenth quality. When you are with this person do you have a sense that someone is at home? I have mentioned Zuigan's test. All of us to one extent or another are living in a dream. The question is how often do we wake up and realize it?

The final test of **PIPs** is: does this person **see the world** objectively, **just as it is,** modestly and without a lot of ego clutter and noise? It is a formidable test because we all view the world in our own unique way, imperfectly.

Brannan: PIPs sounds like a very powerful tool. It would be helpful to give a few examples of its uses.

Gresser: Okay. Suppose you were considering entering into a business partnership with someone. You run a brief character sketch under **PIPs** based on your observations of how this person conducted himself with you and other people and you come up with the following profile.

- **Matching/mismatching**. Does your prospective partner walk his talk? In some ways well, but in other ways poorly. He says he has a code of action, but often he doesn't follow it.

- **Containment**. He is disciplined about not spilling information, but at the same time he is a terrible braggart and a name-dropper.

- **Pain/need**. He is a trained fighter and holds together well when in pain.

- **No assumptions/no expectations.** Basically, you conclude he is a predator. He has a perverse tendency to assume, then presume upon, and finally to consume others.

- **Embraces the 'no.'** He is focused, disciplined, cunning, and persistent. You find he is quite able to give a 'no,' but you also detect a note of condescension, even irritation in his voice whenever he gets a 'no,' with the suggestion that he believes the other party is an idiot for not agreeing with him.

- **Arrogance, vanity and greed.** He is arrogant and vain, and you discover that behind the mask there is a consuming piggish appetite for control and power.

- **Focus.** He has advanced powers of concentration and focus, and an almost elephantine memory.
- *Gravitas.* There is no one behind the voice. Deep down you sense he is a shallow, hollow man.
- **Thoroughly awake and present.** He is on another planet.
- **Sees the world as it Is.** He sees through a glass eye darkly.

Reflecting upon these qualities, the first question PIPs would naturally urge you to ask yourself is: "Why would you ever want to be in business with such a person?" 'Well," you might reply, "he has certain virtues. For example, he is energetic, resourceful, and imaginative. He is a street fighter, which complements my own talents and offsets my shortcomings." On an impulse you might want to enter into this partnership, but **PIPs** would give you pause. If on balance you were to decide to move forward with the partnership despite your reservations, **PIPs** would focus your attention on other important questions. For example, would this person stand by you during the rough and uncertain times when you might really value a strong partner? Would this person deal with the firm's clients generously or in a grasping manner? And so forth.

PIPs would require you to check yourself: "Given this profile, how might this person play upon—even exploit—my weaknesses?" For example, if in drawing your own PIPs profile you conclude you have issues around *gravitas* and **steadiness,** or become particularly disoriented and unfocused around the **pain/ need threshold,** you would want to be extremely careful with this person in high-stress situations, and never look to your partner for nourishment or affirmation. Conversely, **PIPs** would help you better understand how your special strengths— for example, your capacity to listen, presence and trainability—will help you spot the subtle signs and signals of a change of intention that enable you to adjust quickly to his moods as necessary.

By analyzing your opponents and examining yourself with **PIPs,** you will have a powerful tool to take intelligent action **in advance** in all sorts of other situations as well. **PIPs** will help you identify precisely the actions and behaviors that are telltale, and those areas of your own vulnerability that require reinforcement. For example, if you know someone to be devious or a bully, who makes you feel inadequate or frightened, (*i.e.,* loss of *gravitas,* **need, a sense of helplessness** and catastrophe), you can prepare yourself. You can rehearse the script, you can bring someone else along, or you can send a blocker in your place. There are many things you can do to anticipate such situations.

Brannan: It seems to me it is quite difficult to be able to predict accurately our future moods and emotional states which, after all, are sudden and transitory and often bear no direct relationship to the outer world.

Gresser: Yes, I agree. I have noted that things can be going very well in the external world, but then, all of a sudden, we are in a mood, and internally everything is quite dark and melancholy. I would like to return to this subject a bit later when we discuss how to practice.

Brannan: How about situations we don't anticipate?

Gresser: Yes, often these are the most interesting cases, when life suddenly throws us a spinner—for example, a person reveals his or her real character and catches us off guard. **PIPs** will help us see into the character of such situations and guide our response.

I remember some years ago I was conducting a training program on negotiation at a large semiconductor company here in California. After the program, the VP for marketing who headed the group thought it would be cute to

INTEGRITY CORRUPTED

ignore our bills and not answer our phone calls (see PIPs, principles of **matching/ mismatching; arrogance, vanity, greed; failure to nurture** or **to see the world as it is).** Amused by this peculiar development, I waited patiently to see what would happen, remembering Emerson's observation, "The thief (under the law of compensation) steals from himself." Sometimes **PIPs** helps us see that the "right" (simplest and most elegant) move is to do nothing at all. Weeks passed, then months. One day I learned the VP had been fired. He did not attend to the flaws in his character early, and so they surfaced later and in a more corruptive, self-destructive form. I resubmitted my bill to the president of the company and was promptly paid.

Brannan: What about strengths? Can **PIPs** help guide the choice of a partner so that one person's strengths nourish and reinforce another's?

Gresser: Certainly. The best alliances are symbiotic. I know of several partnerships where one person's modesty, containment and steadiness under pressure have provided *gravitas* to the other whose creative energies, buoyed up by a revived sense of trust, have begun to soar. **PIPs** has made both parties more conscious of their individual strengths for their mutual advantage.

Brannan: Let us turn now to *lōgōs*, the final essential skill for a player practicing **The Five Rings**.

Gresser: Okay. But first I'd like to explain a bit about the relationship of *lōgōs* to intuition and reverie.

Brannan: Please do.

Gresser: When we first came up with *lōgōs* for the corporate name, we were only generally familiar with its historical significance. To the Greeks, *lōgōs*, or the word (reason), was the ordering principle of the universe, comparable to the Tao for the Chinese. To live in harmony with *lōgōs* was the goal of all seekers of wisdom. Later in the Gospel of John, *lōgōs* is transformed into the divine word

LŌGŌS

that exists with God and is uniquely embodied in Jesus Christ.

We define *lōgōs* more simply. It is logic, common sense, and intelligence, combined with intuition in action. Thus defined, *lōgōs* is virtually identical with the Chinese conception of integrity (*te*).

Brannan: How is *lōgōs* used in practice?

Gresser: I'll tell you a story of how I once used *lōgōs* in reconnaissance, and after that give one example of how *lōgōs* can help us identify the next best move.

Three years ago I had a legal client who was a very rich man, a visionary, and also a small-time tycoon. He had an ambitious project to develop the San Francisco Bay. How he promised me the world! Opera tickets appeared in the mail, and there were invitations to exclusive dinner parties.

Common sense should have told me to be circumspect, to investigate, to get a better hold on this man and his promises. But I was so enchanted with what he told me—his vision had become my vision—that I didn't pay much attention to what logic urged or my common sense advised.

CREATIVE REVERIE

Somewhere along the way I began to feel uneasy, and I decided to ask my integrity. I should elaborate on this phrase, "ask my integrity," since it involves a bit of technique. The first thing I did was to get fully present within myself. I relaxed, let go, became conscious of the ebb and flow of my breath tides. I allowed whatever thoughts or feelings or images waited below the surface of consciousness to approach. When I began to experience a floating feeling—as if I were just watching a play from the balcony (this state of consciousness is called "creative reverie")—I said to myself, 'What should I know about this person that I may be overlooking?"

Minutes passed, and I continued to relax, just to let go. I was in the zone of nothing special. Suddenly an image appeared, as if from nowhere. A mouth! A fine mouth it was, possessed of white, polished teeth.

"This is rather peculiar," I thought. (I was now leaving reverie.) "What is a mouth with white polished teeth?" So I began to examine the image more closely.

I began with the mouth. It was a large, gaping mouth. A mouth, it occurred to me, is the beginning of the digestive process—something like the First Circle in Dante's *Inferno*. Then I said to myself, "What are teeth?" Well, teeth are the tools of the digestive process, by which we chew up food. I was beginning to have an unsettled feeling in my stomach, but I proceeded.

"What is white?" I asked myself. "Dignified, polished, sophisticated—how interesting!"

So I bundled these associations together and then I said to myself, "My Lord, what can all this mean? What conceivable link can there be to my original question?" And then suddenly, from nowhere, the idea came to me. "The Man is a Polished Carnivore!!" A polished carnivore? Can this be? Let me investigate.

Remember, we do not assume, we only observe when something singular comes up. So that's what I did. I started to pay more attention to his moods and to our interactions, and soon I began to notice all sorts of things that probably were there all along, but I did not see them before—implicitly obvious, I would say—little (in)significant things: the intrusive phone calls, the demands that I put aside important work to accommodate his schedule—like the time he showed up and snatched a half-completed letter out of my secretary's typewriter. Soon I saw a different face behind the mask—an arrogant, grinning, entitled face of a person who, on a whim, would toss aside his promises, dishonor a bill, or betray me. I knew this part of him perhaps better than he knew it himself. And so two to three weeks before he suspended the project and began to quibble about his bill, I was prepared, and so was my firm.

Brannan: Interesting. What lessons do you draw from this case?

Gresser: The key lesson is that we have enormous untapped capabilities and powers that we do not know how to use; and that by a disciplined procedure we can bring logic, common sense and intelligence to bear on important issues, and join these with our intuitive powers when taking practical action. Our integrity is what opens the channel, the connection between conscious and unconscious processes. We receive continuous information and advice from sources that are a part of us, but of which we have only been vaguely aware. Each situation calls forth its own imagery. But we do not follow these instructions blindly. (In this case, it was the image of a mouth.) We return to our intelligence and common sense, always testing, observing like a scientist. And when our intellect does not give us a completely satisfactory answer, we feel our way through. We listen to our bodies and ask, "Does this seem right or not?" and our body will answer.

Brannan: How does this process apply to identifying the "best next move"?

Gresser: Let us return to **The Five Rings**. To find the best next move all you need to do in any encounter is follow this simple procedure. First examine how well you have performed each of the moves in the circle in which you now stand. Have you jumped the sequence of rings or jumped a move? What errors have you committed? If you conclude you have done reasonably well, ask yourself this question: "How can I do even better next time?" This is the analytic function.

If you have played well, celebrate your wins and remember to take the joy and the benefits and to pass them onward, selflessly, without thought of recognition or recompense. This is called **"paying forward."** It is the most powerful technique I know to dispel feelings of helplessness and despair and to enhance self image, clarity and power.

After you have centered yourself in this way, to find the best next move, you need only ask yourself this next question: "Given what I have learned in this situation, what move will best advance my mission and build integrity?" If your analytic mind blocks you, you may decide to bypass it by checking into reverie and repeating the question. An answer, or many answers, will appear if you are patient. They must appear, because you are reconnected, and every answer so conceived will be the "right" one.

Brannan: You know, this issue of "best moves" raises for me a final and perhaps odd question. Suppose your opponents read this book and use the same principles against you and your clients? As a professional person, aren't you a bit concerned about giving your secrets away?

Gresser: It's in my interest that they learn these secrets. What do you mean "against"? In this situation there's no "against"! How am I diminished if my opponents become more effective by enhancing their integrity—if they become clearer about what they want, build missions of service, are not attached or needy, exercise self-control, focus on my pain, and are at ease and adaptable to change? Their "best" move will most likely turn out to be quite "good" for me. If even one player plays this game, you start to enter a realm of magic. Look at the Getz case. With only one set of the parties (ourselves) consciously playing in this way, we produced a landmark result extraordinarily profitable for everyone—the owners, the investing public, the managers, the employees, underwriters, even the Japanese and U.S. governments. We never gave a thought once to trying to reach a "win-win" result. And that was very early in the development of my thinking about these matters. Can you imagine if everyone starts to play the game this way?! Then you will see lightning decisions springing from foresight and wisdom; good humor and sport and surprise everywhere; some sparks, to be sure, but little clawing for personal aggrandizement or advantage, for it will be a roughhouse and creative combat of dragons!

IV

HOW TO PRACTICE

Where shall I take the hit?
What must be sacrificed
and to which gods?
—The Artful Navigator

Just do the important thing that is right before you.
—The Artful Navigator

Too broad? Narrow it. Too vague? Clarify it. Too general?
Be more specific. Too abstract? Be more concrete. Too dense?
Simplify it. If lost in the forest, move toward the sky. If too near
the sun, reduce elevation, return to the earth.
—The Artful Navigator

Modesty. Do simple work. Some of the great martial artists
were clerks in a hotel. We do our work in the world without
much interest in glory. Our ideal is to live inconspicuously in
the town among the people.
—The Artful Navigator

Take the world lightly, and your spirit will not be burdened.
Consider everything minor and your mind will not be
confused. Regard death and life as equal and your heart will
not be afraid.
—Masters of Huainan

Brannan: Julian, you have explained the theoretical foundation for our work, and have outlined the framework of play, **The Five Rings**, and the core skills. But, as we all know, someone can read a book, listen to a tape, go to a seminar, gain a conceptual understanding, and not be able to do very much of anything. The gap between theory and practice is too great. The key is training. What are some of your recommendations as to how a person who is interested in dedicating him or herself to this material can go about attaining real skill?

Gresser: A great Chinese general, Wang Yang Ming, whose profession compelled him to be practical, once observed, "Knowledge without action is not knowledge at all." We study this material by doing it. There are no shortcuts. And the key to mastery is what the Japanese call *kaizen*—continuous improvement at the margin. **The Five Ring** system is the *kaizen* of action.

Brannan: What is the first step?

Gresser: Tracking. Tracking is the first step. To be a great negotiator one must become a great observer and like Cassius see quite through the deeds of men. We can make a science of our daily life. Watch. Here's how.

The first thing I recommend is to keep a **Weekly Log.** See Illustration 5. In form the log is simple. In my design, at the top is the overall weekly mission. Below are the four quadrants of life: professional, personal, physical and spiritual. Underneath is space to record discoveries relating to the overall weekly mission or to more specific goals in each quadrant. There is also space to enter insights and discoveries relating to the missions or, more generally, discoveries that simply open us to joy, wonder and magic. The box on the right provides space to enter instances of **paying forward.**

THE WEEKLY LOG

Brannan: Why did you choose a week instead of a day or a month?

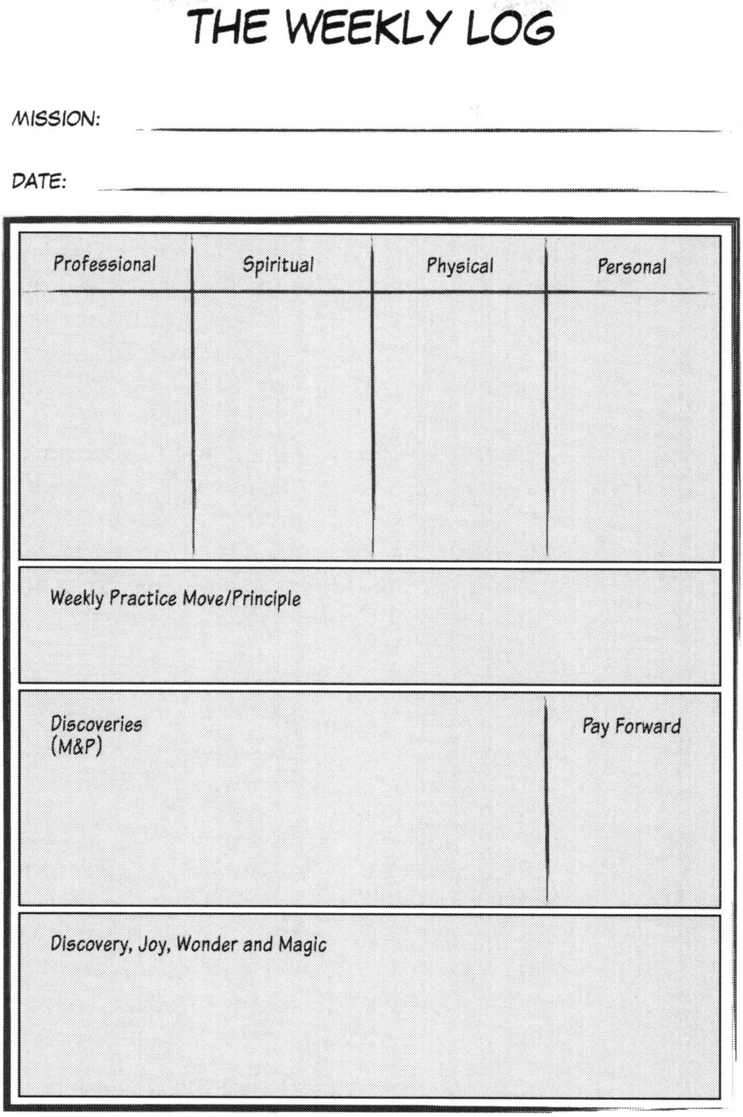

THE WEEKLY LOG

MISSION: _____

DATE: _____

Professional	Spiritual	Physical	Personal

Weekly Practice Move/Principle

Discoveries (M&P)	Pay Forward

Discovery, Joy, Wonder and Magic

Illustration 5

Gresser:　　　Let me make clear the purposes of the **Weekly Log.** The first purpose is to restore coherence. We live lives divided from ourselves. Most people's professional lives are divorced from their spiritual aspirations. Their work pulls against— if not tears apart—their family life. Their physical mission, if there is any, is an afterthought.

The first purpose, then, of the **Weekly Log** is to restore integrity.

The second purpose of the **Weekly Log** is discovery. I have found that every move, every step in a negotiation is a point of discovery—about ourselves and the other players. I have also found there are patterns in the stream of discoveries and images in our life, and this stream runs just below the surface of consciousness, implicit yet obvious, when you train the eye to see it. The **Weekly Log** is designed as a camera to open the eye and to take snapshots of these discoveries.

A third objective is to focus the powers of concentration on a single weakness or strength. We can make far greater progress if we pick one skill or one principle of behavior and concentrate all our energies there, for a space of time, rather than hop like a bird each day to a different flower.

To achieve these three purposes, the **Weekly Log** is optimal—a day is far too short, a month impractically long. After all, who has the patience to concentrate on one thing for a month?

Brannan: I would like to get quickly into the substance of how one actually practices with a **Weekly Log**, but I can't help anticipating that the idea of writing down your "magic" in a box on a **Weekly Log** may simply send shivers up the spine of some artistic and creative people. Aren't you tampering here with something almost sacred?

Gresser: You raise, you realize, the magician's dilemma. There are many conjurers in this world—some of surpassing talent—who can draw out of the mists the most fantastic forms. But can they finish the task? Do they know how to let go, to launch their creation? When air, water, fire and earth meet that is where you must take your stand. Here is where magicians, conjurers and tricksters run aground and often are consumed by their own powers. Great courage and fortitude—integrity—is demanded at this point to resist being pushed around by the elements and to take the action of bringing your creation into the world.

It is the common illusion of some people that order and creativity are incompatible. I know a wonderful woman, a philanthropist, who has supported many worthy causes. Some weeks ago, as we discussed my methods over lunch, she said to me with a wave of her hand, "I don't believe in logic." Can you imagine? Creativity for her is pure mystery that simply flies in through the window.

And yet, when you study the lives of the great creative geniuses—Michelangelo, Picasso, Mozart, Bach, Beethoven, Dickens—and not only men and women artists, writers, and composers, but also scientists and discoverers—you will find that most of them had an explicit method—no, I will go further—they all had a **system**. This is the point Peter Ackroyd makes in his monumental study of Dickens, and it is echoed in Arthur Koestler's classic study of creativity, and by researchers such as Robert Root-Bernstein and Howard Gardner. In my experience the critical guideline in working with the creative forces—and I agree with you that we are working with something most sacred—is profound respect. We can set the boundary conditions through a method—prepare the compost and plant the seeds, so to speak—but then we must step back, leave room, and be careful not to bear down too much. If you treat the Muse as you would your dearest friend, my experience suggests you will be on the right track to knowing each other in a free and exploratory way.

Brannan: It seems there is much art in linking the processes of creativity and effective action. But we should move on. Let's return to basics. How does one actually practice with the **Weekly Log?**

Gresser: After getting clear about your mission, the **Weekly Log** helps you focus on the cases that challenge your skill in each quadrant—a formal

	negotiation, a meeting, a phone call, even a chance encounter are all "cases." Through these cases the game is played, the battle is won or lost.
Brannan:	What is the next step?
Gresser:	After organizing my practice in the **Weekly Log,** I chart the "wave form" of a day. I have discovered that each day has its special pattern, and, more interestingly, as we begin to understand and to settle into its ebb and flow, we can influence in a modest way the course of events we generally assume to be quite outside our control.
Brannan:	How do you mean?
Gresser:	Let me first describe the content of the **Charts** and then mention a few interesting discoveries I have made along the way.

THE CHARTS

I track fourteen indices, many of which may now be familiar. On the top line I trace the flow of "external" events by the hour. Above the line is "positive," meaning something "good" has happened; below it, something unpleasant or negative has occurred. Here and elsewhere I chart ideas, occurrences and happenings that seem to me significant. The external line is the external wave form of my life for this day. The remaining fourteen lines trace developments in the "inner" world. I am interested in the interplay of the inner with the outer.

The second line is the line of emotions. Above are the **emotions** reflecting joy, excitement, triumph and inflation. Below are fears, doubts, negative humors or moods. Sometimes the emotions are tranquil, but at other times they become turbulent, either by becoming inflated or depressed.

Need is the third line, the **sense of ease and time to spare** is the fourth, a **sense of catastrophe** the fifth. I have observed a recursive pattern between them. As **need** goes up, the **sense of ease and time to spare** drops off. When **need** persists, catastrophe appears. None of this, of course, may have any relationship to what is actually happening in the "external" realm. Thus we believe a catastrophe is upon us, when often it is only a phantom, a figment of our emotions and imagination.

Vanity, arrogance, and grandiosity occupy the next line. I have already mentioned the perverse relationship that is possible with these qualities. I know some people who when they get vain, grandiose or inflated, instantly get swatted. Actually, it may be a sign that they are progressing in the practice of integrity. I came upon this discovery working through the **Charts**.

Brannan: Can you give an example?

Gresser: All right. When my creative juices are really flowing, or I have achieved a major break-through in a negotiation, that moment is when I am most vulnerable. If for a second I start feeling that I am superior, brighter, or more entitled, at that very moment, or perhaps even before I become aware, my creativity will start to flag, or I will be out of sync with the move of my opponent, or I will miss an important opportunity. I have created a "distance," stopped listening, and fallen out of touch. I'm sure athletes encounter this same phenomenon on the tennis court or the baseball and football fields. I meet it in the arena of negotiation.

Brannan: What comes next?

Gresser: The **ability to manage the trolls.**

Brannan: The who?

Gresser: (Laughs) The **trolls. trolls,** as you may know, are swart, smelly creatures who live under bridges (often spiritual bridges). Although they seem the stuff of fairy tales, actually **trolls** can take "real" form in moods or humors. They are the melancholy voices that say to us, "Why try to accomplish that or really anything at all? You're not up to that. Why even try. You're over the hill." Professor Michael Ray of the Stanford

ABILITY TO
MANAGE THE
TROLLS

Business School refers to these unpleasant creatures as the Voice of Judgment. There is also an excellent book on the subject by Richard Carson called *Taming Your Gremlin*. A sense of humor is one of the keys to dealing with the **trolls**. Your ability to laugh at yourself and to be present when they're around sends the **trolls** squealing away much like garlic routed the Devil during the Middle Ages.

Seeing the world as it really is is the next element. As need drops and the emotions settle down, the world becomes clearer, friendlier and more simple.

The will (or volition) to combat helplessness is the next. Particularly in these times of turbulence and uncertainty, when almost everyone feels alone and powerless, the Will to combat helplessness can be a guide through the darkest days.

The ability to attend, *gravitas*, steadiness, and trust in the connection are the next set of variables. When you work on steadiness and *Gravitas* you begin to trust in your native capabilities, and then you regain hope and come out to see the world.

Life force or vitality (meaning physical, mental and spiritual energy) is the next element. The Chinese call it *qi*, the Japanese *ki*, and the Indians *prana*. You can feel when the *qi* is flowing and then you know you are in the integrity state.

Pay forward is the next variable. When need and arrogance are down and my life force is engaged, I feel abundant. Giving freely without any thought of recompense, I express my power.

Discovery, joy, wonder and magic is the next variable. When you feel vital and you sense the connection to the world around you, the connection becomes palpable. It is reinforced in every moment. You don't have to do anything. You can feel it in your bones. Just let your eyes be dazzled.

Sense of effectiveness. This is the last element. No matter how wild the weather is,

I can keep my hands firmly upon the wheel. I have seen such seas and I have made it through before.

Brannan: And what have you discovered in your tracking?

Gresser: I have discovered that the outer and the inner are independent, and yet connected intimately. Things can be proceeding magnificently in our outer life, while all of a sudden a mood takes over and we are out of sorts. Although this insight may seem commonplace enough, it is of vital importance to negotiators, because it refocuses us on objective reality: things may seem topsy-turvy, but are they really? How truly insignificant are many of the cares that now seem so important to us? Like the wind, most of them are passing vanities, signifying nothing.

The second insight for me is more remarkable. I have found that by restoring "integrity" in the inner, it is possible to influence the outer.

Brannan: Let's take this more slowly. I'm not sure I follow what you're saying.

Gresser: Look, every good sports psychologist or martial artist understands that by developing certain psycho-physiological powers we can affect external events. The movie, *Chariots of Fire*, is a good example. Coach Mastrobini worked not only on Harold Abrahms' physical body so that he could endure the rigors of the race, but equally importantly, the Coach worked on his character, and as a result Harold Abrahms became an Olympic champion and years later the Elder Statesman of British sports.

I have discovered that when things "go south" on the external line, by restoring integrity on any line in the inner, the "system" somehow recalibrates, and then the external becomes positive too.

Brannan: How does it become positive?

Gresser: In many ways. We can get a phone call from an old friend whom we have not seen in many years. A conflict gets resolved. A contract we have been seeking comes through. Someone dear to us has a great success. The universe seems to be laughing. "I see you!" it says, "but don't take any of this too seriously." And so we don't.

Brannan: How do you mean, "any line?"

Gresser: Any move that restores integrity—for example, exercising the **will to combat helplessness**, becoming less arrogant, **paying forward**, or simply attending, appears to be sufficient to begin to turn the Wheel a degree or so, and that shifts the field. This seems to me to be of enormous significance in these chaotic times, because it says we have more dominion over our life than we ever supposed possible. We have the power to change course instantly whenever we will it, and we can begin right now with little things. It is a discovery that brings hope.

Brannan: It might be helpful to demonstrate this relationship between inner and outer psychic processes with one of your charts.

Gresser: Okay. Here is an illustration of what I call the "wave form" of a day. Now please understand I make no claim to scientific exactitude, only that I and others with whom I have worked have found it helpful to trace the daily patterns in the ebb and flow of integrity.

The first thing to notice on the **Chart** (Illustration 6) is that this day started off as many days, with "nothing special." The player attempted four phone calls and was unable to make contact. The external line is flat.

Coincidentally, however, there is already movement in the inner realm. The **emotions** are starting to plummet. Melancholy and a depression are coming on. Need is on the rise. The **sense of ease and time to spare** is off kilter. Catastrophe is brewing. The **ability to manage the trolls** is in disarray. The player has momentarily forgotten everything he or she once knew about troll management. The **vital life**

force is draining out, and the player's **capacity to see the world objectively as it is,** like Humpty Dumpty, sitting on its head. And for what justifiable reason? No reason.

Next. Around 9:00 a.m. the player says to him or herself, "Enough! I'm not going along with this travesty." Here is the Exercise of Choice—the Act of Will! Now watch. A new inner process begins to stir. The **ability to attend,** *gravitas,* and **steadiness** regroups. Once again the player is beginning to **trust in the connection.** His/her **life force** also revives. **Vanity, arrogance, and grandiosity** (for many of our daily terrors are really just forms of vanity and grandiosity) begin to subside. The **sense of effectiveness,** this player's capacity to grapple, is also strengthening.

Things get even more interesting between 10:00 a.m. and 12:00 p.m. On the external line the player starts to receive some positive feedback. A key business contact he/she has been trying to reach is at home and the conversation produces a good result. Next, a former client offers to provide invaluable assistance on an ambitious project. Then the player's partner enthusiastically supports a new strategy. You see the mists are lifting. The player is starting to enjoy this mysterious process.

One hour follows the next along this general pattern. A little falling off occurs toward the late afternoon as the player's energy flags. Perhaps some overconfident coasting has set in. And then upon returning home after a pleasant meeting with a colleague, a surprise is waiting: a message from a prospect over a project the player has given up and long forgotten. "We want to do the deal! Can you help us?" the message says. "How can this be? It is so wildly unanticipated," the player asks him or herself.

What conclusions can we draw from this example?

First and most basic, we can play at any point upon the Wheel, and that will be precisely the perfect point! The gate is always open,

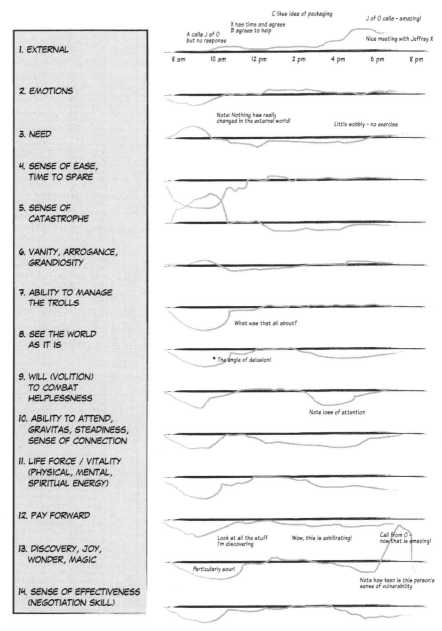

* *The angle of delusion refers to the discrepancy between external events and our ability to see them clearly*

Illustration 6

especially when things are murky and look impossible. That's exactly when you're close— when things are most intimate and you can look inside them. Because each moment, each situation, is essentially non-linear yet continuous, and that's what makes it so interesting.

The second point reinforces the first: The downturns, the dark places in our life, they also have a structure. Winter, too, is an orderly process.

The chart implies the third point. If you were to follow the patterns over days and weeks, I believe you might discover, as I have now done for several years, that the process proceeds in spirals. The basic issues of dark and light roll up, day by day, except that the waves are different and so are the faces.

There is no need to be a passive actor in this process. I have found that when we "hold integrity" as this person has done, as the waves crest and crash about us, the next round in the cycle becomes richer and even more vibrant and friendly. It takes time, but the opening will be there if you can stay conscious enough to embrace it.

To put the same point slightly differently, what I am saying is that there is a fertility in weakness, that the dark times ground us and set off the light, and that the pain we all have to one degree or another has a wonderful energy when we know how to harvest it.

The charts are like a mirror. They are one point of reference. We can use them to learn to love our life a little better—as Rilke writes, "to learn to love the questions" without our overly identifying with them.

Brannan: You mentioned one other discovery.

Gresser: I have found it is possible to "change" the Past, if by the "Past" we mean our memories and our interpretation of it. And if this is so, we can also rewrite the Future which is colored and shaped by the past.

Tracking our progress and our mistakes in the **Weekly Log and the Charts,** we continue to train over the weeks and months. Gradually our integrity deepens. As I have suggested, integrity involves a certain plasticity or trainability of spirit. One of the great attributes of this spirit is the ability to look around corners, to see the light side of dark things, and the shadow in the good. With this eye we can go back and trace the history of things that have been. And what do we find? We find, from the advantage of a developed integrity, that events that once appeared perverse (below the external line) may have seeded many good things. We give thanks to these reverses of fortune, because if they had not happened we could not have become what we are.

Brannan: Charting the wave form of one's life seems a fascinating exercise but what is the essential benefit from the point of view of the practice?

Gresser: If the **Weekly Log** builds integrity in the four quadrants of life, the **Charts** help us see what wondrous things can happen when the inner and outer selves become as one. If the secret to piloting through chaos is presence—when we can be belly-to-belly with our darkest terrors, and they give way to light—then the ability to trace the process, to bring it back before our face, so that we can say, upon reflection, "Yes, this has really happened!" may be the essential tool in our entire arsenal.

Let us move on to one last way to measure the process. I refer to the **Action Log.**

Brannan: The **Action Log** has served me well.

Gresser: Like the **Weekly Log**, the **Action Log** (see Illustration 7) serves several functions. Each **Action Log** contains ten decisions which comprise the essentials of **The Five Rings** system. These decisions address: What we want, our mission, actions and behaviors, the decision makers and their process, pain, budget, agenda, our presentation, discoveries, wins and losses, and finally **pay forward**. (Please note: The key actions and behaviors in the **Action Log** are separately listed and do not have to be "in step" with each

THE ACTION
LOG

other.) The **Action Log** records not only where we "stand" in each negotiation, it also helps us focus. In using the **Action Log** I recommend picking one principle or move at a time in tracking performance in a specific encounter.

ACTION LOG

NAME OF OTHER PLAYER(S) _____ DATE _____

Decision 1. What do I really want? _____
Decision 2. Determine the path of action (mission) _____
Decision 3. Set Goals for:

Action(s)	Behavior (No need)
1. Discovery questions	1. Relax
a.	
b.	2. Listen and Observe w/Empty Mind
c.	a. Am I thoroughly awake and present?
2. Check point	3. No Assumptions/Expectations
3. Take notes	4. Nurture (do not fear the 'no')
4. Investigate assumption	5. Focus
5. 'No'	6. Use Your Pain to Find Your Power
a. Recognize other players' <u>right</u> to say 'no'	
b. Exercise your right of 'no'	
6. Assess your own budget	
(time x energy x money x emotion)	
7. Cultivate the Will	

OTHER PLAYERS

Decision 4. Determine the other player's principal pain(s) _____

Decision 5. Determine the other player's budget _____
         (Time x energy x money x emotion)

Decision 6. Uncover the real decision makers and their process _____

Decision 7. Seat a valid agenda:
   a. Problems _____   d. What I want _____
   b. My concerns _____   e. What happens next _____
   c. Other player's concerns _____

Decision 8. Did I present my case only after making Decisions 1 through 8? ☐ Yes ☐ No
   a. If no, how leaky was I? _____

Decision 9. Analyze Your Wins,   Decision 10. Pay the Benefits Forward
         Errors & Discoveries

Illustration 7

I find it useful for a player each week to track 5 times he or she practices a particular principle or move, and what are the results; then 5 times in a similar situation the player doesn't bother to practice and the results. And finally, 5 times the player neglects to practice, but then catches the error midstream, adjusts, and consciously deploys the move or principle, and the results. Although there is nothing absolute about "5," it offers a useful way to provide an initial meaningful sampling.

A final use of the **Action Log** is to seize the initiative.

As I have mentioned, every negotiation affords an opening. I play, you respond—it really doesn't matter what you do—if I have integrity, I will hold the "initiative" in the counter play. This is why the analysis of wins and errors in Decision 9 is so essential. The **Action Log** is a tool to help us find the "winning" counter move.

Brannan: Julian, I would like to raise a practical concern now that you have explained all the ways of tracking and measuring the process. I believe many people will find much merit in the overall spirit of your approach and in some of the techniques. But who has the time to practice in this way? Most people have families to take care of or pressing business priorities. Do you really believe they will make room in their lives to dedicate themselves seriously to the extent your system seems to require?

Gresser: This, of course, is a critical question, and here is the best way I can respond to it. The method does require an investment of time and effort and creative energy, especially in the beginning. Like the martial arts or any sport, or really any enterprise in life of value, one cannot become an expert in a day. Steady practice is essential. The good news here, however, is there is immediate reinforcement. This is important because no one need take anything on faith. You can instantly derive benefit from practicing any of the principles and moves, and by paying attention to the results. Tracking the process is actually less time-consuming than might first appear. Preparing a **Weekly Log** or the **Charts** takes only 15-20 minutes. Each **Action Log** is about the same. If time is limited, I recommend focusing the **Action Log** on important negotiations and using the **Charts** when things really become turbulent. There is also a natural learning curve which has this curious side effect: the entire process tends to become second nature and internalized. Without taking the time physically to prepare an **Action Log**, you naturally begin to think and act with greater clarity or in terms of **missions of service** staying present, looking for the **pain** points, holding together, **paying forward,** and enjoying the play of inner and outer processes. Personally I have found the **Weekly Log, the Action Log** and the **Charts** continuously useful, but also I have a curiosity about prowling around in such things. A final key point: it's not the length of time you practice that matters, but rather the seriousness of the practice. As you progress you can accomplish in 15 minutes what might have taken you two to three hours several years before, and with a greater sense of ease and play.

Brannan: I think it would be useful at this point to summarize the essentials of the practice.

Gresser: I agree. They are:

- Practice at first in low-risk situations. Enjoy the process of tumbling.
- Keep a record of your "wins" and "losses." Explore their causes.
- Study how to seize the initiative by the re-reaction.
- Pick one behavioural quality, one move or principle each week and concentrate your efforts here, on this single element.
- Become curious about the "hits," **pay forward** the gains.

- A few mottoes:
  - Integrity is built through modest and simple acts.
  - Every moment, every situation presents an opportunity for training.
  - Continuity is power
- Be serious and practice hard; do fewer things but do them more deeply; penetrate and taste the authentic flavor.
- Practice everything with everything. In an integrity system every move you make connects to every other, so that any incremental improvement in one immediately and at the margin enhances the integrity of all.

In my own practice, I have trained myself each night to review before my mind's eye these five questions:

- What are the points of beauty of this day? We so easily pass them by and then we forget. I find that it is in beauty that we can revitalize and recreate ourselves.
- How shall I express them?
- What have I discovered?
- By what case?
- How can I embody this discovery more fully?

To me the truly wonderful things in life—how we meet our loved one, for example—come like a summer's day without our bidding and seem to bear no relationship to anything we have done before. And yet we can create the conditions by modest, steady attention each day to our integrity: paying attention to what we have learned from the drama, polishing, polishing, polishing.... If we can do this, only this, I have found that even the most mundane tasks or encounters become interesting and meaningful and will reveal, if we are disposed to look, surprises and their special touch of magic.

V

THE LŌGŌS NETWORK

Glendower: "I can call spirits from the vasty deep."
Hotspur: "Why so can I, or so can any man; but will they
come when you do call for them?"
—Shakespeare—Henry IV, Part I

"Fantasies these will seem, to such as are able to call my
beginning an ordinary effort."
—T.E. Lawrence

Brannan: We have come very far. It may be useful in this
last section for our students and others to have a
sense of our personal vision, of the path that lies
before us.

Gresser: Let us summarize where we are. We began
with the predicament of many people today
who feel that the ground under their lives is
beginning to shake. The thread that can lead us
through the labyrinth is integrity, and integrity
is a trainable skill. The path must be one of service, which is called the mission. The process
of carrying out the mission, *i.e.,* the negotiation,
never ends, and the secret to holding steady
and moving through chaos is to come to grips
with the universality of pain. For when we can

stay present to our pain and the pain of others, the process of navigation becomes the vehicle of our transformation.

Brannan: It seems you are narrowing the concepts of "path of service," "pain," and "transformation" primarily to business settings which really are a far cry from the true sacrifices and real suffering these terms carry for many people. For me, "path of service" suggests people like Mother Teresa or Albert Schweitzer who at great personal risk have selflessly given of themselves, and through that process have discovered a deeper reverence, satisfaction, and fulfilment in life. Is it really appropriate to use these same words to refer to cases like Getz or Flanagan, which involve people who simply acted intelligently in challenging business situations and were well remunerated?

Gresser: I do not mean to dishonor or in any way to trivialize by some of the business examples I have used the profound contribution of people like Mother Teresa or Albert Schweitzer. They and many others less celebrated are extraordinary people who have done extraordinary things, and their work can be an inspiration to us. But not everyone can be Mother Teresa or Albert Schweitzer or feel their special kind of calling. And yet I believe there are many people who hope to find in their work a way to be of some use and help to others. Of course, businesses solve this problem by giving to charities, and many people do community service on the side. What I am saying, which may be radical, is that it is not necessary to split off what you do to earn a living from the deeper sense of satisfaction and fulfillment I am speaking of. Everyone has some level of loneliness and pain. The cultivation of integrity, whether through the mission, the **practice of presence, paying forward**, or whatever, is a way to connect to and allay that loneliness and pain, and in that process we can find new meaning, satisfaction, and refreshment in work.

If good works were limited to the Mother Teresas of the world, I fear we would be in a sorry state since there are so few of them. But who is to say what will be the cumulative positive effects of thousands of chance interactions among people who might start to act and think in this way? I believe we must extend the concept of service to the daily activities of people if we are to cope with the changes fast coming on us.

Brannan: What kinds of changes?

Gresser: I see rough weather ahead. One doesn't require a special gift of prophecy to foresee increasing misery as more and more people around the world go hungry, as the living environment is destroyed, as ancient and new diseases run rampant, as militant fundamentalism, bigotry, and violence snuff out those who call for temperance, beauty, and reason.

Brannan: And yet so many people appear to be indifferent to all of this—they are too busy, too preoccupied.

Gresser: There is too much suffering in the world to be preoccupied, to live superficially. Although the problems at times seem overwhelming, I believe there is a practical basis for hope.

With regard to the vision of our enterprise and the path before us, there are three premises on which we might productively begin:

- First, a serious and concerted effort to restore integrity is necessary individually, within organizations and communities, at the national level, and among nations. Integrity has been much impaired.
- Second, technology can make a constructive contribution in the development and diffusion of the essential skills.
- Third, the problems before us are so overwhelming—we are too interconnected—for each of us to solve them alone. We must invent new ways of helping each other move through.

Brannan: You and I place great store in technology. I wonder if we are overstressing its role?

Gresser: We live in an Age of Information, of Digital Super-Highways, and Virtual Cyberspace. But are these things bringing us greater comfort, well-being or happiness? I think not. In many ways the tools we are producing are producing more noise, more confusion, more alienation and fragmentation. Are we any wiser because we have computers and our electronic networks?

I agree with you that the tools are not the answer. People, not technology, will bring about the beneficial changes I foresee. But the tools can help.

Brannan: How would you like to proceed?

Gresser: I would like to begin with a classical model which is curiously pertinent to the problems of this troubled age.

Brannan: Fine.

Gresser: Long ago, it is said, in ancient China people lived close to the earth (the *Tao*) and tilled the soil in both its physical and metaphysical sense (meaning character or integrity). In each village you could hear the dogs barking and the cocks crowing, but no one intruded on his neighbor. Formal rules and morality had little use in this society, because people lived in a natural way in harmony with themselves and each other. The leader was a balanced and complete person (in Chinese, *junzi*—君子), one who was skilled both in the martial and the peace-loving arts. He or she (for the Taoists did not discriminate against women) ruled by example, not by cold command or punishments.

Of what relevance is the Taoist model to these confused times? I believe in many ways. It is modest and frugal, which has appeal in this era of privatization and fiscal conservatism. It is skeptical of avarice or incompetence, especially in leaders. Thus it returns political power to the town and village. It respects the voices of local communities everywhere to express themselves. It honors character. And at its core are timeless human values such as the solidity of the family—of such political concern today—that uphold integrity and reaffirm life.

I believe we can engraft this classical model right on the limbs of modern society and the medium will be an imaginative use of technology.

Brannan: How in the most practical ways do you believe computer technology can help this metamorphosis?

Gresser: I would like to discuss how computers can help people acquire the skills of integrity by serving as a virtual executive coach.

This is particularly useful in solving the problem of "fall-off" which plagues everyone who goes through a workshop or seminar. How much do most people really remember two or three weeks after a workshop? Very little. How many participants can really put into practice what they have learned? Few indeed. These are skills—true life skills—that depend as much upon the hand as upon the head. Development of integrity is like the martial arts. You cannot obtain a black belt in a weekend. Continuous practice **in system** supported by coaching is key.

There are three areas where computer technology can help us overcome the limitations of our own physical and mental faculties. The first and most obvious is memory. In training it is invaluable, as I have said, to track and to review our discoveries so that the new skills, the new learning, is assimilated. But who has the memory to keep on top of all of this? If you ask anyone, "On this very day three months ago, what was your most important discovery?" few people would have an answer. And yet if you were to ask the average thinking person, "How unimportant are your discoveries?" she would protest and tell you, "Why, they are the stepping stones that give meaning to my life!" Why then do we squander what is most precious?

If the computer, this electro-mechanical apparatus, has any virtue, it has memory. Perhaps then it can serve as a modern, less poetic version of Mnemosyne (Memory), who in Greek mythology was the mother of the Muses. Computers can help us recall all the points of beauty and discovery that have been put away and long forgotten but which are embedded in their electronic minds. They give us a second chance to relive these memories.

There is another significant use of computers not generally observed. Coping with the challenges of this age demands every bit of our ingenuity and creative vitality. Since these resources are not inexhaustible, the question is how can we conserve and deploy them most efficiently? The first issue is: how do we account? In business today many people have time or money management systems. But how many have a means to keep track of effort, or even more importantly, can account for their "expenditures" of creativity? No one I know in business, much less in family life, "accounts" for expenditures of creativity. And yet by ignoring this most precious of all resources we unconsciously assign a value to creativity and that value is 0. It is startling to consider that almost everyone in business today is misallocating resources by not "pricing" expenditures of creativity. In less taxing times such laxity can pass unnoticed. Not in these times.

We have developed a simple and reliable way to use the computer in measuring and recording expenditures of time, effort, financial reserves, and creative emotion (vitality) in the form of **integrity budget units** (**IBUs**). When first organizing the life mission a player sets the **IBUs** in the life pie and then inputs expenditures in cases under **The Five Rings**. With one click a player or a team can instantly bring up on the screen a bar graph of the original **budget** and the amount of **IBUs** consumed as of that date. By tracking expenditures in any project or case

	the computer helps to prevent waste and to use our "gifts" more efficiently.
Brannan:	I hope you do not expect, Julian, that economists are going to flock to us with open arms.
Gresser:	Perish the thought of flocks of open-armed economists! No, we are not looking to come up with a breakthrough in economic theory. Rather we are continuously searching for a practical and easier way to help people make more effective decisions. We have only limited resources. The best we can do is help find a way to use them more wisely.

This subject of wise decision making raises a third, even more intriguing application for computers. I believe the computer can help us encode the wisdom of the world and make it easily available to all who desire to draw upon it.

Brannan:	Many ideas are bundled up into this last statement. I think it would be helpful to explain them one by one.
Gresser:	Okay. The first step is to make the link between integrity and wisdom. We have characterized integrity as a principle of nature that can be understood and cultivated through diligent practice. You remember the example of the unicelled creature surrounded by a toxic field—how this little thing would take practical steps to hold onto its sense of connectiveness, coherence, wholeness and vitality—its integrity. This decision to hold integrity will be a "wise" decision. The path of wisdom and the path of integrity are the same. If integrity is a skill, then wisdom also is a trainable skill.

Let us discuss how the computer can encode wisdom and make it available to us whenever we are in greatest need of it. In our discussion today we have touched on many key words— integrity, the five core values, **The Five Rings, PIPs**, *lōgōs*, *gravitas*, the **principles of matching/ mismatching, containment and abundance,** and so forth. Based on all these keywords and concepts, we can construct an integrity index, and with this index we can build a data base incorporating all the insights pertinent to each category.

But now something interesting happens. First, we have a way to record our own best thoughts, insights, and discoveries. This is not trivial, Tod. If one looks around today at all the problems, one might easily conclude that there is little wisdom in the world. But I do not believe this is true. There is much wisdom. I have found the day laborer, the taxi driver, the poor and disenfranchised have as much wisdom in their hearts and souls as the powerful, the rich, and the well-educated— indeed often more because they are less encumbered—but most people, irrespective of class or status or education, do not know how to find their own wisdom. The computer can help train and refine the skill.

This indexing system now provides an easy means for a company, firm, or foundation to take stock of everything that is good and noble in its history, then encode these principles for its management and employees in concrete cases, animating them perhaps by multimedia techniques so their "lessons" can be absorbed in interesting and enjoyable ways. By means of this "wisdom audit" an organization can revive its vision, recreate itself, and gain a strong competitive edge.

Stretching the applications of indexing even further, we now have a way to scan all the great works of literature and art (even music) and to find there the essential insights from the viewpoint of integrity. We can store these insights within the computer's memory—the wisdom database— so that players anywhere can instantly obtain coaching on demand on any issue.

Brannan: It might be entertaining to show how Shakespeare, by this method, can become your personal coach.

Gresser: Fair enough. Shakespeare was not only a great poet and playwright. He also looked deeply into the nature of things. Suppose you want some help in dropping assumptions or expectations, or in developing your vigilance in dealing with the **trolls,** or in becoming-more aware of your own vulnerabilities. You "click" upon any of these headings and instantly a picture of Shakespeare appears. (Actually the program can be designed so that either you "click" or Shakespeare contacts you—E-Mail from Shakespeare!) Then in his own words (given the advances in multimedia it will require little effort to design software so that a verisimilitude of Shakespeare actually speaks to you) the master counsels you through his alter ego, Banquo in *Macbeth*.

> *"But 'tis strange:*
> *And oftentimes, to win us to our harm,*
> *The instruments of darkness tell us truths,*
> *Win us with honest trifles, to betray's*
> *In deepest consequence."*

We are playthings, Shakespeare is warning us. There are truly baleful forces in the world and we ignore them at our peril. Assume nothing!

If we can extract the deepest insights from Shakespeare, we can do the same with Goethe, the Bible, the Baghavad Gita, Leonardo da Vinci, Lincoln, Gandhi, and all the great figures of history, living and dead, and from literature, the epic heroes, the wisest people, and they can all, by means of the computer, become our friends and teachers! If we had the financial means, we could construct for every country its Wisdom Genome—the core of its contribution of wisdom to humanity—to be updated continuously and made available, as a birthright, for everyone.

THE WISDOM
GENOME

Brannan: What role do you see the Worldwide Web, the Internet, and communications networks of the future playing in this process?

Gresser: Although, Tod, you probably have much better insights on this question than I, perhaps I can summarize some important observations we have made to date training people in The Five Rings via electronic networks.

We are building The Lōgōs Network—a community of people around the world who are dedicated to developing integrity through *lōgōs*. Already we have up and running an Electronic Conference/Training Hall called LogosNet which is linked to the Internet. At present the main areas of activity are the East Asian Negotiators' Alliance, the European Negotiators' Alliance, the Environmental Leaders' Roundtable, and **The Five Rings** Forum. The idea is to include in each of these substantive areas leading specialists, as well as players around the world who are involved in international or domestic negotiations, marketing and sales, project management, reengineering, creativity and invention, alternative dispute settlement, and a host of other issues. The Information Super-Highway is ideally suited to launching this experiment in international learning and skill-development along the lines we are contemplating.

Brannan: Before you touch on the substance, it may be useful to address up-front two important concerns many busy people have today about networks. I refer specifically to the widespread perception that a network is a form of lonely hearts club; and second, especially for people in business, that to contribute ideas or information to a network—even a private conference group—risks giving away a strategic competitive advantage.

Gresser: These are serious practical considerations. With regard to the first objection, it is true many networks have degenerated into gab groups, and even worse, into opportunities to pander child pornography or violence. The abuse is inherent in the medium. If the users are degenerate, the network will also be degenerate. But most networks are not this way. In our venture, because everyone who participates will possess a common method, a code of communication and a personal dedication to cultivating integrity, the work of these groups can be focused, effective, and creative.

The second objection appears a very real concern for business people. I have a friend, a prominent lawyer and scholar, whom I would like to involve in some way in our efforts. His first reaction was, "I will have to think carefully about what my firm will say. The worst case would be that by participating I might breed legions of competitors!" This is an old way of thinking. Whenever we open our mouth in a seminar or a symposium we are giving away something. The question is what do we get back? Some people will not understand, but others will. They will see that when the goal is integrity, the return is only enhanced for everyone by each new entrant to the Network.

I could make this point more concretely by citing some examples of how a modern community on the general lines of the Taoist model might evolve out of The Lōgōs Network and other allied networks imbued with the same spirit.

The first important observation we have made, quite startling to me as I am still learning about computers, is that it is possible to train hundreds, even thousands of people in an instant. This is because we always work on basics. A player logs on: "Help me with **no assumptions**. I understand the concept," he writes, "but I cannot put it into practice." I or someone else types in a few coaching tips, and then click! a hundred other people who are struggling with this same issue can be helped.

On the same lines: Another player is about to enter a critical stage in a negotiation (**Ring 4**) and hesitates to grant her opponent the opportunity to say 'no.' "I understand the principle. I read the tutorial in the software program. I have even practiced in low-risk situations. But still it seems unnatural. I'm afraid," she writes. Her inquiry resonates with many others. But then ten people reply, "I didn't believe it either. But here's what I did and look at the results," writes one. "Try this," writes another. "The software doesn't quite make this clear, but if you do it in this way, it is really powerful. I have found that people appreciate not being pushed." So the first player who is struggling with **'no'** takes their advice to heart, makes a decision, and takes the action. That's the key, the Act! Perhaps she stumbles. So what? She has a hundred—over a thousand—comrades-in-arms who are rooting for her. She **will** succeed in the end, if she persists.

Deploying the Network for reconnaissance is another use. "I am negotiating a joint venture with the Hung Yueh Petroleum Company in Beijing," logs on an American businessman. "Has anyone developed a **PIPs** on the decision makers?" Instantly a player in London responds, "This may be helpful to you," and sends him a **PIPs** in code. The American businessman immediately gains an edge.

The Network could bring help to environmental groups even in the most remote areas of the world, and thereby possibly shift the balance of power in a critical way. Take for example the class action suit recently filed by a group of indigenous people in Ecuador against one of the huge U.S.-headquartered multinational oil companies. The complaint charges that the oil company's wastes are destroying their rain forest habitat, and also are poisoning their drinking water and food supplies. **The Five Rings** method will provide this group with a new and powerful tool to develop and to coordinate strategies with their U.S. counsel and concerned environmental organizations, conduct reconnaissance, and concentrate all their resources on raising the price (pain) to the oil company of not taking responsible action.

The third insight, which became immediately obvious once we established LogosNet, is that one person's success encourages others to succeed. A player, a venture capitalist, comes to a training workshop. He is trying to persuade a bank in Hong Kong to continue its support to one of his firm's portfolio companies. He uses **The Five Rings** and "wins" the negotiation. The bank stays in. It is worth a few million dollars to him. With his permission I write up the case (preserving the anonymity of all parties). Everyone on the Network immediately learns of his victory and, more importantly, sees how he concretely worked the system. "If **he** can do it, I can do it," each person says to him or herself.

Paying forward is also wonderfully enhanced by the Network. Ten players have wins. Some modest, some great. They log on: "We wish to pay our gains forward," they write, "they have brought us much joy. Who knows of cases of great need where we might be of some help?" From across the world instantly come the replies: This player knows victims of an earthquake in Greece. A negotiator in Chile logs on about a family he knows with a child who is deformed because his mother took thalidomide. A group in Brazil appeals for help in its fight to preserve the rain forest. The general counsel of a leading pharmaceutical company writes that his firm is a member of the Make-A-Wish Foundation, that he knows of a child in New Hampshire with an inoperable brain tumor who wants to break the Guinness Book of Records on get-well cards before he dies. The connections are made and countless selfless actions taken, quietly and unobtrusively, falling as the gentle rain from heaven.

Brannan: What then is the question?

Gresser: The question is when will the transition begin from this Age of Noise to an Age of Wisdom? It seems we have waited a very long time.

Can a single person change the course of history for ill? It appears so. At least a single individual can precipitate the change. Did not a single madman by a single evil act—the assassination of Gandhi—change irrevocably the course of India's history? What about a single generous act? Why then cannot a single act of kindness, warmth, and cheer reverse the course of evil? What about a hundred acts by a hundred people, or who knows how many by what number of countless unheralded acts of goodness over time? What might be their effects? Where is the threshold that, once breached, could bring a watershed of beneficial change?

There is a very interesting movie, *Weapons of the Spirit*, which I recommend strongly to all those who are interested in these matters. It describes life in a small French town in the Pyrenees during World War II. It was a town occupied mainly by Huguenots, which perhaps provides a clue, because these were people inured to struggle and hardship, who throughout their history had dedicated themselves to compassionate service. In every other town in the area the Jews had been shipped off to concentration camps, but in this town the Jewish community went on living a normal life, without going into hiding, raising children, sending them to school, attending to daily chores, and burying the dead. In the center of the town the Gestapo made its headquarters, but for some reason they took no notice of the Jews who were right under their noses.

"We did what we had to do," explained some old men and women in the town. They were interviewed years later by a Jewish photographer who as a child growing up in the town had himself witnessed it all. There were no plots, no sabotage, no subterfuge. "We did what seemed right and natural at the time, that was all." And the Gestapo, for this brief moment, either failed to see or would not act.

The producer of *Weapons of the Spirit* described what happened in this town as a "conspiracy of good"—a shaft of light in a dark and gruesome period.

Please scan

That is our goal: to set in motion such conspiracies of good and see if, together, we can help Fortune turn her Wheel.

Brannan: To where could this ultimately lead?

Gresser: I do not know. I am content to enjoy the mystery of it. My feelings are expressed in this passage by Albert Camus, which responds to your question of where things could lead.

Brannan: What did Camus say?

Gresser: "Great ideas come into the world as gently as doves. Perhaps, then, if we listen attentively, we shall hear, amid the uproar of empires and nations, a faint flutter of wings, the gentle stirring of life and hope. Some will say that this hope lies in a nation; others in the men. I believe that it is awakened, revived, nourished by millions of solitary individuals whose deeds and works every day negate frontiers, and the crudest implications of history ... each and every person, on the foundation of his or her own suffering and joys, builds for all."

Book II

THE EXPLORER'S MIND

Prescript—21st Century Humanism and the Quest for a More Abundant Life

In these times we seem, like Dante, to have entered a dark wood where our basic "systems"—financial, technological, ecological, and social—are falling apart. Our primary sources of protection—government, religion, family, schools—are unreliable. Even nature itself appears in rebellion and is no longer a place of refuge. Most people around the world are struggling barely to survive and millions more fear for their future and sense that opportunities for themselves and their children are vanishing.

Yet new discoveries in brain and other sciences, powerful new information/communication technologies (ICT), and new collaborative modes of social engagement suggest a global stirring toward a brighter age, where each of us can pursue and realize a more abundant life. We are near a shift in how we think and reason, how we learn, how we engage with one another, what actions we can wisely take, and where they might lead us.

In the physical realm, a recently published book, *Abundance*, by Dr. Peter Diamandis and Steven Kotler,[11] asserts that the present dramatic changes in ICT will deliver in the next few years to every person on the planet the fundamentals of life—water, food, shelter, energy, health care, education, and political freedom. The focus of Book II is on the Explorer's Mind—the intersection of brain, mind, and consciousness—itself a state of natural abundance. The Explorer's Mind is a next frontier, the logical companion of the Age of Prosperity which the authors of *Abundance* predict.

The concept of the Explorer's Mind, which is defined in the next chapter, has a clear lineage in Buddhist teachings, in particular Zen and martial arts, although the core insights are recognized in virtually all the wisdom traditions. What is perhaps fresh, and the contribution I seek to make in this book, is the elaboration of these core concepts in a new way of observing the world—that is, multidimensionally and with kindness, which has traditionally been associated with spiritual practice. I have found that the Explorer's Mind has many practical uses in approaching a broad range of existential challenges confronting the world today and, as I will show, the New Media (the Internet, the World Wide Web, and smart devices) provide an ideal medium for beginning the conversation.

Just as the rise of commerce and attendant economic prosperity provided a necessary foundation for the birth of Italian Humanism in the thirteenth and fourteenth centuries, it is conceivable that the coming Age of Abundance will awaken a New Humanism and Second Renaissance in the twenty-first century. During the first Renaissance, people rediscovered and reentered the world of secular inquiry and self-reliance which flourished in classical antiquity. People in Western Europe came to look at life as did people in ancient Greece and Rome, which is to say that they ceased to think and feel as cloistered medieval men and women and started to think and feel like modern people in the spirit of a new life.[12]

A Second Renaissance will have its own form and twenty-first century Humanism will flower in its own unique fashion. The **Past, Present, and Future** (Editor's note: Throughout Book II when referring to special realms introduced in Chapter II the author elects to capitalize and to render bold for emphasis.) will be linked in new ways; today's technologies are different and vastly more powerful. The problems are also different: in particular, the deterioration of the natural environment and the capacity for planetary self-destruction. The first Renaissance was confined largely to Western Europe, but the New Humanism and the Second Renaissance of the twenty-first century will draw upon the thought and legacy of both East and West and must harvest the vast untapped human potential of China. The epic of our time will be fueled by an ancient form, storytelling, formatted and transmitted through the Internet and legions of smart devices, but also (as was once customary) from parents to their children, by elders to the community, across circles of fire.

One way to introduce the Explorer's Mind is by understanding how we manage uncertainty, which seems to me the source of much suffering and also opportunity. If we can learn to think about and work with uncertainty in a new and imaginative way, we may be able to induce a shift. The Explorer's Mind provides a point of leverage.

I

ACCEPTANCE

A pilgrim called Lingyun stopped his journey to observe a peach tree in full bloom on the opposite side of a canyon. The record of his encounter survives to this day:

> *For thirty years I searched for a master swordsman.*
> *How many times did the leaves fall, and the branches burst into bud?*
> *But from the moment I saw the peach blossoms,*
> *I've had no doubts.*[13]

Uncertainty

On March 11, 2011 an earthquake measuring 9.1 on the Richter scale rattled the city of Fukushima in northwest Japan, toppling office buildings and farm houses, capsizing boats, and bringing an eerie silence. Shortly after, the waters rose and a roaring tsunami struck the city. Like some fearsome dragon the waves fell upon six nuclear power plants, crippling four, and causing some (as if in evil league themselves) to explode and release a spume of radio-active gases into the air and surrounding rice fields. The poison-ous cloud spread rapidly throughout the region, and in a matter of days the seismic-tsunami-nuclear-environmental catastrophe morphed again into a national economic crisis, as one Japanese auto-parts supplier after another collapsed and other industries nose-dived. Twenty-thousand people are estimated to have perished or been seriously injured in the Fukushima earthquake. It will likely take thirty years to clean up the wreckage. Meanwhile, 20 million tons of toxic debris, estimated to be 2,000 miles long and 1000 miles wide, emanating from Fukushima's nuclear power plants and surrounding towns, is heading across the Pacific toward Hawaii and is reported already to have reached Alaska. Cascading catastrophes like Fukushima, which experts acknowledge as possible but extremely unlikely, now occur with increasing frequency.

We are more connected than we imagine. Few people have heard of the Cascadia Subduction Zone which is a crack in the earth's crust, roughly sixty miles (100 km) offshore and running eight hundred miles (1,300 km) from Northern Vancouver Island to Northern California. It has produced large earthquakes repeatedly throughout geological time, the last reported over 310 years ago. Seismologists believe the next is overdue. A 9.1 Cascadia quake would not only cause massive destruction in the Pacific Northwest. It would likely also trigger a sympathetic reaction in the San Andreas Fault along California, which in turn would power tsunamis down through Mexico and out across the Pacific onto the shores of Japan, Indonesia, Hong Kong the Philippines, New Guinea, Australia, and New Zealand. Cascadia's tremors could also produce seismic reactions in China.[14]

Even seemingly trivial events or limited emergencies can have rapid and gigantic consequences. On August 14, 2003 a minor power failure at a few lines, managed by the First Energy Corporation in Ohio, exploded in nine seconds into a massive blackout affecting millions of people in the Midwest, New England, New York, and parts of Canada.[15] Iceland's financial crisis beginning in 2008 precipitated financial emergencies across Europe, whose ripples continue today.

The causes of these catastrophic ripple-effects are complex, but certainly our overdependence on technology is a critical factor. We are all in the same boat, because our systems—both natural and man-made—are now over-coupled, overloaded, and overwrought. This applies to climactic, ecological, seismic, economic, financial, informational, and even psychological systems. As the Yale sociologist Charles Perrow writes, accidents under these circumstances do not require a specific human error, they are intrinsic to the structure, and they are ordinary.[16]

The essential problem with overtaxed, tightly-coupled systems is that there is no easy way to interrupt or shut down errors. They can proliferate within and jump across systems, multiplying and compounding their destructive impact. At the same time, systems that are chronically overtaxed lose their capacity to adapt to stress and change. There is, of course, a balance point. In human biology, for example, some significant level of tight coupling is essential to life force and resilience. But excessive coupling produces rigidity, and loose coupling results in dissipation of energy and weakness.[17]

Charles Perrow's work focuses on normal accidents. But the deterioration and vulnerability of the present infrastructure becomes even more troublesome when we account for the likelihood of terrorism and other forms of intentional sabotage. In a recent report, federal officials at the U.S. National Institutes of Health (NIH) are drafting a plan to regulate access to a pair of studies on a deadly strain of avian flu virus—H5N1—which the NIH itself financed at Erasmus Medical Center in the Netherlands and at the University of Wisconsin-Madison. Researchers at these centers created mutations in H5N1 which rendered it highly transmittable between laboratory animals. The H5N1 strain has thus far been deadly in 60 percent of cases involving humans, and if the strain is widely released, experts estimate that millions of people will die. In explaining why the results should be disseminated in forthcoming issues of the journals *Science* and *Nature*, the acting Chairman of the National Science Advisory Board, Paul Keim, attempted to reassure the public by pointing out that replicating the experiment would require significant expertise in genetic engineering in order for terrorists to develop a virulent strain. As will be seen shortly, this is a dangerous and untested assumption, especially when we understand the capacities of "creative amateurs."[18]

The average person's circumstances today mirror the breakdown of our technological systems. We live with a paradox of overdependence within a wilderness of new connections. Even as we are more and more electronically coupled, networked, and linked, we seem increasingly out of touch with things that matter most. Our own circuits are overloaded by a rising Everest of information and the speed by which everything takes place. Time itself seems to be compressing and often our deepest needs—for intimate connection, for meaningful work, and even decent healthcare—go unmet.

There are patterns in the breakdown of our own psychic integrity.

- A pervasive sense of anxiety, fear, despair, and hopelessness.
- An increasing appetite for violence and aggression.
- A widespread exhaustion (both physical and existential).
- A loss of inner silence, sanctuary, and space to pause, rest, and re-create ourselves.
- A feeling of being empty and satiated at the same time.[19]
- A desperate need to control.

- A struggle against uncertainty and the fundamental reality of change itself; hence a need to constrain, limit, and narrow.
- A need to simplify everything as either black or white; intolerance for the rainbow of shades, colors, and nuances; a tendency toward fundamentalism in its various forms.
- A tendency to constellate every occurrence, to find false linkages, dark meanings, and conspiracies everywhere.

The breakdown affects values, interests, and priorities:

- A disdain for empiricism and in its place the naïve and superstitious belief that our thoughts must be true simply because they occur to us.
- Linguistic sloppiness—a reduction of complex ideas into commercial sound bites, a fatuous reliance on clichés, and other artificial supplements for thought, what Conrad called the "old tired words."
- A declining appreciation of ideas as valuable in themselves, especially big, exciting, and dangerous ideas, which for the last several centuries have transformed science and societies.

The breakdown is further expressed externally in:

- An increasing instability in personal relationships and business alliances.
- An increase in drug and alcohol abuse and other forms of addiction.

Authors Diamandis and Kotler add a new dimension to this gloomy picture in their description of the amygdala, a tiny, almond-shaped organ in the brain whose primary function is to modulate primal emotions of rage, hate, and fear:

It's our early warning system, an organ always on high alert, whose job is to find anything in our environment that could threaten survival. Anxious under normal conditions, once stimulated, the amygdala becomes hyper-vigilant. Then our focus tightens and our fight-or-flight response turns on. Heart rate speeds up, nerves fire faster, eyes dilate for improved vision, and the skin cools as blood moves toward our muscles for faster reaction times. Cognitively, our pattern recognition system scours our memories, hunting for similar situations ... and potential solutions (to help neutralize the threat). But so potent is this response that once turned on, it's almost impossible to shut off; and this is the problem in the modern world.... We're feeding a fiend.[20]

We are all affected—high and mighty, poor and humble—although the poor as always will suffer disproportionately. If these trends are uninterrupted, the quotient of human misery is likely to rise sharply within the decade.

Societal collapse, as described above, provides one storyline, one version of the world.[21] But it is only one. Another version of the reality, another story line, is offered in the recent book, *Abundance*. According to the authors Diamandis and Kotler, the accelerated development of exponential information communication technology (ICT) combined with the beneficial effects of the other trends they cite are so powerful that widespread societal abundance within a generation is virtually certain. For example, the exponential graph drawn from *The Singularity is Near*, a treatise by Ray Kurzweil, extrapolates the continuation of Moore's Law over the next century. It indicates that by roughly 2023 the average one-thousand-dollar laptop will be able to communicate at the rate of the human brain, and within another twenty-five years at the brain-power of the entire human race.

Thus the crucial difference between these two versions of reality—abundance or collapse—seems to depend upon our assessment of probabilities. Moreover, it would seem that a cause of much suffering in the world is our anxiety about the future, which is to say, uncertainty. If we knew with greater certainty and clarity in which direction we were heading, we could likely think ahead, plan, and adapt.

We are so accustomed to viewing uncertainty as an adversary, might we be missing something interesting and more vital, something below the surface? What if doubt were to become our ally and uncertainty a source of creativity and strength? Is it possible that uncertainty can help us re-establish our connection to what is primary and essential? What if the border between certainty and uncertainty is far more subtle and blurry than we suppose?

How we manage uncertainty affords an interesting way to introduce The Explorer's Mind. For if we can learn to think about and work with uncertainty in a new and imaginative way, we may be able to induce a shift. We may be able to reinforce the positive developments envisioned by Ray Kurzweil, Peter Diamandis, and other writers while dealing soberly with the darker, less optimistic forces at play. The Explorer's Mind provides a point of leverage.

The Explorer's Mind Defined

I will define what I mean by "The Explorer's Mind." It is a dynamic state of consciousness which is alive, immediate, and always different. We are accustomed to thinking about "mind" as an abstract extension of the brain or intellect and located somewhere in the head. But Explorer's Mind combines intellect (head), heart, and hand, which aligns it with *integrity*, or the *lōgōs*. As explained in the next chapter, Explorer's Mind enables us to voyage into realms of human experience which have not generally been understood to be connected with each other.[22] By "exploration" I follow the Latin root, "to search for," as in a hunt or quest. Exploration for me encompasses not only the quest to discover new territories in the external world, but also the largely unknown and unmapped terrain of our own minds. The Explorer's Mind is concerned equally with both domains and has the capacity to reflect upon and to explore itself. The Explorer's Mind can extend infinitely.

Lingyun and the Peach Blossoms

The story at the headnote of this chapter is an example of a *koan*. A *koan* in the Zen tradition is a kind of puzzle which guides us in our exploration of uncertainty and is used to precipitate awakening. You might think of it as a gate into another realm of consciousness. In Japanese, the character for *koan* (公案) literally means "public case." There developed over the millennia, originating in China, a repertoire of such stories with commentaries by various masters conversing with their students (adepts). The repertoire of *koan* classics has been passed down as aids for study and practice. There are thousands of these gates. The story of the pilgrim Lingyun and the peach blossoms introduces some of the qualities of the Explorer's Mind.

We meet the pilgrim Lingyun in the present story at the point of his awakening. He has journeyed for thirty years and just now, looking across the canyon, he sees a peach tree in exuberant full bloom. He is overwhelmed. Perhaps the first point to observe is the suddenness of the process. His awakening strikes him suddenly out of nowhere. He cannot anticipate it. He has no control over it.

Lingyun is a patient man. His search has taken him thirty years. The years of his life are like leaves on the trees; they put out tender shoots in spring time and are then scattered. But now, he has a chance. His quest is answered. Lingyun's discovery is an event in the outer world—the peach trees in their loveliness. But his awakening is an internal one. A part of Lingyun, himself, which is the peach trees, finally begins to blossom. This *koan* uses a particularly image, but in the Zen tradition anything will do: a pebble hitting bamboo, for example. As Shakespeare reminds us, "Ripeness is all."[23]

Lingyun's sense of uncertainty, his doubt, has vanished. Doubt about what? We are not told. How many times did he pass a similar peach tree in bloom? Perhaps he was so preoccupied with the affairs of his life that he had eyes but did not see, he had ears but could not hear. Now his doubts are reconciled. He experiences the world, innocently.

The *koan* celebrates the beauty of life and its bounty. How could he ever doubt? How could he ever forget? Lingyun experiences a sense of profound connection. The inner and outer worlds are as one. He is fulfilled. The Explorer's Mind has become Lingyun's sanctuary.

Survival

Lest the reader conclude that the Explorer's Mind is some esoteric Zen concept, the following survival stories lend insight into a more general human capability to cope with uncertainty, or to transform uncertainty into certainty during crises. From reports of survivors it seems that when we humans swing over the abyss and know that we will die at any moment, everything else is stripped away. We do what we must.[24] We don't have the luxury or space to allow the terror of uncertainty. The following two accounts suggest that uncertainty, rather than a source of anxiety, was in fact a spur toward survival.

The Sacred Chamber[25]

Joe Simpson found himself upside down in an uninhabited snow-covered mountain in Peru, with a broken ankle from a fall at nineteen thousand feet. He might have panicked, but he didn't. He didn't pay attention to his thoughts, or those of his buddy, Simon Yates: "You're fucked, matey. You're dead." In *Deep Survival*, Lawrence Gonzales describes how Simpson took charge of things within his own power, namely himself, and left the rest behind. There was no self-pity. He focused on the rhythm and the pattern of raw data—bend, hop, rest—step by painful step, until he and Yates, ever so slowly, managed to pick their way down the slope of the mountain. But they miscalculated. Simpson went straight over the cliff, dangling, unable to reach the six-foot wall where he might plant his ax. Recognizing the hopelessness of the situation, Yates cut him loose to save his own life and to spare Simpson the horror of freezing to death on a rope.

Simpson landed with a huge concussion on a slick and snowy bridge above a black abyss. High above, writes Gonzales, he could see the hole he had punched through the snow and a sky "furious" with stars. Exhausted, dehydrated, hypothermic, and frostbitten, he fell asleep. Officially he was dead.

In the morning he awoke with a revelation:

> A pillar of gold light beamed diagonally from a small hole in the roof, spraying bright reflections off the far wall of the crevasse. I was mesmerized by this beam of sunlight burning through the vaulted ceiling from the real world outside. It had me so fixated that I forgot about the uncertain floor below and let myself slide down the rest of the rope. I was going to reach that sunbeam. I knew it then with absolute certainty. How I would do it, and when I would reach it were not considered. I just knew.[26]

Suddenly he was filled with energy and optimism: "For all its hushed and cold menace, there was a feeling of sacredness about the chamber, with its magnificent vaulted crystal ceiling, its gleaming walls encrusted with ... myriad fallen stones." He returned to his routine, accomplishing the micro-goals of clambering out of the crevasse, up an enormous cone built from the snow sifting in from the outside, deep at the bottom, narrowing at the face of the hole. He emerged twelve hours later into the sunbeams and "a beauty I had never experienced before."

Yet he was dying. His energy was gone and his will was slipping away. He was unable to move. He had ten hours of daylight left. With his last remaining life force, empowered by an iron will and a rage that refused to consent, he struggled down the mountain with no idea of where he was heading. Yates was packing the burros at the base camp and moving out when he heard a weak yell at a distance from the camp. It was Simpson. He was taken down the mountain on a donkey and lived to tell his story.

Lost at Sea[27]

Louis Zamperini, an Olympic runner and an American flyer in World War II crashed in the middle of the Pacific Ocean when the engine of his plane gave out. In her best-selling book, *Unbroken*, Laura Hillenbrand describes how he survived forty-seven days on a life raft, surrounded by twenty-foot sharks, without water, food, or shelter, exposed to a merciless sun, with an injured comrade dying by his side. To survive, he had to become fiercely resourceful.

Please scan

They had no drinking water, so Zamperini devised a way to harvest rainwater, catching it in a canvas sheath and siphoning it into cans. They trapped and ate small sharks with the remains of sea birds they had captured. When a Japanese Zero's bullets strafed the raft, puncturing the air chambers and tossing them overboard, they fought off the sharks, found an air pump, and patched the raft with canvas, glue, and sandpaper. They built a tarp from canvas into a large sheet to shield them from the sun. Although their bodies were failing, their minds remained supple and resilient. Hillenbrand writes, "In his mind he could roam anywhere and he was quick and clear, his imagination unfettered." His memory remained nimble and he was able to recall details from his distant past.

Joe Simpson's and Louis Zamperini's survival depended upon maintaining an attitude of sufferance, objectivity, and even indifference to their mortality. Although their lives hung precariously in the balance, they were simply too busy surviving to waste precious time struggling with worrying about uncertainty. In short, Joe Simpson and Louis Zamperini were able to construct an alternative version of reality, a fiction of certainty within a sea of uncertainty, which enabled them to survive.

Trust the Connection

When I enter Explorer's Mind, I have a sense of being "online." It is a very clear and distinct sensation. My primary experience is energetic, of being vitally alive. This is closely associated with the sense of tapping into an energy field. This is called a *"qi*-field" in the Chinese martial art of *qigong* (氣功). I describe it in the next chapter. Once this energetic coupling is established, the ideas start to flow—first one, then another, then groups of them tumbling out. Life seems to flow easily, there is no impediment. Interesting dreams—flying dreams or dreams with pythons—arrive naturally. Synchronicities—surprising coincidences—abound. They come so frequently I have the odd sense of a private conversation going on in which I am only partly involved—I am an amused observer or a part-time guest. But the deepest sensation is one of gratitude: gratitude for the gift of life and the chance to do something useful while I am here.

As I can now enter this Explorer's Mind easily, I have learned to trust the connection. But connection to what? It turns out this connection has a direct bearing on the main theme of this chapter: the interplay of certainty and uncertainty.

In the *Heart Sutra*, one of the most profound Buddhist scriptures, it is written:

Avalokiteshvara, the Bodhisattva of Compassion, meditating deeply on Perfection of Wisdom, saw clearly that the five aspects of human existence are empty, and so released himself from suffering. Answering the monk Sariputra, he said this:

Form is nothing more than emptiness,
emptiness is nothing more than form.
Form is exactly empty,
and emptiness is exactly form.

The other four aspects of human existence—
feeling, thought, will, and consciousness—
are likewise nothing more than emptiness,
and emptiness nothing more than they.

All things are empty:
Nothing is born, nothing dies,
nothing is pure, nothing is stained,
nothing increases and nothing decreases.[28]

The *Heart Sutra* provides an insight into the relationship of certainty and uncertainty. Just as form and emptiness co-exist, interpenetrate, are one and yet are separate, so also, perhaps, certainty and uncertainty are in a continuous and emerging dance, one residing within the other. In a sense this is a restatement of the Greek philosopher Herakleitos' "unity of opposites." He wrote, "Opposites cooperate. We know health by illness, good by evil, satisfaction by hunger, leisure by fatigue." The idea also approaches Werner Heisenberg's famous Uncertainty Principle, which states that it is impossible simultaneously to measure the present position while also determining the future motion of a particle, or of any system, small enough to require quantum mechanical treatment.

The practical application of these abstract notions for the explorer is to stand somewhat apart and not to be caught in the trap of certainty versus uncertainty—in other words, not to conclude that either one or the other is absolute reality. The following two stories illustrate the observing Explorer's Mind and then show how you can verify these abstract notions usefully by yourself.

Bodhidharma Meets Emperor Wu

Sometime in the fifth or sixth century, Bodhidharma, the twenty-eighth patriarch, who is credited with bringing Zen Buddhism to China, met the Emperor Wu of Liang.[29]

Emperor Wu was proud of his support for the monasteries and his knowledge of Zen. He questioned the master, expecting to get some credit:

"What is the main point of the holy teaching?"

"Vast emptiness, nothing holy," said Bodhidharma.

Somewhat irked, the Emperor continued,

"Then who are you, standing before me?"

"I do not know," replied Bodhidharma.

No point, nothing holy, in fact no-thing at all.

In working with this *koan* don't try to solve it intellectually. If you try to do this, you usually don't get anywhere fast. It is designed to block your intellectualizing processes. More effective and far more fun is simply to hang out with it. You can take any piece, for example, "vast emptiness, nothing holy," or "I don't know." You simply allow your mind to rest in not-knowing, with no struggle, and let the world of vast emptiness, nothing holy, come to you; and when it decides to appear, you maintain your attitude of not-knowing. Very easy. No struggle. The Explorer's Mind simply attends.[30]

But it would be an error to infer that the Explorer's Mind is a passive or languid state. For at times, Explorer's Mind can strike like lightening steel.

Martial Arts

Martial artists across all cultures have cultivated Explorer's Mind in the face of uncertainty with extraordinary discipline. In his advice to the swordsman, Zen master Takuan Soho points out that "unfettered mind" must extend throughout the body and not be allowed to be cornered in any one place. "When facing a single tree (opponent), when the eye is not set on any one leaf and you face the tree with nothing at all in mind, any number of leaves is visible without limit. But if a single leaf holds the eye, it will be as if the remaining leaves will not be there."[31]

An astonishing examples of unfettered mind is the following account by Trevor Leggett, one of the highest ranking early judo experts and an astute student of Zen and the Japanese martial arts.

When the rebel army swept into a town in Korea, all the monks fled except the Abbot. The general came into the temple and was annoyed that the Abbot did not receive him with respect. "Don't you know," he shouted "you are looking at a man who can run you through without blinking?" "And you," replied the Abbot calmly, "are looking at a man who can be run through without blinking." The general stared at him, made a bow, and retired.[32]

In other words, the Explorer's Mind is also no-mind. The Abbot's practice had reached so advanced a level that the imminent certainty of his demise and the uncertainty of transcending it merged, and all that remained was vast emptiness. In the Abbot's consciousness, the general's sword could pass through without his blinking, because nothing was there, nothing to pass through.

Please scan

Acceptance

Although the *Heart Sutra* suggests it is about heart or compassion, the western reader may feel something remote and cold in it. This has caused at least one commentator, the Korean Zen master Mu Soeng Sunim, to write of the Great Transcendent Heart Wisdom Sutra (its full name in Sanskrit is *Maha Prajna Paramita Hridaya Sutra*): "Although Hridaya means 'heart' here, in the title of the Sutra, it is used in the sense of 'core' or 'essence' rather than the physical organ." In my personal practice I have experienced vast emptiness as opening my mind/heart to feelings of compassion, kindness, and generosity of spirit. I have found a way to express these same ideas more concretely and to engage the heart directly. It is to accept and to work with what is and with kindness.[33] It seems to me this gentles the cold abstraction of vast emptiness. If we can learn to accept what life delivers, we have a way to step around the Scylla and Charybdis[34] of certainty and uncertainty, we simply attend to the work before us. If we can apply intelligence with heart (kindness) to the task at hand, we are acting with integrity, we are piloting through chaos. In my experience, this decision to enter Explorer's Mind is an act of personal choice. I have been able to track an interesting pattern which I refer to as "adversity's spiraling and creative wave form."

Adversity's Spiraling and Creative Wave Form

I have noticed in my life that adversity can follow a spiraling and creative wave form. In Illustration 1, as we descend the terrain becomes darker and thicker. We struggle and at times we can even regain ground. We have a break, a little light in the thickness, but then we falter and fall deeper into despair. At last we approach the point where Shakespeare's King Lear says, "The worst is not, so long as we can say, 'This is the worst.'" We plunge. Then there is nothing, only the abyss. We have no other choice but to surrender, to accept, to be kind to ourselves, and to forgive. We simply are. At this point, at first imperceptibly, a slight shift occurs; the terrain changes. It softens; a first glimpse of sunlight far on the horizon, the flicker of an insight, then another, and another. We begin to sense our collecting powers inside our pain. That is the point, we regain our connection. At last sunlight breaks through and with it a great coiling creative thrust. In the end of the cycle we find ourselves on higher peak than when we started. The spiral has its own natural pace and often it takes more time than we are willing to tolerate. But these natural cycles in some sense are uninterested in our personal time agendas. I have learned that if we can develop a sense of humility and patience with the process, this is one way to pass through uncertainty, disappointment, and despair.[35]

The same pattern applies equally to survivors in desperate situations as it does to people in ordinary difficult and even calamitous situations. I have a friend who made some unwise decisions in business. He purchased a house way above his means. He started a company without carefully assessing its prospects for financial success. He made some foolish investments. He trusted the wrong advisors. He found himself in terrible financial straits. He could have buckled, he could have gone under, but he persevered—not always elegantly, mind you, but he kept going. He is still struggling, but he appears to have gotten a foothold. He has leverage to climb out of the abyss.

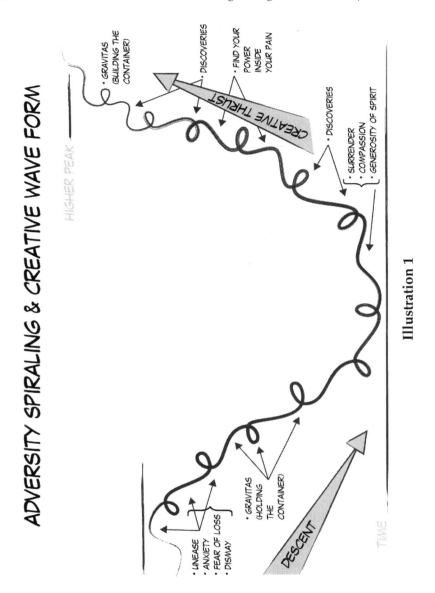

ADVERSITY SPIRALING & CREATIVE WAVE FORM

HIGHER PEAK

- GRAVITAS (BUILDING THE CONTAINER)
- DISCOVERIES
- FIND YOUR POWER INSIDE YOUR PAIN

CREATIVE THRUST

- DISCOVERIES
- SURRENDER
- COMPASSION
- GENEROSITY OF SPIRIT

- LINEASE
- ANXIETY
- FEAR OF LOSS
- DISMAY

- GRAVITAS (HOLDING THE CONTAINER)

DESCENT

TIME

Illustration 1

Adversity's spiraling and creative wave form does not always bring a happy ending. I have another friend who was diagnosed with a lymphoma in his youth. It was quiescent for many years. But it returned. By then, he had a wife and two children who depended upon him. He fought his cancer like a tiger, like Achilles. But it was not to be. He died and he never reached any peak of greater understanding or power. Life is not always clear or fair or as simple as the

Adversity Spiral illustration suggests. But I still believe we can try to work with the hand we are dealt. I'm not sure there is a better way.

Unexplainable Connections

Along the path, at times, something magical happens. These odd occurrences hint at deeper connections with the natural world which western scientific minds can scarcely imagine. Here is one such singular report in *The Atlanta Gazette* on July 25, 1998.

> The State Minister for Environment has today announced in respect to the recent devastating cyclone in Bangladesh in which six hundred people drowned: A dolphin took hold of a baby, who had been swept out to sea at the village of Ukhia by a tidal wave during the height of the April 29 cyclone. The baby was delivered back to shore, eighteen miles from Ukhia where the villagers pulled the child from the dolphin's mouth and took it to a district hospital. The infant is said to be recuperating.

In Buddhist terms, we might attempt to explain this story as a tender mercy of the Goddess of Compassion (*Kuanyin*). She, whose ten thousand eyes and arms reach out to the suffering in the world, takes the form of a dolphin. But our attempt to explain may not satisfy those who will demand scientific proof. It seems it is one of those mysteries Victor Hugo refers to in *Les Miserables* "which God reveals at night to eyes that remain open." We do not scrutinize but simply let our eyes be dazzled.

The Explorer's Mind seeks to discover the essence of things simply. As I rewrite this chapter, Angela brings me a *tanka* (Japanese short poem), which conveys in four lines what it has taken me thirteen pages to describe:

> I hold a bowl of tea in my hands.
> In its green color I can see all of nature.
> I close my eyes to contemplate the hills
> and the pure water running in my heart.[36]
>
> —Sen Soshitsu

Exercises: Exploring Uncertainty

1. Biofeedback—Learning to Relax Control

You can easily verify the principle that the world advances by relaxing control. Simply purchase a disposable biofeedback unit which measures the temperature in your hands. Now, try to force your hand temperature to rise by attempting to control it. What happens? Next, just let go. Relax control, let out the clutch, and simply repeat the following autogenic phrases: "I am letting go," "My hands are warm," "My hands are heavy," "The flow is easy." What do you discover about gaining "control" of the temperature in your hands? What deeper principle might be at work?[37]

2. Managing the Mind in Uncertainty—A Collaborative Experiment

Managing the mind in uncertainty need not be as formidable as it seems at first glance. You just have to turn the horse's head toward home; you don't have to demand that you be home in a hurry.[38] Here is a simple practice:

- Please re-read the sections in this book which deal with the following "moves": **presence, No Assumptions, No Expectations, negative capability, not-knowing, the will, steadiness, and resilience,** and more generally, the chapter, "How to Practice."

- Next try with one move and practice using the **Field Notes** which you can soon print out from the Explorer's Wheel web site (www.explorerswheel.com). I suggest the move of simply focusing on being present while working with the situation you have before you.

- Then look for scenarios where circumstances in your life suddenly appear and grab you, where things appear painfully uncertain, where you want everything to be different than it is, when you struggle with reality. Run the following experiment: Record three times this week when you held steady (Holding Integrity) in the face of uncertainty and what you discovered. Then, three other times this week when you panicked, how that felt, and what you learned (Falling Off). And finally, three other vintage times, when you panicked, thought all was lost, but then recovered your balance and integrity (Recovery).

- You may want to supplement your inquiry by tracing the process with the "Gyroscope" an online version of the graphs, described in Book I, Chapter IV, or simply refer to the Adversity Wave Form.

- As you record your wins, it is important to pay them forward. (Please refer to the earlier section in the book and the "coaching tips" on **pay forward.**) You may want to jump ahead and read the section on the "Butterfly Effect," a global initiative to explore the ripple effects of generosity.

- Please pay attention to the details. I recommend that you keep an Explorer's Log of your discoveries. The processes we are discussing are subtle; the seeds of awakening germinate quietly according to their own pace and timing— but then one day there is a sign.

- Readers may enjoy having a look at Lynne McTaggart, *The Intention Experiment*, 2007.

II

THE EXPLORER'S WHEEL AND THE EIGHT-FOLD NOBLE PATH

"Nothing is too wonderful to be true, if it be consistent with the laws of science."
—Michael Faraday

I did not understand at first that the Explorer's Mind enables us to find connections of anything to anything and everything with everything. In physics, a wormhole is a theoretical tunnel or bridge, a shortcut, between different dimensions in space/time.[39] Through Trusting the Connection, the Explorer's Mind leads us into a wormhole of the psyche, a new way of thinking "intertidally" outside our comfortable vertical silos of specialization. I believe this ability to think intertidally, to find close connections between bodies of knowledge and experience which appear far apart, will become an increasingly important resource for our challenged species.

The astronomer Carl Sagan once observed, "Extraordinary claims require extraordinary evidence". If we are to embark on a journey as bold as traversing a wormhole, physical or psychological, some framework or vessel may prove useful. The Explorer's Wheel in Illustration 2 can provide the vessel. The Wheel in many cultures combines the symbolic content of the circle with the idea of movement, becoming and passing away. The author's intention behind calling his image "Explorer's Wheel" is to highlight its secular, non-denominational character, while keeping the process inclusive and inviting to possibility.[40]

The reader will note that the Explorer's Wheel has the distinctive fluid shape of a spiral. When a courier was dispatched to the Florentine painter Giotto (1266?-1337) requesting a sample of his work for Pope Benedict XII, the painter created a perfect circle in red ink. The courier asked Giotto whether that was the only sample of his work the Pope was to receive. Giotto replied that the image was "enough and too much."[41]

In Japanese the spiral wheel is called an *enso*. The *enso* evokes power, dynamism, charm, humor, drama, and stillness. The Japanese master Keizan Jokin (1268-1325) observed, "When you strike space it echoes, and thus all sounds are manifested; transforming emptiness to manifest myriad things is why shapes and forms are so various. Therefore you should not think that emptiness has no form or that emptiness has no sound. When you investigate carefully on reaching this point, it cannot be considered void and it cannot be considered existent either."[42] Book II Chapter IV will couple modern technology to this ancient form in the idea of a "smart *enso*."

Please scan

The Explorer's Wheel is built on a series of eight, theoretically infinitely expanding, domains. It was only after I began to explore the literature on the number "8" that I began to understand its significance. In the Chinese classic, *The I Ching*, the *Chinese Classic Book of Changes*, 8 or *Pi* is the hexagram Holding Together, or Union, which unites the Abysmal Water with the Receptive Earth. 8 is also the foundation of the Buddha's 8-Fold Noble Path. Thus, the number 8 appears to be a portal into union or connection.

The *I Ching* speaks in an oracular and parabolic language, which often defies logic and invites us to apprehend intuitively. The hexagram states:

> Holding together brings good fortune.
> Inquire of the oracle once again.
> Whether you possess sublimity, constancy, and perseverance.
>
> What is required is that we unite with others, in order that all may complement and aid one another.

Water fills up all the empty places on the earth and clings fast to her. Water flows to unite with water, because all parts of it are subject to the same laws. So, too, should human society hold together through a community of interests that allows each individual to feel him/herself a member of the whole. Fundamental sincerity is the only proper basis for forming relationships.

As you can see, the Explorer's Wheel has the following structure. The particular configuration I have selected is based on a personal, an aesthetic and intuitive preference. The Reader may prefer a different sequence. Arrange the realms in a way that is most congenial for you. At the center, I have placed Explorer's Mind because that is the center in my cosmology. However, you can freely enter through any gate. I have placed the Past at 6:00 o'clock and the **Future** at high noon. For me, their balancing energies "hold" the structure. Beauty appears at 11:00, Discovery/Invention/Innovation at 3:00, Connecting to Humanity at 5:00, the Networked Brain/Mind at 7:00, Life Force at 9:00, and Wisdom at 1:00. Each inner circle forms its own 8-point matrix. Fill in the essential elements as you discover them. Each of these will point you to what is personally interesting to you, opening new and evolving patterns without end. You can explore each of these realms as deeply and richly as you fancy. I have found that when I begin in one realm, I soon find myself in another. For example, the Realm of Beauty can morph into a Realm of Wisdom or Discovery. You can explore serially or meditate upon the central core, Trust the Connection, and all eight quadrants simultaneously. It doesn't matter. It's up to you. Let's begin the journey into the **Past**.

CONNECTING TO THE PAST

The ancient Greek poet Agathon (~ 441-401 B.C.) observed, "Even God cannot change the Past." Agathon's statement implies that the **Past** is a distinct, inflexible, linear, dead "thing," separate from the living Present. Is he correct? What, after all, is the **Past**? There may be another way to think about it.

The **Past** may better be viewed as a *potpourri* of largely subjective experience, strongly colored by emotions and untested assumptions, augmented by our creative imagination, conflated, translated and explained to ourselves in unexplored stories which themselves are edited, revised, expurgated, mixed up, and largely forgotten, as the experience we once had fades from memory and consciousness. These fragments of experience—the data—are stored in images–visual, auditory, olfactory, kinesthetic, synesthetic, and so on—which suddenly appear, often unbidden, in response to a stimulus in our present lives.[43] We "re-member" or "re-collect" meaning, gathering the fragments and reassembling them, unlike Humpty-Dumpty, who was unable to put all the pieces together. At this point in the sequence our creative imagination fueled by emotions gets to work. We reinterpret the data and produce new stories which we attempt to bring into conformity with the version of reality we favor at any particular moment.

If one strips away all the emotions and subjective content, one might still argue that the **Past** at its core is based upon "facts."[44] But even solid facts are far from secure. As the optical illusion in the footnote suggests, our sturdy and reliable world of "facts" may be

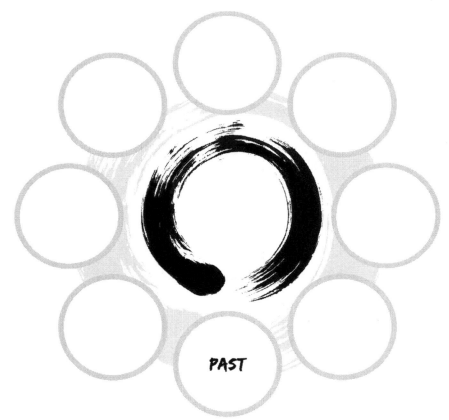

PAST

Illustration 2

built on shifting sands.[45] Cognitive bias predominates. We see what we want to see, or are directed to see, or are most comfortable with seeing.

In a famous experiment by Daniel Simmons and Christopher Chabris, the subjects are asked to watch a one-minute video of two teams of three players each, one in white shirts, the other black, as they weave around each other tossing basketballs. The viewer's task is to count the number of tosses by the white team. Without warning, after thirty five seconds a man dressed as a gorilla enters the room, walks directly in front of the players, thumps his chest, and departs. A full fifty percent of the subjects did not remember seeing the gorilla even when asked if they saw anything unusual. The experiment has been repeated with consistent results.[46] If our own living ocular proof is fallible, as this experiment suggests, how much more elusive are the story lines which are locked away in the closet of our memories.

Please scan

Might it be possible that what we perceive as the "dead" past can actually come "alive," while a large part of our daily lives may actually be already "dead?" Can we choose when we are alive or dead? Is it possible to live simultaneously and creatively in **Past, Present, and Future**? Here is a curious story which may provide some insight. It is a classical tale from ancient China, but its deep question is about what is real, and what isn't, and is as fresh as it was over fifteen hundred years ago.

Alive or Dead?[47]

Daowu and Jianyuan went to a house to offer condolences. Jianyuan struck the coffin with his hand and asked, "Alive or dead?"

Daowu said, "I'm not saying alive, I'm not saying dead."

"Why not," Jianyuan asked.

"I'm not saying, I'm not saying," Daowu maintained.

On the way home Jianyuan became belligerent,

"Say something immediately, Teacher, or it will be the worse for you."

Daowu said, "Hit me if you like, but I'm not saying." Jianyuan hit him.

After Daowu passed on, Jianyuan went to Shishuang and told him the story.

Shishuang said, "I'm not saying alive, I'm not saying dead."

Jianyuan said, "Why not?"

Shishuang said, "I'm not saying, I'm not saying!"

At this point Jianyuan awakened.

Exploring the Story

Is there something about saying, naming, or defining that takes life out of this moment? Something about "not-knowing" that holds its mystery? If uncertainty is a form of not-knowing and not-knowing is the birthplace of all that is possible and creative, why then need we fear it?

Jianyuan held on tight to his personal version of reality. He had to know the answer to his deep question: "Alive or Dead?" It had become an obsession, as if there was some-"thing" to know. He struck his old teacher. But Daowu was compassionate. He refused to steal his student's opportunity for awakening. "I'm not saying, I'm not saying." Awakening takes time. Many years after Daowu died Jianyuan sought out Shishuang, another master, and asked the same question. The question refused to leave him and he received the same reply. But this time, he is ready. "Alive or Dead?" No theory. BAM! It is right now. Are you alive, Jianyuan, or dead? It's your choice. It's our choice. Not-saying is a Zen way of pointing to what Albert Einstein called the "mystery."

If we can alter how we interpret the **Past**, might it also be possible to influence the effects of our past actions in the **Present** and the **Future**?

One benefit of being truly alive is that we are no longer captives of the hungry ghosts of our own imaginations, which enables us to cancel, at least in part, the consequences of past actions. In Christian terms this is called "redemption." In Buddhism, it is called becoming "akarmic," liberated from our karma.

No one understood this better than Charles Dickens in his classic story, *A Christmas Carol.*[48] The tale is about an old miser, Scrooge, who lives alone, "solitary as an oyster." After many years of being mean to everyone, on Christmas Eve he has a series of odd encounters with "spirits" from the "other side." One of them is the Ghost of his late partner, Jacob Marley. The meeting takes place in Scrooge's dank flat on a cold London night. Rattling his fetters with a horrible noise, Marley's Ghost says to Scrooge, "I wear the chain I forged in life. I made it link by link and yard by yard; I girded it on by my own free will, and of my own free will I wore it. Is its pattern strange to you?" The chains are Marley's actions while alive.

"But why do spirits walk the earth, and why do they come to me?" asks Scrooge. "It is required of every man," the Ghost returns, "that the spirit within him should walk abroad among his fellow-men, and travel far and wide; and if that spirit goes not forth in life, it is condemned to do so after death. It is doomed to wander through the world ... and witness what it cannot share, but might have shared on earth, and turned to happiness."

After encountering other interesting spirits, the Ghost of Christmas Present and the Ghost of Future Christmas, Scrooge at last awakens from his slumber, as did Jianyuan. It is a bright and snowy Christmas morning. Scrooge's spirit, like the fresh snow, is light as a feather, and as Dickens, his creator, writes, from then on he no longer needed to resort to spirits, alcoholic or otherwise. His spirit is free to "work kindly in its little sphere, whatever it might be, to find its mortal life too short for its vast means of usefulness. Though some people rolled their eyes when they beheld the change in him, his own heart laughed and that was enough for him".

At those times when my own mind is light, I have discovered that my relationship with the **Past** appears to change. The dark stories soften, or perhaps I see them with fresh eyes. The **Past** becomes closer, more intimate, and events and people long forgotten suddenly reappear in new and often helpful ways. It seems that a curtain parts and two worlds which once appeared separate are one. The relationship of our mind to the **Past** may be far more adaptive, plastic, and dynamic than we generally suppose.[49]

CONNECTING TO WISDOM

The Explorer's Mind and **Wisdom** are linked by space, vast spaciousness. In this sense, the Explorer's Mind moves in the opposite direction from conventional academic knowledge, which in many cultures has been associated with filling the mind to the brim with facts. Although "knowledge" may be assembled and accumulated, it seems that **Wisdom** requires a different skill set: attention, patience, empathy, and a retreat from pre-conceived, conventional notions.[50] Here are some of the attributes of the Explorer's Mind which link it to **Wisdom**.

Illustration 3

Spaciousness in a Cup of Tea

Nan-in, a Japanese master during the Meiji era (1864-1912), received a university professor who came to inquire about Zen. Nan-in served tea. He poured his visitor's cup full and then kept pouring.

Aghast, the professor exclaimed, "Stop! It's already full, no more can go in!"

Amused, Nan-in replied, "Like this cup, you are so full of your own opinions and speculations. How can I show you Zen unless you empty your mind?"[51]

Mercy and Kindness

Wisdom is closely allied with love and forgiveness. As Shakespeare writes, it blesses both giver and recipient: "it is mightiest in the mightiest: it is enthroned in the heart of kings." Explorer's Mind is reflected in Nelson Mandela's choosing not to incite a bloodbath against the white Afrikaans who had imprisoned him for twenty-seven years in Robben Island, but rather to call for reconciliation. No one expressed this quality more powerfully and poetically than President Abraham Lincoln in his Second Inaugural Address.

> With malice toward none; with charity for all; with firmness in the right, as God gives us to see the right, let us strive on to finish the work we are in; to bind up the nation's wounds; to care for him who shall have borne the battle, and for his widow, and his orphan—to do all which may achieve and cherish a just and lasting peace, among ourselves, and with all nations.

Lincoln is the historic archetype of intelligence, vision, practicality, and compassion. If we listen closely to the Second Inaugural Address, we can discover Lincoln's sense of timing, sequencing, and steadiness, which are also attributes of **Wisdom** and the Explorer's Mind. Lincoln was deeply connected to the tragic cadence of his time, a period of profound uncertainty and turbulence. It is said that his mind worked slowly and thoughtfully (negative capability) but with the power of a bear trap.

But **Wisdom** is not solely the domain of great historical figures like Mandela and Lincoln. Perhaps few people today have heard of Mattie Stepanek, but those of us who first encountered him in his various television appearances can never forget him. Matthew Joseph Thaddeus Stepanek (July 17, 1990—June 22, 2004), known as Mattie Stepanek, was a young American poet who became a peace advocate and lobbied on Capitol Hill on behalf of peace, people with disabilities, and children with life-threatening conditions. He suffered from a rare form of muscular dystrophy, *dysautonomic mitochondrial myopathy*, and died before his fourteenth birthday. His sister and two brothers also died from the same disease during early childhood. You don't need to read further. Simply point your phone and listen to this brief excerpt of Mattie speaking and you will understand.[52] In his moving tribute to Mattie, his friend, former president Jimmy Carter, observed at Mattie's funeral, "We have known kings and queens, and we've known presidents and prime ministers, but the most extraordinary person whom I have ever known in my life is Mattie Stepanek."[53]

Please scan

Although Explorer's Mind often works at a different pace from Internet time, when called upon, it can move with lighting speed, learn, and adapt. Hakuin Ekaku was a famous Zen master, accomplished artist, and poet. Here is one of my favorite Hakuin stories:

The Gates of Paradise[54]—Trainability

A *ronin* (masterless samurai) visited Hakuin and inquired, "Is there really a paradise and hell?"

"Now why would a beggar-faced fellow like you ask such a silly question? What lord would have you as his guard?" observed the master.

Enraged, the ronin drew his sword.

"Here open the gates of hell," noted Hakuin.

At these words the ronin perceived the master's teaching, sheathed his sword, and bowed.

"Here open the gates of paradise," Hakuin smiled.

Hakuin's story illustrates three points simultaneously about the qualities of the Explorer's Mind. First, Hakuin's mind itself is steady in the face of danger. Like Joe Simpson or Louis Zamperini or the Korean abbot, he does not give in to panic, which is really the voice of delusion. One might say he is rooted to nothingness, to the earth. Right (wise and compassionate) action, unimpeded by worry, flows naturally in the stream of things. Second, Hakuin's steadiness creates an opening for the *ronin*. There is a field-of-mind effect. In this case, the *ronin* is also an explorer with a deep question: Where is paradise and where is hell? Hakuin's question sparks a critical moment for discovery. But the *ronin* is also a remarkable person. Probably he has pondered his question for a long time. He has the capacity to see the error of his ways: his rage against what is, against reality, and he is willing to change course—in an instant. His conflict with Hakuin is really the outward expression of the war within in his own mind. He at last finds the gates of paradise: the aware and tranquil mind.

Demanding Evidence—The Empirical Quality of Explorer's Mind

It might seem paradoxical that Explorer's Mind can act instantaneously in some situations and insist on empirical evidence in others. But that is its nature. Moreover, you don't have to be a Zen master like Hakuin, or a martial artist, or a natural genius like Lincoln, to learn wise balance. There is a simple but elegant move you can practice to begin: you simply don't need to believe your thoughts or your emotions—your worries, fears, and terrors, or the conceits, vanities, and grandiose stories—none of them. If your brain produces some outrageous panicky story, you can insist on the evidence. You can be scientific about the process, just as Carl Sagan recommends. Although Sagan was referring to extraordinary and often unfounded claims in science when he observed that great claims demand great proof, his dictum applies equally to the whispering of the panicky mind.

Because we are accustomed to believing the scary stories we tell ourselves, it is difficult for many of us (the author included) to parse sober reality from our own internally-generated propaganda. Here is a technique that may be useful.

Byron Katie, in her powerful process of personal inquiry which she calls, "The Work," poses five questions:[55]

Please scan

- How certain am I that the story I am telling myself is true? (Can I be 100 percent certain?)
- How does the story I am telling myself make me feel?
- Who might I be without the story?
- What if I were to turn the story around?
- What are the chances that the opposite of my story is equally plausible?

In practicing this technique I have made the following interesting discoveries:

- Almost invariably I cannot confirm the veracity of the story I am telling myself.
- Telling myself scary stories makes me feel awful.
- I become free when I simply don't believe the stories.
- It is easy to imagine the opposite of what I am telling myself.
- Not only is the opposite at least as plausible, in my experience the voice of panic rarely, if ever, proves true.[56]

By putting stories or pre-conceived notions to the test in this way, uncertainty can become your friend and doubt your ally. They preserve our sanity. There is a marvelous scene in the movie, *Doubt,* where a ferocious head nun, portrayed by Meryl Streep, is convinced that an independent minded (doubting) priest (Phillip Seymour Hoffman) is sexually abusing a young black choir boy. The scene is a parochial school in the Bronx. Her protective rage and his disdain reach a fierce climax in a final confrontation in her office, when he demands proof and she bursts out indignantly, "I need no proof. I have my certainty!" But as we learn, her certainty is the source of her suffering, and her coming to doubt, the beginning of her finding peace of mind.

The Explorer's Mind, as noted, is ultimately empirical. We learn to strip away the stories, the rage, the hurt, and to observe the world innocently just as it is. In struggling with our demons, we continuously ask: "Why should I believe you now? What is your proof? Have your teachings ever proved true before? What if **this time** I try something different?" The embodied wisdom of the Explorer's Mind may require no more than this slight shift in attention.

BEAUTY AND AWAKENING

As Umberto Eco has ably demonstrated in his *History of Beauty* (2007), definitions, perceptions, and the appreciation of **Beauty** have changed over the centuries and across cultures. The cliché is accurate: **Beauty** does depend on the eye of the beholder. But is there something more? Is there also an immutable quality of **Beauty** that transcends time and culture? I believe there is, and that **Beauty** opens us to deeper, universal undercurrents and connections.

The sixth century Ionian philosopher and mathematician Pythagoras of Samos is generally credited with the idea that the planets

Illustration 4

and stars behave according to mathematical principles and work in concert to produce "heavenly harmonies" inaudible to human ears. A century later, Plato maintained that **Beauty** exists on an abstract plane as a perfect form. Is it possible that there is a resonant frequency of these subtle harmonies which we can apperceive and experience as "**Beauty**?"[57] Albert Einstein expressed the relation of **Beauty** to science as mystery.

> The most beautiful experience we can have is the mysterious. It is the fundamental emotion which stands at the cradle of all true art and science. Whoever does not know it and can no longer wonder, no longer marvel, is as good as dead, and his eyes are dimmed. It was the experience of mystery—even if mixed with fear—that engendered religion. A knowledge of the existence of something we cannot penetrate, our perceptions of the profoundest reason and the most radiant beauty, which only

in their most primitive forms are accessible to our minds—it is this knowledge and this emotion that constitute true religiosity; in this sense, and, in this alone, I am a deeply religious man.[58]

A Paradox

To the ancient Greek philosophers, and to this great man of science, **Beauty** is experienced as remote and unreachable. But for many people, like the pilgrim Lingyuan, **Beauty** is direct and immediate. In this section, I wish to show that the apparent paradox of the remoteness and immediacy of **Beauty** is the same as paradox of certainty and uncertainty discussed earlier; that the opposites are actually aspects of each other, and of one, and that the paradox can be reconciled by a shift in consciousness which I am calling the Explorer's Mind. In fact, our discovery of **Beauty** in the ordinary and unnoticed **is** the awakening of the Explorer's Mind.

Beauty in Nature

Our primary connection to **Beauty** has been through Nature, and our sense of awe and wonder is likely unchanged since the dawn of our species. Indigenous peoples retain this living, immediate connection with **Beauty**. The Navajo, for example, have a special ceremony called the "Beauty Way," which is designed to restore balance and harmony by reestablishing the link to the Natural World.[59]

With dew about my feet may I walk
With beauty before me may I walk
With beauty behind me may I walk
With beauty above me may I walk
In old age, wandering on a trail of beauty, lively, may I walk
In old age, wandering on a trail of beauty, living again, may I walk
It is finished in beauty
It is finished in beauty.

The naturalist John Muir expressed it this way:

Climb the mountains and get their good tidings.
Nature's peace will flow into you as sunshine flows into trees.
The winds will blow their freshness into you, and the storms their energy, while cares will drop off like autumn leaves.[60]

Beauty and the Arts

In a famous letter, often attributed to Goethe, the poet once observed that Bach listened in on God's conversation with Himself. If this is so, Bach was able to transcribe by his genius this celestial conversation. As a musician I have discovered that **Beauty** in music has certain magical properties that correspond perfectly to and arouse specific emotions and energies. Some examples:

- If I want to connect to bounty and generosity, I listen to the final choral of the first Bach Cantata (*Gott ist mein Konig* BWV 71).
- For triumph: (Handel Organ Concerto, concluding chorus from *Esther*)
- For hope: (Mozart arias from the *Marriage of Figaro* and *Cosi Fan Tutte*)
- For steadiness: (Handel overture from *Sampson;* Bach's *Well Tempered Clavier*, especially Volume II, No.7, E-flat Major fugue of bells.)
- For liquid diamonds: (George Frederic Handel, Suite No. 2 F Major, Allegro)
- For Promethean energy and power: (Mozart's *Jupiter Symphony;* Mozart Piano Concertos nos. 20 and 24, especially Daniel Barenboim)
- For mad frenzy: (Beethoven, *Kreutzer* Sonata; especially Itzhak Perlman and Vladimir Ashkenaszy.[61])
- For serenity: (Keith Jarrett, *Shenandoah;* Beethoven, *Moonlight* Sonata)
- For revelation and transcendence: (Handel, *Messiah*, Aria: "I Know That My Redeemer Liveth.")

A Private Reminiscence on Music and Inspiration

I have the memory of my father playing the preludes and fugues of Bach's *Well Tempered Clavier* on the piano before I recall drinking milk. It is one of my fondest memories of him. I turn the wheel and my mind moves fast "backward" fifteen years, and I am standing beside him playing the recorder, accompanying his Bach chorale. He is so alive again I can smell the Bay Rum aftershave with which he would douse his head.

Recently, at five in the morning, I am in my car returning from a business trip. I decide to listen to Book One of the *Well Tempered*

Clavier with Glenn Gould as the artist. I am doing my best to keep both eyes on the road (there are still only a few other drivers) while I simply let my mind rise and fall with the tones and the voices. The image of my father passes by like a cloud. In the cascade of sounds, at some point "I" disappears. Time stops. Only Bach and Gould remain. Soon the *jinni* begins to appear, as if from Aladdin's Lamp. First one idea arrives—a scout—then another, then a burst. I try to keep track, to remember them in sequence. As a writer I am grateful when the Muse speaks—and when she does, I must put everything aside. She won't wait; I cannot stop the flow of ideas, even if I wished. But it is glorious. My experience of **Beauty**, especially in music, is of a heightened energy state. While listening to Bach I have the odd sensation of connecting to his creative life force, across a chasm of two hundred and fifty years, which I can siphon directly into my own living cells.[62]

I have discovered that I can also siphon creative energy in the visual arts. In Paris there is a painting by Pierre August Renoir in the Musee D'Orsay entitled, *A Dance in the Country*. You can see it for yourself with a simple online search. A man is holding a young woman in his arms. She appears ecstatically happy in his embrace. It is a spring afternoon. She looks out and sees us, from more than hundred years ago. Forever will he love her, and she will be forever fair. **Beauty** enables us in this way to discover and awaken to the eternal part of ourselves.

In the wondrous world of the Internet we can today hear the living voice of William Butler Yeats, reading his reverberant poem, *The Lake of Innisfree*. He also steps out of the pages from over a hundred years ago.[63]

Please scan

Cellular Expressions of Beauty

My experience of Bach at a cellular level may not be just poetic fantasy, but rather physiological reality. Recent discoveries in a new field of neuroaesthetics are beginning to provide support for the insight that Beauty is not an abstraction, but rather is experienced in every cell of our bodies. In one important study, Professor Semir Zeki and Dr. Tomohiro Ishizu reported that the brain's medial orbitofrontal cortex appears to respond significantly to visual and audio cues which subjects experienced as beautiful. These parts of the brain, along with the visual and audio cortexes and the caudate nucleus, an important part of the brain's learning and memory system, become highly active.[64]

Dr. Candace Pert, a research professor in physiology and biophysics, has asserted for many years that emotional receptors are alive and distributed throughout the autonomic nervous system, not only in the brain.

> There is a lot of evidence that memory occurs at the point of synapse; there are changes that take place in the receptors. The sensitivity of the receptors is part of memory and pattern storage. But the peptide network extends beyond the hippocampus, to organs, tissue, skin, muscle and endocrine glands. They all have peptide receptors on them and can access and store emotional information. This means this emotional memory is stored in many places in the body, not just the brain. The autonomic nervous system is pivotal to this entire understanding. Its importance is much more subtle than has been thought. Every peptide that I have ever mapped and more can be found in the autonomic nervous system.[65]

In sum, there is a neurological correlate for our emotions, including the appreciation of **Beauty**, which is felt and experienced throughout the body.[66] Is it possible that we are hardwired, predisposed to receive **Beauty** from anywhere and everywhere? The neurochemical receptors within our bodies may be the receiving stations of an even more refined transmission network.

Beauty in Improbable Situations

As the Explorer's Mind reaches outward, it discovers **Beauty** in improbable circumstances. In his Academy award-winning film, *Waste Land*[67] artist and photographer Vik Muniz depicts Brazil's *catadores*—garbage pickers who mine the treasure from the trash heaps of Rio de Janeiro's Jardim Gramacho landfill. These are the forgotten, the human discards of Brazilian society, who are the victims of injustice, indifference, and cruelty. Through his interviews and skill, the director portrays their everyday lives with tenderness, dignity, optimism, and joy in a way that ennobles them and touches our hearts. His film won many awards and was very much a collaborative undertaking. The proceeds from the sales were returned principally to the participating artists and the community and stimulated an artistic revival. However, for me what is most beautiful about this film is the director's ability to connect us to their lives and, through them, to our common humanity. Muniz lets light upon their faces, their laughter, and their tears.

Please scan

Beauty in Nothing Special

A cold wind rises, momentary flecks of iridescent brightness, and we vanish from the stage. Is there **Beauty** in our departing this earth, as on our arrival? Can we find **Beauty** even in nothing special?[68]

Takuan Soho (December 24, 1573 – January 27, 1645) was a Zen monk, calligrapher, painter, poet, gardener, and tea master. He was a friend and teacher of the great swordsman/artist Miyamoto Musashi. He seems to have been unaffected by his fame. On his deathbed he instructed his disciples: "Bury my body behind the temple, cover it with dirt and go home. Read no sutras, hold no ceremony. Receive no gifts from monks or laity. Let the monks wear their robes, eat their meals, and carry on as on normal days." At his final moment, he wrote the Chinese character for *yume* (夢, dream) put down the brush, and died. Today Takuan lives on in the humble Japanese pickle, *takuan*, which bears his name.

CONNECTING TO LIFE FORCE

In the Chinese language the character for life force, or vital energy, is *qi* (氣) written with the ideogram of breath passing in waves over rice growing in a paddy. Hence, the derived meaning of *qi* as the living source of nourishment. The same idea of a life energy or the breath of life is found in many cultures: Greek (*pneuma*), Japanese (*ki*), Sanskrit (*prana*), Hawaiian (*ha*), Navajo, (*nilch'i*) Lakota (*ni*), and Hebrew (*n'shamah* or *ruah*).[69]

The primary sources of *qi* are:

- Original *qi* which is inherited from parents or the universe
- Breath *qi*, from respiration
- Dietary *qi* from what we eat and drink
- Internal *qi* as it flows inside the body through special channels which in Chinese medicine are called meridians

The world's cultures which have discovered the "subtle" *qi* energy—meaning that it cannot be fully measured by current Western scientific instruments—have developed elegant systems to cultivate it.[70] The Chinese art of *qi* training and practice (*qigong*) cultivates the *qi* with three objectives: warfare (especially as an energetic shield against external attack), healing, and wellness maintenance (including as a barrier against pathogens).

Illustration 5

The foundation of *qigong* is connectedness. When the *qi* is blocked, disease results; when the *qi* flows naturally, health and vitality ensue. Connecting to life force is *qigong*, and follows the basic principles of connecting to the **Past** and to **Beauty**.[71]

Qigong practice begins and continues with discovering and re-establishing our connection to the earth. Most people appear to hover over the earth when walking, absorbed in thoughts, and lose their connection to the ground. Therefore "rooting" is a deeply beneficial training. The most immediate way to experience this connection, and to strengthen and to recharge your *qi*, is to practice *zhan zhuang* (standing post), which Ken Cohen, a leading *qigong* teacher in the West, refers to as *qigong*'s "million dollar secret." The basic elements of the technique, almost verbatim from Ken Cohen, are:

- Hold your rounded arms out in front about two to three feet in front of the chest at shoulder level, fingers pointing toward each other, elbows pointing downward, arms about six inches from your body, as if you are embracing a beach ball or a tree trunk.
- Relax.
- Root—sink your weight and *qi* through the feet into the ground—like a tree with deep roots.
- Keep feet parallel, flat on the ground.
- Keep your knees gently bent.
- Maintain the spine straight and long.
- Keep your chest relaxed, not distended or depressed.
- Hold your head suspended, imagining a string lifting your head.
- Keep your eyes slightly open with a soft and peaceful gaze.
- Breathe through your nose; let the breath become slow, long, deep, smooth, and even.
- Keep your mouth slightly open, with the tongue touching the palate.
- Stay open with direct and peripheral awareness.[72]

There is a simple and elegant *qigong* practice called the "Inner Smile," which is an effective way to cleanse the mind and restore peace and happiness. The formal practice was first published by Mantak Chia.[73] Elizabeth Gilbert, author of *Eat, Pray, Love*, learned a similar practice from her Balinese teacher, Ketut Liyer, in her first encounter. "Why they always look so serious in yoga? You make serious face like this (he demonstrates), you scare away good energy. To meditate, only you must smile. Smile with face, smile with mind, and good energy will come to you and clean away dirty energy."[74]

Please scan

Connecting to Nature's Life Force

I began to understand the importance of connectivity through *wushu* training with Master George Xu as we practiced in Golden Gate Park. I still remember him, a true fighter, and the story he told me one day of his encounter on the Shanghai Bund with a lady *gongfu* "master." This lady was challenging all opponents, claiming she could kill anyone by paralyzing them with her powerful *qi*. "Go ahead and kill me," he told her. I asked him what he would have done if she had proved the real thing. "I am a *wushu* man. I am ready to die," he replied. And then, almost parenthetically, "Anyway, I wanted the taste of it." He taught me method: You don't strike an opponent with your fist alone. Your fist is part of your arm, your arm is connected to your shoulders, which are connected to your hips, your legs, your ankles, your feet, and your feet are deeply connected to the earth. The earth energy (*qi*) coils, rises, and explodes though you. You don't strike him. The earth strikes him. Trust your connection to the earth.[75]

One day I was in my garden practicing *zhan zhuang,* and I began to trace the limbs of the trees, as if I were doing a slow *tai chi chuan*, the dance-like Chinese inner martial art. I fancied that the limbs of the trees were moving, in slow time, along with the branches which were nodding in the wind. Instantly I could feel the energy of the earth and the trees rise up through my body. It was a glorious sensation. Since then whenever I feel depleted, I imagine driving my electric (body) vehicle to the nearest service station (a tree) and recharging its battery.

From these insights I developed my own form of *qigong*, which I call "tree-gong." The practice is simple:

- Select a tree whose power and energy resonate with yours.
- Imagine yourself deeply setting down roots, by letting your energy flow into the earth through your *yong quan* (bubbling well) points at the center of the insteps of both feet.
- Connect your roots to the roots of the tree.
- Assume the *zhan zhuang* stance.
- Enjoy the practice as long as you like.
- See what you discover.

I have since extended the technique to the ocean and sky by exploring the idea of "sea-gong" and "sky-gong," following similar protocols. You can invent your own free forms. The point is that ALL this vital energy is available to you, and it's FREE. You simply need to know how to tap in: Root, relax control, and connect. The great Zen master Yumen observes, "Medicine and disease cure each other. The whole universe is medicine."[76]

CONNECTING TO DISCOVERY, INVENTION, AND INNOVATION

The Explorer's Mind begins with a sense of surprise and wonder. No one captured the thrill of discovery and exploration better than Mark Twain.

What is it that confers the noblest delight? What is that which swells a man's breast with pride above that which any other experience can bring to him? Discovery! To know that you are walking where none others have walked; that you are beholding what human eye has not seen before; that you are breathing a virgin atmosphere. To give birth to an idea—to discover a great thought—an intellectual nugget, right under the dust of a field that many a brain-plow had gone over before. To find a new planet, to invent a new hinge, to find a way to make the lightnings carry your messages. To be the first—that is the idea. To do something, say something, see something, before anybody else—these are the things that confer a pleasure compared with which other pleasures are tame and commonplace, other ecstasies cheap and trivial. Morse, with his first message, brought by his servant, the lightning; Fulton in that long-drawn century of suspense, when he placed his hand upon the throttle-valve, and low, the steamboat moved; Jenner, when his patient with a cow's virus in his blood, walked through the small pox hospitals unscathed; Howe, when the idea shot through his brain that for a hundred and twenty generations the eye had been bored through the wrong end of the needle; the nameless lord of art who laid down his chisel in some old age that is forgotten now, and gloated upon the finished Laocoön; Daguerre, when he commanded the sun, riding in the zenith, to print the landscape upon his insignificant silvered plate, and he obeyed; Columbus in the Pinta's shrouds when he swung his hat above a fabled sea and gazed abroad upon an unknown world! These are the men who have really lived— who have actually comprehended what pleasure is—who have crowded long lifetimes of ecstasy into a single moment.[77]

What if each of us has the potential and could have the opportunity to become a Columbus, a Madame Currie, or an Armstrong? How many such moments of discovery might fire our collective genius? What wicked problems can be solved, once we put our collective minds to them?[78]

Wicked problems—the really nasty complex problems produced from tightly coupled systems[79]—will rarely be solved by domain experts palavering with other experts in their narrow silos of specialty. Here are the elements of an alternative discovery/invention/ innovation process based on the Explorer's Mind and networked creativity. The Explorer's Mind offers a broader lens to approach these complex problems and the negotiation/navigation model, discussed in Book I, may provide an effective means to disseminate and guide breakthroughs to their highest and best uses.

Inventing for Humanity[80]

- **Assemble the Discovery Team(s)**

Every Discovery Expedition has a Discovery Team, which ideally includes: 1) domain experts; 2) scouts—intuitive individuals who can think about any problem imaginatively; 3) analysts—persons with strong analytic skills; 4) facilitators—persons who are skilled in team building, interpersonal relations, and mediation. They help to hold the center.[81]

- **First Clues: Discover=Uncover; Invent=Find**

The first hint is contained in the Latin derivation of the word, "discover" (Latin: *discooperire*, to reveal, uncover, disclose). We think of "inventing" as coming up with something new, but here also the original Latin meaning is to "find" (*invenire*). Even the word "create" has the same sense, at least in German: *schöpfen*, to ladle out from a great sea of potentiality. Let us pause to reflect on the implications. The deep discoveries exist already, within our own minds, perhaps just beyond our grasp. This insight alone can strengthen the Will and give us hope when we are blocked. Realizing that a solution exists already in itself can influence the probabilities of success.[82]

- **Formulate the First Generation "Core Discovery Puzzle (CDP)"**

All great strategy begins with crafting the essential problem. I prefer to call it a "puzzle," because although it may be knotty, nonetheless it is an opportunity, and puzzle evokes play and adventure. It is useful to begin with domain experts. They have the scientific or technical knowledge and usually a lifetime's experience with the issues. We will honor and credit their experience, but we must not be bound by it. The knowledge of experts can establish the baseline of the expedition.

Illustration 6

It is not always easy to define precisely the CDP. One technique is to ask an expert to define the CDP. Then provide the context by asking such questions as "How far have you come?" Where do you ideally want to end up?" "How would you describe some important milestones along the way?" "What has to happen for you to reach these milestones?" and so on.

- Identify and Explore Limiting Assumptions—Our assumptions limit our ability to see by our assumptions. This is explained in an earlier chapter of this book.[83]
- Find the Fallacy and Cognitive Illusion.

Albert Einstein once famously observed, "Whether you can observe a thing or not depends on the theory which you use. It is the theory which decides what can be observed." It may therefore be useful at the outset to examine rigorously the cognitive underpinning of the theory or story we are running to solve the problem.

The words we employ to describe the world contain embedded assumptions and fallacies. Simply exposing the fallacy may produce a breakthrough. For years ornithologists misclassified black swans as a different species of bird because they were black and obviously could not be swans—until someone had the smart idea that it might be possible to have a black swan. For years polio was considered a form of influenza and many children died because they were misdiagnosed and ineffectively treated. In the philosophy of language this is called "the problem of classes," *i.e.* assuming "a" cannot be "b" because it does not possess all the core characteristics of "a"; or the reverse: "a" is "b" because it shares some, although not all, of "b." Both premises assume "a" ("things" like "swanness," or "polio") exists in nature and fail to acknowledge that "a" is an abstraction, separated from the underlying empirical data[84].

In an important book, *Thinking Fast and Slow*, Nobel Laureate Daniel Kahneman systematically identifies common cognitive illusions as "false" beliefs that we intuitively accept as "true." These errors in perception pervade decision-making in government, business, and many other areas of life. These include:

- The Illusion of Validity: the false belief in the reliability of our own judgment.
- The Illusion of Understanding: the false belief that something is true because it has been confirmed by the past.

- The Illusion of Availability: a biased judgment, based on a small sampling, yet spurred by memory which happens to be readily available.
- The Bias of Endowment: our tendency to value something more highly when we own it than when someone else owns it.

Following Dr. Kahneman, the Discovery Team is well advised to scrub systematically the basic theory, metaphors, key words, and other building blocks of the initial and future generations of the CDP.[85]

- ## "Translate" the CDP into Metaphors and Stories

Is it possible to "translate" the Core Discovery Puzzle so that anyone can understand and play with it, even someone with no technical training? One way of democratizing a technical scientific problem is to express it as an image, a metaphor, or a good story. Our minds love good stories. Here is an example:

Some years ago I was on a train heading for Yale Medical School with my brother, who is a viral oncologist. We were visiting his friend, a prominent researcher of mad cow disease. I asked my brother, "Can you encapsulate the CDP of mad cow disease so a smart kid might instantly grasp the issues and even contribute to a solution?"

"OK, I'll give you three scenarios," he replied. "You have a house. Scenario 1—Someone flies over the house and drops a bomb. The house collapses. Scenario 2—Someone lights a match to the house and the house burns up. Scenario 3—The house collapses. In Scenarios 1-2, the causes are clear, *i.e.* bomb and match. In Scenario 3, there does not appear to be an external cause. What's going on? The smart kid responds with delight: "Dad, it's obvious. The termites woke up!"

The smart kid is not programmed to think the way experts are. His mind is innocent. He is naturally endowed with Explorer's Mind.

Now suppose the mad cow researcher also has an Explorer's Mind. Rather than dismissing the lead as childish nonsense, she translates the kid's lead back into the technical language and context of medical science. She returns to an earlier line of research, some creative "hunches" she has ignored, and six months later she makes an important discovery, which has eluded her and others for years.[86]

I am not suggesting environmental factors are the cause of mad cow disease. I have no knowledge and make no such claim. I am simply offering a way to enlist the creative capacities of a large segment of the "disenfranchised" population—kids or retired people, for example—

who are excited by science and want to explore without inhibitions. They too can enjoy contributing to the Discovery Expedition.

• Enlist Creative Amateurs

Many of the heroes and heroines of science have been creative amateurs who have labored on, unheralded and unknown, driven by the sheer exuberance of the quest: Gregor Mendel, who developed the science of genetics; Michael Faraday, a clerk in a London book shop, with virtually no formal education in science, who revolutionized our understanding of electricity; Srinivasa Ramanujan, an impoverished Indian mathematician, who influenced mathematics from string theory to crystallography. Even Pasteur and Einstein were not formally trained in the fields in which they made their most important discoveries. The more we investigate, the more we will find creative amateurs contributing significantly in many fields of science.[87]

As an attorney I have personally represented many creative amateurs who have developed breakthroughs in wave-powered electricity, wind energy, distributed desalination, waste-to-biofuels, waste-to-energy, cost-efficient energy storage, solar-powered mass transit, and a small, vastly more efficient motor. None of these inventors were professionally trained experts in these fields; many did not have college degrees. Most have faced extreme difficulties in being recognized. Such creative amateurs offer a reservoir of talent, waiting to solve the knotty problems of our age.

• Deploy the Discovery Engine

Technology and various methodologies can also contribute in solving complex scientific and other problems. I have organized some of the best of these into a coherent system, a Discovery Engine, which can be focused on the CDP. Three prominent examples among many are the following.

a. Discovery Engineering is an electro-encephalogram (EEG) biofeedback system which enables explorers to work with "creative reverie." This, in turn, is a natural state of consciousness, which every person experiences just prior to sleep and just upon leaving pre-sleep (hypnagogia) wherein an unconscious part of the mind suddenly becomes available. Perhaps the most famous historic example of a scientific breakthrough in creative reverie is that of the discovery of the organic structure of benzene by the Belgian chemist Fredrich August Kekule. The breakthrough arrived in the midst of a reverie dream of a snake swallowing its tail (Ouroboros), which formed a hexagon. Kekule's prepared mind noticed the signal he was being given by the striking image of the Ouroboros and his genius was to link it to his unsolved scientific challenge. EEG bio-feedback training teaches us how to enter creative reverie at will and tap the imaginative powers of our mind, and then systematically to "decode" its signals.[88]

Reader's Compass—Exploring Creative Reverie

For readers who would like to have a first taste of creative reverie, all you need to do is keep a pad of paper by your bed and pay attention as you slip into sleep. At the border you will encounter a liminal state of relaxation and detachment, a state of just watching, a sense of the world floating by. I like to imagine myself in a great theater, with my mind a screen, and I am here to watch the show. Suddenly, images arise—visual, auditory, olfactory, kinesthetic, tactile, synesthetic (refers to crossover senses, *e.g.* seeing a sound, etc.)—unbidden, and so life-like they cannot be distinguished from ordinary "reality."

I invite you to jot down these images. The same experience of creative reverie can occur just emerging from sleep as well. If you encounter such images in a dream-like sequence, coming out of sleep, I invite you to write down your dreams, in as great detail as you can but in reverse order, which will enable you to remember the entire sequence. There is an interesting literature on the interpretation of hypnagogic imagery and related dreams which you may enjoy exploring.[89]

b. Lead user innovation—is an entirely different procedure developed by Professor Eric Von Hippel at the Sloan School of MIT. Von Hippel has shown that many important technical and other challenges can be effectively addressed by identifying people in other, sometimes remote, fields who have struggled with and solved these issues. He reports that especially when the uses are non-competitive, the inventors are willing to share their secrets.[90] Lead user innovation is an excellent example of "horizontal" thinking, or "exaptation," a term coined by Steven Jay Gould and Elizabeth Vrba. One example is when an organism develops a trait for a specific use that then gets hijacked for a completely different function.[91]

Please scan

c. Triz—refers to the theory of creative problem solving developed by Genrich Altshuller in 1946 and later taught in many engineering academies in the old Soviet Union. Triz has become an integral part of the engineering curriculum in engineering schools in twenty-six countries. Triz masters have shown that solutions to many complex engineering problems can be systematically generated by reference to a standardized procedure, analogous to a mathematical formula. From a Triz perspective, the solutions to most engineering problems are "inevitable."[92] In a way, Triz and discovery engineering stand at opposite ends of methodologies for enhancing powers of discovery. Dr. Altshuller originally developed Triz to elevate scientific problem solving above the level of randomness in conventional brain storming. Discovery engineering harvests the creative randomness of the psyche through the insouciance of dream-like reverie. Randomness is considered a virtue.[93] When combined with other procedures, these methodologies constitute a formidable resource for innovators.[94]

- **Enhance Search, Analysis, and Tracking through Collaborative Business Intelligence Networks (CBINS)**

The Discovery Team has at its disposal many new tools for search, analysis, and tracking, among the most advanced of which is Intellipedia, the collaborative search engine developed by the U.S. intelligence community. A variety of other collaborative intelligence tools will permit the Discovery Team and other participants to map the "mind flow" of ideas, applications, and contacts, modeling these connections in the way the brain processes patterns.[95] It is also now possible to rank the reliability of such intelligence, as explained in the final chapter.[96]

- **Gain Leverage Through Collaborative Innovation Networks (COINS) and Open Innovation**

The Discovery Expedition can gain powerful leverage by drawing upon the resources of a wide range of strategic relationships, generated by COINS, a term originated by Peter Gloor in his book on *Swarm Creativity*.[97] One of the principal advantages of a COIN is that it aligns and tightly couples inventors (technology push) with users (market pull), thereby creating powerful feedback loops and accelerating the time-to-market of conceptual breakthroughs to commercially viable products and services. COINS are ideally designed in combination with concentric circles of strategic alliances within a framework of open innovation.

As shown in Illustration 7 there is now ample evidence that most of the commercially important inventions and innovations from

THE FOURTH QUADRANT

1600 - 1800

Illustration 7

1800 until the present have been developed under a non-market/networked/open innovation framework.[98] This is further corroboration of the increasing importance of collaboration in a networked world and of the importance of developing new models of intellectual property to support such collaboration.

- **Devise and Apply a New Model of Intellectual Property (IP)**

Contributors to Discovery Expeditions must be able to trust that their intellectual contributions will be fairly rewarded, otherwise they will tend to hold back their best ideas. The present legal structure for IP does not optimally encourage creative collaboration.

An improvement on the present model would encourage participants in the "inner" Discovery Team to optimize their IP portfolio by pooling their ideas in cross-licensing agreements and, preferably, by "mega-patents," which combine all inventions in one or a few "super patents." The attribution of profits and other credit can best be addressed by contract, not by weakening or balkanizing the patents. The integrity of the framework is optimally maintained by an "alliance charter" that addresses the deep issues—such as the parties' expectations, sense of equity, protocols of communication, and emergency scenarios—which standard legal agreements do not. Wherever possible, disputes should be addressed by mediation, rather than more formal legal processes such as arbitration or litigation.

The contributions of "outer" circles of participants are best addressed by offering them a wide range of financial and other rewards, prizes, citations, and public acknowledgement. Since 2001, much good work has been done on establishing a "Creative Commons," especially in the area of copyright protection. The Creative Commons license and methodology offers a stable and tested platform for sharing ideas within the context of a Discovery Expedition.[99] Because many significant scientific and other current challenges demand new combinations of diverse talents and skills, the development of legal and meta-legal innovations to foster collaborative discovery, invention, and innovation may prove as valuable to society as the underlying breakthroughs they help to accelerate.

• Incentive Prizes

The authors of *Abundance* provide a further useful dimension to my proposed model—the power of incentive competitions. Incentive prizes have a venerable history. In 1714 the British Parliament offered 20,000 pounds to the first person who could devise a way to measure accurately longitude at sea. In 1795, Napoleon I offered a 12,000-franc prize to anyone who could invent a way to preserve food which would feed the French army on its Russian campaign. Incentive prizes, including Peter Diamandis's famous X Prize, operate by a few clear principles. First, large incentive prizes raise the visibility of a particular challenge and create a mind-set that it is solvable. Second, such prizes break bottlenecks. Third, they generate broad networks and provide a powerful incentive for top talent to become engaged. Lastly, they provide a strong financial opportunity for the winners. To these attributes, I would add that such prizes help to build international bridges. As of this writing,

I am working on establishing a China X Prize to be funded by China's 100 Top National Champions, who have the vision to reach out and work collaboratively with the rest of the world in tackling its most pressing challenges.[100]

Summary

We are proposing an alternative, more inclusive model of the discovery, invention, and innovation process, which we believe will enable us to address a wide variety of the hitherto intractable problems now confronting the world. The model has these distinguishing features:

1. The operating premise is that the discoveries exist already in inchoate form. We suffer from a species of blindness in not seeing them.

2. The focus of our intense concentration is upon a series of precisely defined Core Discovery Puzzles which are transformed, translated, democratized, and refined as the Expedition proceeds and generates insights and solutions.

3. A unique peripheral vision is achieved by horizontal thinking encouraged through the Explorer's Wheel.

4. Powerful leverage is produced by effective collaboration delivered through Collaborative Business Intelligence Networks (CBINS) and Collaborative Innovation Networks (COINS).

5. Impedance in the system, produced from now dysfunctional notions of intellectual property, is optimally addressed by a new legal model, drawing upon the Creative Commons and other collaborative IP models.

6. Participants are provided a means to cultivate and reach toward their higher potentials while working together to "invent for humanity."

One of the interesting beacons along the journey will be the frequency of synchronicities and serendipities—in other words, ostensibly non-causal, curious, chance occurrences which have special meaning or significance to the discoverers. Carl Jung and others suggest that synchronicities reflect a deep connecting principle expressed in universal symbols or "archetypes."[101] The presence of synchronicities is one sign that the trail is "warm." Chance, it seems, favors the connected mind.

Illustration 8

CONNECTING TO HUMANITY

In the West the concept of "mind" is still generally viewed in the popular press and also by many scientists as an abstraction. It is conceived as an extension of the intellect, which is deemed to be located in the physical brain. In Eastern philosophy—and as developed in the integrity model in the first edition of this book—the mind is an integral concept of head, heart, and hand. For example, the word *kokoro* (心) (in Chinese and Japanese the alternative pronunciation is *shin*) really means "heart/mind."[102] The Explorer's Mind incorporates these meanings and when it "connects" to humanity, it does so in this non-dualistic integral way.

In his famous essay "*On Compensation,*" the American transcendental philosopher Ralph Waldo Emerson wrote:

In the order of nature we cannot render benefits to those from whom we receive them, or only seldom. But the benefit we receive must be rendered again, line for line, deed for deed, cent for cent, to somebody. Beware of too much good staying in your hand. It will fast corrupt and worm worms. Pay it away quickly in some sort.[103]

This is a restatement of the Indian practice of *Karma Yoga*, beautifully and simply expressed by Vivekananda: Don't hold on to the fruits of your labor; do work that helps others, and your mind will be free.[104]

Butterfly Rescue

I came upon a related series of inventions which are embedded in this book in a curious way.

I like to keep a watchful eye each day for its special points of beauty, which themselves become *koans* (subjects for meditative reflection). I will go back in time eight months ago. I am meandering around my garden and I look up and there is a stunning gossamer maze, glistening in the sunlight. It is a gigantic spider web. The designer is not home. Transfixed I ask, "How can spiders possibly contrive a web between two trees at a distance of eight feet?" After all, I presume, spiders do not fly. It seems miraculous. In the Age of the Internet, we have a university library at our finger tips, and so I look for the answers. I now understand how spiders can vault across improbable spider distances. The *koan* points the way to deeper questions. For example, how can a human mind learn to vault across vast mind distances?

Some months later in the late afternoon, I see a Monarch, royally basking against the yellow patina on the eaves, as if it has a world of time. I have always had a special feeling for butterflies. I recall the famous passage by the Chinese philosopher, Chuang-Tzu (*pinyin*, Zhuangzi), which presents the wonderful challenge of ambiguity to the Explorer's Mind. Chuang-Tzu asks that we step into different orders of reality.[105]

One day about sunset Chuang-Tzu dozes off and dreams that he has turned into a butterfly.

He flaps his wings and sure enough he is a butterfly! He completely forgets that he is Chuang-Tzu.

But then he awakens and realizes to his dismay that after all he is only Chuang-Tzu.

But wait! Is he really Chuang-Tzu dreaming he has transformed into a butterfly, or is he in reality a butterfly dreaming he is Chuang-Tzu?

Meditating on the Monarch, the thought appears: How long do butterflies live? I learn that Monarchs are especially long-lived, because of their long-range migrations to wintering roosts in south-central Mexico, a uniquely environmentally favored location. During these hibernations, they are able to suppress the synthesis of juvenile hormone, which inhibits aging.[106]

Another late sunny afternoon in my garden. My wife calls out, "Hurry, a butterfly is caught in a huge spider's web. It's probably already dead." I rush to see what's happening, and there the poor thing is trapped in the branches of a tree about ten feet from the house. It weakly flaps its wings. Obviously it is exhausted. It waits for the return of the spider and its fate, to be eaten.

I find a ladder and my wife suggests I go up with a mop and knock at the web. The butterfly tumbles down on top of the mop, stunned. I cup it in my hands. It rests for a precarious moment, hovering between life and death, and then, just as in the fairy tales, it flutters its wings and, with a swoop, soars triumphantly over the treetops.

I suggest to Angela, "Why don't we establish a local club, The Butterfly Rescue, with the goal of helping children and others in desperate need? And Angela tells me about these little boys, ages eight and nine, whose parents were killed only a week before in a head-on collision with an SUV, leaving them paralyzed below the waist, and their kid sister, age six, also seriously injured. When this chapter was written, they had succeeded in raising only $200,000 in oil-rich Texas.[107] Perhaps we are all, in our brief lives, deep-down, butterflies—vulnerable, beautiful and ephemeral. I pledged at that moment to do what I can to assist in such calamities, and Book II, Chapter IV, takes the first step in outlining a practical strategy.

I go back to the Internet and I start researching Butterfly Effect and I am told that in chaos theory, the **butterfly effect** is the *sensitive dependence on initial conditions*, where a small change at one place in a non-linear system can result in large differences to a later state. The effect derives its name from the theoretical example of a hurricane's formation being contingent on whether or not a distant butterfly has flapped its wings several weeks before.

Please scan

And then the idea comes to me, The Butterfly Network and its Butterfly Effect Experiment. The elements:

- Enter by clicking the Butterfly Icon, which is an icon empowered by SmartCodeFx Solutions.[108]
- This takes you to a menu of options, and by one click you can direct funds to a cause of your choice. A prominent example is See Your Impact. There are thousands of other noble causes.[109]
- There is also a daily series of graphics, organized as a social networked game, displaying the ripples of The Butterfly Effect around the world, with lights flickering on a rotating globe, indicating how near we are to a global tipping point.[110]

In his 2007 book, *Blessed Unrest*, Paul Hawken traces the evolution of a global movement of movements. It has no name. The individual initiatives share no charismatic leader, they have no unifying ideology, no single root or segment of society predominates. They coalesce opportunistically into larger networks, and then dissolve. What they do share is a kinship with the earth and a fervent desire to heal her wounds and to restore justice. At the time of writing, Hawken estimated there were at least 130,000 such organizations. Although largely ignored by politicians and the media, their influence is growing. Their numbers may have doubled in the last five years.[111]

Please scan

The latent power of these networks can be more fully appreciated when the thread of the Explorer's Mind takes us to new discoveries in the plasticity of the human brain and the coming impact of computer networks that run and communicate by light.[112]

CONNECTING TO THE NETWORKED NEUROPLASTIC BRAIN

In 1913, Nobel Prize winner, Santiago Ramon y Cajal noted in his masterpiece, *Degeneration and Regeneration of the Nervous System*: "In

Illustration 9

adult [brain] centers the nerve paths are something fixed, ended, immutable. Everything may die, nothing may be regenerated. It is for science of the future to change, if possible, this harsh degree." And there the axiom stood until the current revolution in neuroscience. Some of its most relevant findings for our inquiry are as follows.[113]

Core Assumptions

- The basic assumption and metaphor that the brain is a hard-wired "machine" are incorrect and inapt.
- Quite the opposite: The brain is an amazingly adaptive, resourceful, and "neuroplastic" organ: an open system. In brief, the brain can change itself.
- The brain is subtly networked. Contrary to what was previously thought, various localized centers of the sensory

cortex—the "visual" or "auditory" cortex, for example—are in fact plastic processors, connected to each other and capable of processing and adapting to a wide range of signals. As neuroscientist Paul Bach y Rita notes: "I can connect anything to anything."

- Contrary to accepted medical doctrine, even after substantial brain tissue dies, the brain can actually recover. Moreover, we don't require a whole brain to have an intact whole mind. Dr. Norman Doidge reports one patient who was born with half a brain and was able to regenerate and recruit other parts of her brain and go on to lead a whole and full life.

New Frontiers

- Neurological development can continue even in old age, although not as rapidly in older animals as younger ones. Cognitive decline can be reversed by the right mental exercises; even Alzheimers may be mitigated or slowed down.
- Both the central (autonomic/brain spinal cord) and peripheral nervous system are neuroplastic; they have the capacity to rewire themselves and alter the communication patterns of approximately one hundred billion neurons.
- Plasticity is competitive and subtractive. If we stop using mental skills, we do not just forget. The brain's real estate is deployed to other uses. In short, if we don't use it, we lose it.
- The ablest group of neurons is selected to do the task. According to Nobel Laureate Gerald Edelman, the competition is ruthless among neuronal operators to see which ones can most effectively process signals. When we learn a new skill, our brains can recruit new operators, which vastly increases their processing power, provided they can create a roadblock between the operator they need and its usual function. It has been shown that when a signal neuron develops a long-term memory, it can go from 1,300 to 2,700 synaptic connections.
- Plasticity is also collaborative. After two or more areas begin to interact, they influence each other and form a new whole. Neurons that fire together, wire together. It is possible to induce nerve cells to regenerate by the systematic use of limbs or other parts of the body, which have been programmed for learned disuse. By relearning forgotten

actions, Dr. Edward Taub and others report promising results with spinal cord injuries, Parkinson's, multiple sclerosis, and even arthritis.

- We can even influence which genes are expressed and which are not. The first "template function" allows genes to replicate and is currently thought to be beyond our control. However, the second, or "transcription function," controls when a gene is "turned on." It is then able to regulate the production of new proteins which, in turn, alter cellular structure and function. The transcription function is influenced by what we do and think. There is even evidence that this altered transcription function can be passed across generations.

- Action coupled to internal vision is the key to rapid neuronal development. For example, obsessive-compulsive disorders can be interrupted by re-labeling. By reframing a problem, patients can literally "change the channel" and produce new networks. Hence the second rule of the new neurology: Neurons that fire apart, wire apart. By not acting on their compulsions, patients weaken the connections and thus learn to heal themselves.

- Networks are "sticky." The very same properties which enable plasticity also serve to establish patterns, especially in later life when most people lead more restricted lives that can lead to rigidity. Reprogramming the circuits requires difficult and repetitive work.

- "Your own body is a phantom," observes V.S. Ramachandran, "one that your brain has constructed purely for convenience." Dr. Ramachandran is the first physician to perform the seemingly impossible operation of successfully amputating a phantom limb.

- Mental review and practice may produce similar neurological results in the brain as actual physical practice.[114] From a neurological point of view imagining an act is tantamount to performing it.

- Memories themselves are plastic, as Freud observed. They, too, can be rearranged and re-transcribed.

- "Anticipatory neurogenesis" is also possible. We can actually produce or recruit new nerve cells by repeatedly dreaming future scenarios. Foresight, or the capacity to extract a theme from a series of events before they unfold, is associated with the right frontal lobe, to which neurons from other parts of the brain can be recruited. Pre-cognitive ability can be neurologically enhanced, and neurological development can enhance pre-cognitive abilities.[115]

- Chaos, at least to some extent, appears to stimulate neuronal growth. The noisier, the more disorganized the brain (at least up to a point), the smarter we are. Chaos enables the brain to assimilate new information and to respond to changing situations in new ways. Like dreaming, chaos makes new connections possible.[116]

Culture

- Culture affects brain function. Throughout our lives we learn a set of ancestrally developed skills and abilities. We reproduce our culture through brain activity, but we can also create new brain circuits that did not exist in our ancestors. The critical difference between chimps and humans lies in the gene which controls neurogenesis. The human cortex alone has thirty billion neurons and is capable of making one million billion synaptic connections. According to Nobel Laureate Gerald Edelman, the number of possible neural connections is ten followed by at least a million zeros. (The number of particles in the known universe is ten followed by about seventy-nine zeros.) All electronic devices rewire the brain. Because our nervous system is plastic, it will take advantage of this compatibility and will merge with electronic media, making a single, larger system.

Please scan

The fundamental message from the current research in neuroscience is that we are already deeply connected through the networked brain. In fact, our brain is a network of connections—one hundred billion nerve cells reaching out to each other forming connections, approximately one thousand trillion of them, or approximately the number of leaves in the Amazon rain forest.

READER'S COMPASS—POINT OF PAUSE AND REFLECTION ON THE MERGER OF NEURONAL AND ELECTRONIC CIRCUITRY

I do not intend to imply that the overlap of electronic and brain circuitry is necessarily a wonderful development. Although I see the potential, I also appreciate Ken Cohen's warning, "I take this as a dire prediction of loss of autonomy, the devolution of conscious-ness as it will no longer be shaped by the challenge of nature; and a continuing deterioration of empathy because people will increas-ingly resonate with soulless machines, rather than with each other or the natural world. We already see the effect of such rewiring in the decrease of creativity, improvisation, and play among children and an increase in narcissism and entitlement."

How can these perspectives be reconciled? Readers are encour-aged to send your thoughts and ideas to: (www.explorerswheel. com).

What then of the mind? Is mind simply an artifact of the brain, an über-computer; or is it something more? In his book, *The Sin-gularity is Near*, Ray Kurzweil[117] engages in an imaginary debate with the philosopher John R. Searle around the key issues of reductionism and materialism. Kurzweil points out that the poten-tial of the brain's computing power is vast, largely untapped, virtually unlimited, and, in an odd way to put it, *sufficient*. Per-haps, the implication of V.S. Ramachandran's observation, "your body is a phantom, one that your brain has constructed purely for convenience," is that all of our fancied reality is no more than a contrivance of our brains, and even this "our" is our creation. Yet if this is so, then the mystics and sages and the scientific reduc-tionists may both be making the same point when they suggest that everything that exists, or may ever exist, lies dormant and possible within "us."

Yet suppose the story does not end but rather begins here. What if the brain is a step-down transformer in physical form of some-thing far more subtle and profound? What if the brain is a part of, but only a subset of, Mind? (Here "mind" is capitalized to suggest the interpenetration of energy field(s) larger than our individual brains.) How does Mind enhance brain function? And what are the implications for the survival, or the next stage of evolution of our survival or the next stage of evolution of our species, if our brains and minds should decide to transform themselves?

During many years of Zen practice, *qigong*, and various mar-tial arts, I have had numerous curious experiences. Perhaps the strangest was a seminar my colleagues at Discovery Engineering International (DEI) and I once did for the Office of Technology Assessment (OTA), with several participants from the Defense Intelligence Agency (DIA). The purpose of the program was to give the staff of the OTA a first-hand experience of discovery engineering so they could provide an initial assessment to Congress on interesting technologies, as required by OTA's enabling legislation. This was around 1984, a period when Senator Clairborne Pell and others in the Congress and the federal government were interested in Russian paranormal experiments, in particular telekinesis, psycho-kinesis, or the remote control of physical instruments by remote brains or minds.

The protocol, as developed by DEI, was to introduce participants to our EEG biofeedback system. After one to two preliminary sessions on the machines in which the participants learned to work with creative reverie and "incubate" discovery questions, we engaged in a free session simply for the fun of exploration. The instructions to participants were to record their images and at the conclusion of the session to note them down without discussing them among themselves. Afterward, we planned to facilitate their interpretation of the images. As we waited for our clients to complete the assignment, we noticed that one member of the DIA team was circulating a paper which was causing the other members much delight. When we inquired, the team members confessed that their colleague had been peering into their minds and recording the images they were experiencing, which he then illustrated in the paper circulating among them. When my DEI colleagues and I asked how he was able to do this, the DIA team readily replied that they had learned it from some Native American tribes which had developed the practice into a fine art form. They informed us that they regularly "practiced" in this way and it was great fun. This was the most curious example of what our DEI team came to call "shared states of consciousness."

Most people assume that you are either conscious or you are not. But it may be that our brain, or mind, has the capacity to experience different levels of consciousness, including sharing these states simultaneously with others, and that our brains or minds are networked in subtle ways. Although participants reported identical images in every training program DEI offered between 1984 and 1986, and some images in considerable detail, the experience at OTA was the most singular.

The OTA experience occurred in present time. But might it be possible, as Shakespeare's Macbeth inquires "to look into the seeds of time, and say which grain will grow and which will not?" What if the "seeds" and "grains of time" are our living brain cells, growing in present time in anticipation of, and already connected with, a plurality of possible futures?

III

CONNECTING TO
THE FUTURE

*Alice laughed: "There's no use trying," she said; "one can't
believe impossible things." "I daresay you haven't had much
practice," said the Queen. "When I was younger, I always
did it for half an hour a day. Why, sometimes I've believed as
many as six impossible things before breakfast."*
—Alice in Wonderland

*"My suspicion is that the universe is not only queerer than we
suppose, but queerer than we can suppose."*
—J.B.S. Haldane

What could be more improbable and more taboo than to foresee
the **Future?** In Greek mythology Cassandra, the daughter of King
Priam of Troy and his wife Hecuba, was so beautiful that Apollo
fell in love with her and bestowed upon her the gift of prophecy.
However, when she did not return his love, Apollo placed a curse
on her, so that no one would believe her predictions. Her tragedy
of deep understanding and impotence is said to depict the human
condition. With the passing of the ancient world and its reverence for inquiry, curiosity became a sin (*libido scienti*), consistently
condemned by the church fathers—most famously in the trial of
Galileo. Even today an exploration of the **Future** is dismissed by
the high priests of science as "unscientific" or "pseudoscience."
The unstated, uneasy premise may even be that methodologies
presuming to probe the **Future** tread on a domain of "forbidden

knowledge."[118] Such biases are important because, as Kahneman and others point out, they can preclude serious inquiry and distort perceptions of what we see.[119]

The odd thing is we regularly predict the **Future** in some domains of activity and often with considerable accuracy. However, as noted at the beginning of this Book II, a shift is occurring of such complexity and at such a rate of change that these models and processes, powerful as they are, cannot account accurately for, nor help us to cope effectively with, the compounding stresses on the systems upon which we have come to depend. A new map may be helpful.

This chapter first sets a baseline by examples of how we are already working successfully with the **Future**. Second, we will suggest how our understanding of the **Future** very much depends on our state of consciousness—that as we begin to observe the world from multiple dimensions, the Explorer's Mind, our experience of

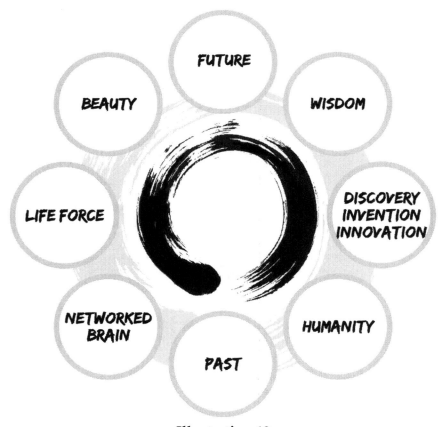

Illustration 10

the **Future** alters and our creative options increase. Third, we will introduce several methods which when combined will powerfully amplify existing techniques. Finally, we will apply this framework to a significant unsolved problem, the prediction of earthquakes, which the experts tell us are catastrophes just waiting to happen.

Modern Risk Assessment, Predictive Analytics, and Corporate Strategy

In his important book, *Against the Gods*, Peter Bernstein argues that bringing risk under control is one of the central ideas which distinguish the modern era from the distant past.[120] In fact, techniques and procedures such as probability analysis, sampling, regression to the mean, game theory, scenario planning, and others all seek to guide present actions by estimations of the **Future**. These and other procedures are now commonly used in a broad range of human endeavor: by stock analysts in making investments, surgeons in performing operations, engineers in building bridges, entrepreneurs in launching businesses, and astronomers in exploring the heavens—all seeking to manage the constant companion of risk. Predictive analytics has become a serious discipline.[121]

One field with a practical foot in the **Future** is business strategy. Professor Jim Schrager, a top corporate strategist at the University of Chicago Business School, has identified four key components of his Behavioral Strategy Model, which draws upon the earlier work of Herbert Simon in artificial intelligence.

- Representations—by which he means how a problem is conceived, mapped, and expressed. Professor Schrager places great emphasis on formulating and continuously refining the most powerful questions, which will guide the subsequent discovery process.[122]
- Patterns—the trends, story-lines, data, and knowledge points by which experts derive solutions. Dr. Schrager observes that the patterns stem directly from the representations of the problem. Hence, the solution is highly dependent on how the initial problem is represented or defined. As noted, this line of thought is consistent with Einstein's observation that in science the theory governs what will be observed.
- Memory Links—Dr. Schrager points out, citing the earlier work of the narratologist Roger Schank, that we recognize the patterns through the stories we tell, which are indexed and encoded in snapshots or "gists."

- Practice—What distinguishes experts, Dr. Schrager concludes, is their ability to frame issues and to rapidly find the relevant patterns, which they can recall, process, and apply more powerfully than the rest of us.[123]

Explorer's Mind and Consensus Reality

The present consensus about the **Future** is based on several important premises. First, the **Future** is a "thing" distinct in itself which exists in nature. Second, this "thing" is separate and can be distinguished from other "things" which we call the **Present** and the **Past**.[124] Third, the direction of Time is linear. The **Past**, **Present**, and **Future** are related in linear Time. Fourth, **Wisdom** is separate from our consciousness of **Past-Present-Future** time. This is the accepted view, the "consensus reality." But what if our consensus turns out to be an opinion, a viewpoint? What if it were possible to experience the **Future** differently, more expansively?

Please scan

We can begin with the Latin derivation of the English word "**Future**." We find the root "*sum*," meaning, "I am."[125] The **Future** tense is expressed in the irregular participle of *esse*, "to be." Similarly, and as noted earlier, the Latin meaning of discover and invent, both of which have the connotation in English of actions pointing to something which is "out there," implies that which is out there exists already, right here in the present. It is only a matter of seeing it.

Many people who have ecstatic or epiphanal experiences report that the **Present**, **Past**, and **Future** collapse simultaneously into one continuous living experience. For example, when Charles Dickens awakens Scrooge from his visits into the **Past**, **Present**, and **Future**, he exclaims in a delirium of joy, "I will honor Christmas in my heart and try to keep it all the year. I will live in the **Past**, **Present**, and **Future**. The Spirits of all three shall strive within me. I will not shut out the lessons they teach." "Time before him," Dickens narrates, "was his own to make amends in."

When we cultivate the Explorer's Mind, our experience of the **Future** modulates. The **Future** comes closer. It takes on different shapes. "Reality" is multi-layered and multi-dimensional, with only the base being the experience of linear time and of a separate **Future**. Each of these different tiers appears to have its own distinct relationship to the **Future**. At times we can work inside of time, as opposed to standing outside of it, as in normal reality. In the Zen tradition, such experiences are largely dismissed as delusional, noisy precursors (in Japanese, *makyo*[126]) on the path to awakening. The Explorer's Wheel provides eight realms in which the reader can experience these different levels of time. We do not discuss in this book the issue of non-linearity of time in science, except to point out, as has been recognized by many others, that ancient insights into human consciousness and modern discoveries in quantum mechanics and other branches of theoretical physics are actually closely aligned.[127]

The following cases introduce tools and processes which will enable us to connect to the **Future**. The first examples are drawn from the field of negotiation. The reader may find them plausible, as they involve the tangible quality of character which is under the ostensible control of the negotiator. The second are variants of scenario planning which couple, in imaginative ways, possible alternative **Futures** to present capabilities. The final set include more esoteric practices, remote in time or space, which some readers may insist demand a higher standard of proof.

Character in Negotiation

The ancients well understood that a person's destiny can be read in his or her human character. In East Asia it is widely recognized that a person's character is revealed by her or his calligraphy. A popular example is the scene in the movie *Crouching Tiger, Hidden Dragon*, when the suspicions of the heroine (played by Michelle Yeoh) are immediately confirmed when she beholds the swordswomen-like skill displayed by her enemy (performed by Zhang Ziyi) in writing her name. It is no coincidence that in Greek the original meaning of "character" is "to etch."[128] A person's character or destiny was believed to be etched on the clay tablets of life. The technique of **Player Integrity Profile (PIPS)** described in Book I, Chapter III[129] is a shorthand way to assess character, based on an analysis of integrity. What is important to point out here is our ability to assess and even to influence the **Future** by working more effectively with the **Present**. The following example illustrates this principle.

In the early days of DEI we organized a seminar at the Fetzer Foundation to introduce discovery engineering to its top management.

The Fetzer Foundation was the brainchild of John Fetzer, the former owner of the Detroit Tigers, an entrepreneur who was interested in supporting research in consciousness and integrative medicine. The president of the Foundation, Ambassador Glenn Olds, himself a polymath and visionary, was a strong supporter of DEI and endorsed a strategic alliance between our start-up company and the Foundation.

After the preliminaries which explained how to use the equipment, the participants learned how to enter "creative reverie," and after concluding the session,[130] recorded their images and experiences. What was striking was the number of images of turbulence and violence—a tornado, a wolf's head, quicksand, swamps, and similar pictures. When we integrated and analyzed these images, a picture emerged of an imminent *coup d'etat.* The Foundation was caught in a morass, upheaval was at its door, and the alpha dog would be decapitated. We summarized our findings in a report to the president, warning him of the impending crisis. Unfortunately, our report was not heeded and, like the predictions of Cassandra, Troy fell. Several months later the entire management team at the Fetzer Foundation was fired in a sudden move by the Board.

The important lesson our DEI team derived from this experience was that the **Future** can be deeply embedded in the **Present**—if we have the eyes to read it and the **Will** to act upon it. If Dr. Olds and his team had run **PIPS** analyses on themselves and the Fetzer Foundation at that time, the **Future** would have appeared before them. It was implicitly obvious.

Interested readers can easily verify for themselves the principle of the **Future** embedded in the **Present** simply by practicing **PIPS** and compiling a statistically significant number of cases.

Reader's Compass—Commentary on the Fetzer Foundation Case

In the Fetzer Foundation example, all the data required to make an effective decision were readily available. The challenge for the management team at that time was for the members to open their own minds and to let down the emotional filters, which we have described in earlier chapters as a deluded sense of "need." They "needed" to stay in a limited comfort zone, running a safer preferred story of reality: all was well, all would be well. They did not listen and they missed the many signals. But their unconscious minds knew far more than they were consciously willing to reveal or concede. Through creative reverie the DEI Discovery Team was able to help them connect to a deeper part of their minds—a part which was less interested in what they thought they needed and more able to observe with innocent eyes. Even when the **Future** was made clear, as the DEI Team did in its report, management did not heed the warning. As a **PIPS** analysis often suggests, a lapse in vision, a failure to listen, and an inability to take effective action are often closely coupled.

Scenario Planning, Day-Dreaming, Appreciative Inquiry and Backlighting the Future

In scenario planning a group of analysts develops game-like simulations of possible **Futures** based on various indicators. The method combines many factors in complex, non-linear ways often to produce surprising results. Scenario planners search for novel insights about the **Future**, deep shifts in value, and disruptive inventions, and then by deploying systems-thinking they produce plausible story lines. Scenario planning is currently used in a wide variety of military and corporate settings.

A more imaginative, although far less well documented, strategy is the methodology developed by my friend, Dr. Elspeth McAdam. Dr. McAdam, who grew up in Africa, is a professionally-trained psychiatrist with a medical degree from Cambridge University. She spends her time in retirement working with street children and people living with HIV in East and Southern Africa, as well as other communities around the world.

Her technique involves exploring the **Future** by day-dreaming it[131] and then by "backlighting." This is a form of dreaming from a desired future, backwards toward the present by a process similar to "appreciative inquiry." Appreciative inquiry (AI) was pioneered by D.L. Cooperrider and S. Shravista in the 1990s. AI looks for the very best of what is and explores what makes this possible, and also seeks to identify the skills and abilities people have that have not been named or recognized before. Elspeth asks her clients to write them all down because she believes this is how identity gets created and expanded. The American educational philosopher John Dewey suggested that identity is actually created through the identification of abilities, skills, and resources. Elspeth encourages her clients to dream **Future** scenarios in which their capabilities are fully and successfully embodied. "We are not interested in being realistic," she observes, "but rather in tuning into the creative grammars that dreaming conversations will bring forth.... We find that the dreaming conversation itself creates the means whereby we become the things that we dream." Once inside the **Future,** her language switches to a **Future/Present,** and the details in painting the dream are the secret. *How* are you able to do this? *With which* colleagues are you collaborating? *What* gave you the idea to do it this way? *How* are you feeling about this situation? The story line, its metaphors and grammar are all important. "There is an ocean of meaning in a drop of grammar," she quotes Wittgenstein. The mood, context, and emotions all color the portrait.

After these embodied **Futures** are vividly displayed, Dr. McAdam guides her clients back in reverse order to the **Present.** It is very helpful to do this with a partner. The backlighting sequence is also managed in a dream-like state. She works with her subjects to trace back, step-by-step, right up to the **Present,** the specific and critical milestones that enabled them to realize their emerging **Future.** At each stage they are re-living in the **Future/Present** the precise details of what is happening: "*What* is the closest point before you arrived at success?" "*What* happened before that?" "*What* challenges are you overcoming?" *How* are you doing that? *Who, where, when, what, why, how,...*?

The details limn the picture, the road map, indelibly in the brain. Many of the young people she works with in the *shantis* of South Africa went on to realize their dreams, especially the King of Thieves, as he was proud to call himself, along with his merry band.

The King of Thieves, with Dr. McAdam's assistance, developed not simply a vision, but also a living plan—we might conjecture a neuropathway, fueled by creative emotions and energy, which altered the probabilities of the venture. And that, based on our earlier summary of neuroplasticity, is perhaps the secret to Dr. McAdam's success.[132]

The **Future,** like the **Past,** becomes part of the practice of the **Present,** not in some vague ethereal way, but right at hand, inside our living brains. By focusing on what is good, and encouraging them to dream more fulfilled and happier lives, Dr. McAdam effectively sidesteps the ethical concerns that some will have with cold techniques associated with manipulating or engineering the **Future.** The Explorer's Mind is ultimately about living fully in this precious present moment which can encompass all that we dream or imagine, even worlds more wonderful and strange than any of us today can suppose.

An Experiment with Time

My first exposure to precognition was in a gift of J.W. Dunne's *An Experiment with Time* from my friend, Roger Fisher, a Harvard Law School colleague and the co-author of *Getting to Yes.*[133] In *An*

Experiment with Time, Dunne reports on a curious discovery he made in his youth. He began to notice that, in his experience, the ordinary time sequence was reversed. In great detail, his dreams appeared to foreshadow events: for example, the volcanic eruptions in Martinique or the arrival of an English expedition in Khartoum. At first he did not believe his own dream record, "The waking mind refuses point blank to accept the association between the dream and the subsequent event." So he began to record the dreams far more meticulously. He observed that the greater the detail, the greater the probability of finding corroborative material in the "outside" world. From his observations, he developed a method and encouraged his friends and others to see if they could repeat his results. They were confirmed. Based on his experience, he wrote a second book, *The Serial Universe,* in which he elaborates his basic thesis that time may not be linear. His books raise the question of whether it might at least be possible to coexist at any moment in parallel universes: one of linear time, and the other not.

Reader's Compass—Commentary on Precognition in Dreaming

Skeptical readers may challenge the validity of Dunne's experiments, which were conducted many decades ago, without scientific controls or protocols. From a contemporary scientific point of view, they are anecdotal—although Dunne, in fairness, did propose a method by which explorers can confirm and replicate his findings by themselves. Unlike cases which focus on the character of an individual explorer, his experiments in time are open-ended, diffuse, and concern events and conditions often outside the personal experience of the dreamers. Following Sagan's axiom that great claims require higher levels of proof, the burden in this case would seem to be on the shoulders of the proponents of pre-cognition. At the same time, it would seem a serious error simply to ignore or dismiss such anecdotes. Moreover, the integrity move of **negative capability**—the ability to tolerate ambiguity without the irritable reach for clarity—may be essential here. A deeper, more systematic inquiry, especially linked to practical applications—for example, in Discovery Expeditions—would seem worth considering.

Remote Viewing

A related body of research and practice explores the potentialities of remote viewing as a means of connecting to the **Future**. One major center for remote viewing research in the U.S. has been the laboratory of Robert G. Jahn, Dean Emeritus at Princeton University's School of Engineering and Applied Science. Along with Brenda Dunne, Robert Jahn established the Princeton Engineering Anomalies Research Lab in 1979 with the mission to study the low-level psychokinetic effects on electronic random event generators. Over more than twenty-five years, Jahn and Dunne claim to have created a wealth of small-physical-scale, statistically significant results that suggest direct causal relationships between a subject's intention and otherwise random results[134].

The basic process begins by a remote viewer (RV) entering a reverie state. The goal is to pick up information from intuition and all the physical senses, filtering out the "noise" of ego, interpretation, assumptions, stories, and the like. The protocol requires RVs to write squiggles on a piece of paper, which come to them spontaneously in connection with the Target. These squiggles are referred to as the "signal line." Next, all senses are tapped for information, again with the instruction not to interpret anything. The suspension of interpretation is a hallmark of the process. Through an iterative process, patterns emerge. At that point the data can be explored for subtle details relating to the physical, emotional, and other aspects of the Target. Targets can include physical objects, people, events, and other subjects of interest to the RV.

According to accomplished remote viewers, the art is "time insensitive," meaning that skillful viewers can zero in on a Target in the **Past, Present,** and **Future** with almost equal facility. The theory is based on an interpretation of quantum physics in which the **Present** is actually formed through a dynamic feedback process with **Past** and **Future.** More recent work published by Courtney Brown and his Farsight Institute posits the theory of "multiple Futures" and "multiple universes."[135] The remote viewing field is bold, complex, and fascinating. Certainly, it resonates with Dr. Haldane's prediction that the universe may turn out to be queerer than we can even suppose.

Reader's Compass—Commentary on Remote Viewing

Remote viewing differs from pre-cognition in that it asserts that the technology can be used to detect targets beyond the normal range of the five senses. It coincides with pre-cognitive dreaming in that remote viewers maintain the same techniques and protocols that will enable them to peer into the **Future** and time travel into the **Past.** For the sake of argument, let us concede the critical premise of the distinct separation of **Present, Past,** and **Future.** In this case, the claims of remote viewers to detect specific remote targets can be explained as a vestigial human power, which contemporary people have long since been accustomed not to use. The fact that the perception is outside-the-skin, beyond our ordinary sense-based capacities, places the same burden of proof under Sagan's axiom on the proponents of this approach. This principle should apply even more to the claims of remote viewers to perceive outside-the-skin, outside-of-present time, **Future,** or **Past** events. A crucial point here is that the field of remote viewing has been systematically investigated by the U.S., Russian, and other military intelligence communities. Much significant classified data may exist which demonstrate the greater reliability of the technology and the startling implications of its foundational premises.

Corporate Strategy Reconsidered

How might Dr. Schrager's Behavioral Model be enhanced if it were possible to approach his same strategic questions from multi-dimensions of consciousness?

- Representation—The formulation or representation of the problem or challenge might differ dramatically, as the Explorer will look deeper and more broadly, orienting himself or herself very differently to the **Past, Present,** and **Future.** The core questions should become more interesting.

- Patterns—Pattern analysis will change. The Explorer will see links and connections—not just on the surface of things, but also identify broader, deeper patterns over longer periods of time. When we use the Explorer's Wheel, the relationships between seemingly remote and disconnected phenomena will become more apparent. This is especially so when the Explorer observes and connects these phenomena from different levels of consciousness. In fact, the patterns never really exist in the "external" world. They are the product of our creative imaginations. As the Explorer's Mind reaches outward into other realms, new patterns will emerge. A kaleidoscope produces even more lovely configurations as the observer is prepared to see them.

- Memory Links—The stories will also change and will tap into shared memory links. The reader will recall the earlier example from Book II, Chapter III, of the DEI training with the Office of Technology Assessment. It is likely that most of us share states of consciousness with other people and with humanity as a whole. Carl Jung referred to these common memory links as "archetypes" which connect us to our "Collective Unconscious." Using creative reverie, Explorers can gain access to these collective archetypal memory banks.

- Practice—The ability to enter into different levels of unconsciousness will improve with practice.

But this capacity transcends technique. When we embody integrity as defined in this book—a state of dynamic balance of eye, hand, and heart—we don't really "foresee" in an ordinary sense. The **Future** flows into the **Present**. We explore and play with it. The **Future** emerges from the journey. We have a different perspective on who we really are.

Anticipating a Mega-Earthquake in California

According to most experts a mega-earthquake on the scale of the Fukushima earthquake is virtually certain to take place in California within the next thirty years. It is likely the earthquake will strike major population centers or strategic localities such as the San Pedro Ports of Los Angeles and Long Beach (POLA/POLB) and the levees in the San Joaquin Valley. As indicated in Book II, Chapter I, such catastrophes now occur with such frequency around the world that they have become the "new normal."

Some Facts

The POLA/POLB are not ordinary ports. Approximately 25 percent of all American and foreign commerce in the U.S. runs through these two ports. There are five separate fault lines in Northern California that put the delta and its levees at greatest risk. Because of the region's soil of sand, clay, and peat, the ground will shake during an earthquake up to ten times as much in the delta as outside it, which will increase the chance of a levee failure. Seismologists predict that there is a 40 percent chance of a "catastrophic" earthquake of 6.7 magnitude or greater in the region in the next thirty years. A significant quake would likely destroy California's levees. A flood in the delta could sink downtown Sacramento under as much as twenty feet of water, cut off Southern California's principal water supply, cripple California's economy (the eighth largest in the world), and disrupt global trade.

Present Paradigm

At present, earthquake prediction is a provenance of government officials and seismologists. It is an expert's problem. The experts have concluded that it is not possible with existing knowledge and technology to predict earthquakes within sufficient time to allow public authorities to implement effective emergency management. As a result, it is a foregone conclusion that losses in lives and property will be enormous. Because no adequate federal or state compensation scheme exists for victims of these disasters, and as the Price-Anderson Act places a cap on the liability of operators of nuclear facilities and other relief, the losses will be borne largely by the public.

A Different Strategy

Our proposal is directed first to Jerry Brown, the present Governor of California, and also to the responsible persons in his administration and the federal government who are concerned with earthquake prediction and emergency management. At the outset I wish to make clear that our proposal is not intended as a critique. California's approach to emergency preparedness is actually ahead of other states. There are many dedicated public officials in California and the federal government who are deeply committed to protect the public. There are thousands of seismologists and other experts around the world who have devoted their lives to finding a solution to the earthquake prediction problem. But the core problem remains urgent, potentially imminent, and unsolved. We are only asking for that the key decision makers be receptive to considering a different way. Our proposal has these elements.

- Scrub the Problem Definition for Biases and Assumptions—Earthquake prediction is not an ordinary problem. In addition to all the intellectual biases and assumptions which must be identified and rigorously explored under the framework set out in Book II, Chapter II, the quotient of fear in this instance is far higher than in smaller challenges.
- Address Candidly the Element of Fear—The scenario we are describing—a single event collapses California's economy and interrupts global commerce—is unprecedented.

Thinking about the "unthinkable" is frightening. Moreover, there is also the matter of guessing incorrectly. A prediction of a major earthquake one month in advance will likely necessitate relocating millions of people, costing billions of dollars, as was contemplated by the Japanese government at the time of the Fukushima earthquake. But suppose the prediction, which most likely cannot be delivered with perfect certainty, turns out to be wrong. The legal liabilities of public officials and others who will be involved could be staggering. Fear will be perhaps the most powerful factor if Governor Brown decides to hold onto the prevailing paradigm and not risk doing anything innovative. For Governor Brown to succeed, he must provide inspired leadership, which will include addressing candidly and constantly the powerful dynamics of fear.

- Launch a Discovery Expedition—I would urge Governor Brown in cooperation with the relevant federal agencies to organize and launch a Discovery Expedition along the lines described in Book II Chapter II. I would define the Initial Core Discovery Puzzle as "How can we precisely predict an earthquake within one, three, or six months at or near strategic locations such as POLA/POLB?" I urge that the full gamut of discovery/invention tools be systematically deployed, including Discovery Engineering, Lead User Protocols, Triz, and other useful methodologies. I would deploy the most powerful pattern recognition technologies available today in connecting the dots and delivering action blueprints based on the data.

- Gain Leverage with Strategic Alliances—The Brown Administration or the federal government will be able easily to garner financial and, even more importantly, human resources and technologies from the private sector. If imaginatively and effectively organized and marketed, many companies, private foundations, and other governments and international organizations will likely contribute resources. A key success factor will be the powerful leverage generated by these strategic alliances and networks.

- Know the Point of Vulnerability—The breakdown in the proposed scenario, if it comes, will likely occur at the point of effective implementation. If the Discovery Expedition seriously deploys all the protocols, tools, and framework described in this book, it is likely that someone, somewhere, will identify an already existing solution or devise a new one. We, the members of the Discovery Expedition, within relatively short time (one to three years) will understand how to predict earthquakes with far greater reliably and precision than we currently do. To employ the language of the integrity model, the problem will not be at the level of the "head." We can agree that Governor Brown, President Obama, their successors, and the other officials who will be involved care about mitigating the suffering of this catastrophe. Thus the problem is likely not at the "heart" level either. The point of vulnerability will be a failure to couple "hand" to head and heart, thoughtfully, decisively, in a timely manner. As in other emergencies, bureaucratic turf wars, failures to share information, ego, and risk tolerance may interrupt the flow, and the window of opportunity may be lost.[136]

- Democratize the Process—The prediction of a mega-earthquake in California is too important a problem to be left solely in the care of bureaucrats and experts, no matter how dedicated they are. The knowledge of experts is significantly limited by how they represent the problem (Schrager), their limited circles of professional associates, the stories they are running, what tools they are using, what biases (mostly unconscious) they are subject to, and what fears or reservations they have about seeing the world differently. Every citizen in California and many others share a common interest in better methods being developed to predict a mega-earthquake in California. Governor Brown and President Obama and their successors have a unique opportunity to transform this highly complex technical problem into a source of continuous societal exploration and learning. The mechanics of precisely how they can do this are explained in the next chapter in the section on "Global Disaster Explorer's Wheels."

Author's note:—As this book goes to press I have become familiar with the remarkable work of John Casey and his colleagues at the International Center for Earthquake and Volcano Prediction (IEVPC/ http://www.ievpc.org/). IEVPC bases its technology on an analysis of precursors among other factors extending over many years and is focusing its predictions of mega-earthquakes with advance notification of a year or more. If effectively supported, the work of IEVPC has the potential to save millions of lives and transform the field of scientific prediction of natural and man-made disasters, and corresponding governmental and private sector emergency response. In light of the fact that most academic seismologists in the U.S. take the position that earthquakes are inherently unpredictable, the "discovery" of IEVPC seems to confirm the principle in the Age of the Internet that breakthroughs may already exist if we have the curiosity to search for them."

The Sum of It

When we conducted a focus group in September 2011 with some young people in Hong Kong, they exclaimed in unison, "Don't tell us about earthquakes and typhoons—that is not what we are interested in. Instead just give us ten minutes of clean air, ten minutes of oxygen; and while you're at it, show us how we can live a happy fulfilled life under such conditions." They are right. In a sense, the prediction of earthquakes, as critically important as it is, will in the end most likely attract only a limited number of people. But what if the prediction of earthquakes, or really any issue which deeply concerns people today, can be transformed into a gate for exploration and new learning? What if every deep question suddenly becomes an on-ramp to discover a happier, healthier passage through this world toward our shared dream of a more abundant life?

A Brief Interlude: How to Cultivate Explorer's Mind

Previous chapters have discussed various aspects of the Explorer's Mind. It may be useful now to pause for a brief interlude on how you can cultivate your own Explorer's Mind, as a bridge to the last section on abundance.

You can approach Explorer's Mind from two directions. Either is fine, because as explained earlier, they are in their essence one and the same.

Emptiness

One practice is simply to meditate on not-knowing. In the Zen tradition, the most basic *koan* is MU (in Japanese, "nothing" or "not", or vast nothingness=space). To discover MU you don't need to do very much. Just find a quiet congenial place in your house or under a tree, and meditate on MU. Inhale MU in an easy way; then exhale MU in an easy way. It is simple. Nothing special. Try for five minutes twice a day during the first week, then ten minutes in the second; aim for thirty minutes twice a day for a month. If your mind wanders, gently direct it back to MU. During the practice you are not trying to find or discover anything. You are simply dwelling in nothingness; it is a respite. This living moment becomes your Explorer's Wheel. When you leave your meditations and enter into the bustling world, see if you can detect MU in anything that appears externally or within your own mind. In other words, see if in the solidness of external "things" or in the insistent artifacts of your mind—your fears, your sense of indignation or betrayal, your high hopes, your disappointments—you can also detect the trace of MU. [136a]

Fullness

You can cultivate an Explorer's Mind from the opposite direction. Here I suggest using the Explorer's Wheel as a scaffolding. As you practice, Explorer's Mind may become second nature and you can dispense with the scaffolding. Please take a moment again to observe the Explorer's Wheel. As discussed in the previous chapters, you can enter any realm and simply dive as deeply as you wish, or you can contemplate the Explorer's Wheel as a whole. You may find at first that a part of you rebels at this last idea, protesting, "It is too much, I feel overwhelmed." This is the voice that belongs to the part of our minds which has been programmed by society to think in narrow silos.[137] We're not supposed to be able to connect everything to everything. But suppose we can? Suppose it is part of our natural endowment, a gift at birth to every one of us.

In exploring this proposition, you don't need to force or bear down or think about anything. It is really about passive observing. In the Chinese language this is called *wuwei* (無為), the art of action by non-action, of accomplishing much with less. Allow yourself simply to relax into the Explorer's Wheel, and observe from the inside out. The key is to play with it, to have fun. I suggest you keep an Explorer's Log, and I'll give you a hint: note any changes you detect in your vital energy, your creative life force. Please e-mail your ideas or discoveries to the Explorer's Wheel web site (www. explorerswheel.com).

IV

ABUNDANCE

*Blessed is he who learns how to engage in inquiry, with
no impulse to harm his countrymen or to pursue
wrongful actions, but perceives the order of immortal
and ageless nature, how it is structured.*
—Euripides, Fragment from an unnamed play,
fifth century, B.C.E.

The Age of Abundance envisioned by Peter Diamandis and
Steven Kotler rests on a single proposition: we are already blessed
by a cornucopia of natural resources and opportunities, which our
powerful new technologies are currently harvesting. They cite six
important drivers for their optimism. First is the law of exponential
integration (Moore's Law) which will continue to drive down the
costs of information and communication technologies (ICT) so they
become ubiquitous. Second is the convergence of these technologies with a myriad of other technologies, products, and industries
which will deliver to everyone the essentials of a more abundant
life: clean air, food, water, affordable energy, health care, education,
and political freedom. Third is the active involvement of millions of
creative amateurs, which they call "Do-It-Yourself" entrepreneurs,
who are continuously innovating. Fourth are the contributions of a
new generation of "techno-philanthropists" like Bill Gates (Microsoft), Pierre Amidar (e-Bay), Richard Branson (Virgin), and Jeff
Skoll (e-Bay) who are helping to finance the coming prosperity.

Fifth are the emerging multi-billion-dollar markets, which have become available through the rapid diffusion of ICT, especially within poorer countries. Lastly, multiplying "virtuous circles," as these various forces work in synergy[138], will deliver prosperity and happiness to millions of people in unexpected and wondrous ways.

The one domain which Diamandis and Kotler do not mention is the nexus of the brain, mind, and consciousness, which today is experiencing its own revolution. In this book we refer to this liminal zone as the Explorer's Mind. We have suggested that the Explorer's Mind is itself a natural state of abundance and benevolence, whose cultivation, to follow the same logic in *Abundance*, only awaits the careful application of intelligence and knowledge. This chapter produces a new educational model of personalized self-learning and societal learning, based on other currently available technologies not cited in *Abundance*. What if an awakened human consciousness or Explorer's Mind were to guide the promising trends and patterns cited by the authors? This next convergence has the potential to transform global society in orders of magnitude beyond the authors' present predictions.

Your Explorer's Wheel—Personalized Self-Learning

The purpose of your Explorer's Wheel is to help you design and pursue a more abundant life[139] and also to have fun along the journey. I will provide here some introductory thoughts on the specifics of the structure and beneficial applications of the Explorer's Wheel in personalized self-learning. I suspect that even by the time this "living" book is published, the platform will be more advanced.

The benefits of this new model of self-learning will likely occur from individual explorations expanded through a large array of connected networks. On the personal front here are a few specific examples.

- Intertidal (multi-dimensional, stereoscopic, holographic) Thinking (consciousness)—As explained in Book II, Chapters II and IV, each of us is learning a new skill, *i.e.*, how to think and explore more deeply and broadly—two seemingly opposite approaches that are, in fact, aspects of each other. If our thesis of connectivity is correct, then as explorers you and I will gain insight into a wide variety of fields by learning one process—Trust the Connection—and applying it in as many areas as our curiosity takes us. This is another way of expressing the holographic character of the inquiry.[140]

- Intelligence—Intelligence is not just a matter of smarts. The integrity model advanced in this book emphasizes a dynamic balance between intellectual gifts (brain power), compassion and empathy (heart), and practical action (hand), which will keep you, the explorer, steadily on course. Attention to practical application produces powerful learning feedback loops.

- Creativity and Inventive Power—Creativity and inventive power tend to arise from the interplay of solitary exploration enhanced at times through collaboration and access to resources. In a prelude to her book, *Quiet: The Power of Introverts in a World That Can't Stop Talking*,[141] Susan Cain writes that geniuses from Issac Newton to Steve Wozniak required silence, solitude, privacy, and autonomy to accomplish their best work. As Wordsworth said of Newton, "A mind forever/Voyaging through strange seas of Thought/alone." True, Steve Wozniak's primitive new machine, the Altair 8800, the ancestor of the personal computer, would have never seen daylight if he had not teamed up with the wizard, Steve Jobs, and the simpatico band of engineers in the Homebrew Computer Club. But the spark of invention came from Steve Wozniak's solitary vigil. In his words, "inventors and engineers are almost like artists; in fact, the best of them are artists and the best of them work alone."[142]

- Wheel Velocity and Momentum—The system will monitor the velocity of Your Wheel and that of the entire network and furnish you with a report. In this way you can have a sense of how you are contributing to the momentum of the enterprise and how its intelligent energy is increasingly available to you.

- Create Your Own Luck—A talented young advisor to our project, Kyle Ricento, suggested the idea of "Creating Your Own Luck" as an app. This is a fascinating application of the Graph Program introduced earlier in this book and the skills you will develop over time. As you explore the principle of connectivity, you may find that synchronicities start to happen. Don't pay them too much heed. Just continue to practice steadily and your fortunes may shift. There is no way to force or to control the process. You simply play and have fun with it.

- Using the Explorer's Wheels to Help Others—As part of the Master Explorer's Wheel there is a special realm, Connecting to Humanity, which includes the Butterfly Effect. As noted, **paying forward** recalibrates all elements to your advantage— your sense of possibility goes up, your worries recede, your vision and focus sharpen, expectations are no longer so important, and your vital energy and resilience soar.[143]

- Personal Learning Networks—Along with your friends you can create your own Personal Learning Network (PLN), a new learning environment where you and other explorers can dream and reflect back the **Future**, articulate your visions and goals, and tell your stories. As Dryden and Vos note in their book on learning networks: "For the first time in history, we know how to store virtually all of humanity's most important information and make it available, almost instantly, in almost any form, to almost anyone on earth. We also know how to do that in a great many new ways so that people can interact and learn."[143a]

- Designing Your Own Wheel—We will provide the tools so that you can design Your Personal Explorer's Wheel under an open source license.[144]

New Educational Technologies

Your Personal Explorer's Wheel and your affiliated networked wheels can incorporate some of the exciting new educational tools and resources. The Khan Academy is an example of a non-profit organization whose mission is to become the world's first free virtual school. The mission of Salman Kahn, the Academy's founder, is to enable anyone, anywhere in the world, to have the same access to learning. The Kahn Academy makes its library of 2,700 videos available to its network of partner schools, along with special software which enables each student to learn at her or his own pace and style.[145] Another example is game technology. The authors of *Abundance* note that "games outperform textbooks in helping students learn fact-based subjects such as geography, history, and physics, while also improving visual coordination, cognitive speed, and manual dexterity. Surgeons and pilots trained on video games perform better than those who were not."[146] The Explorer's Wheel is an ideal platform to design "The Game of Life," which uses the gaming world to help train explorers for their journey in the "real" world.[147]

ICT Meets Enhanced Consciousness

As ICT converges with the new brain science, the implications for humanity will be profound. Here are three important nodes of convergence where the impact on your Personal Explorer's Wheel and Personal Learning Network will be immediate and transformational.

Optoelectronic Computing

Imagine Times Square in New York at the height of rush hour—hundreds of cars waiting to pass through the intersection. Now imagine, for a moment, that it is possible for every car to proceed directly through the intersection, passing through any car in its way, without collision, friction, or congestion. That capacity is available in another domain right today—immediately. It will be delivered through continuous interconnected parallel optical networks designed by Lightfleet Corporation, which is headquartered in Camas, Washington. In a nutshell, it involves 3D networks processing virtually unlimited bytes of information and knowledge, without wires—based solely on light. According to Lightfleet's CEO, John Peers, a recent commercial prototype licensed to Microsoft processed 600,256 bytes of information per second, per channel (with thirty-two channels currently operating) at 95 percent efficiency. We are only just beginning to explore the implications for dramatically increased processing speed, cost savings, reliability, raw computing power, and a plethora of new versatile applications. Optoelectronic networks using Lightfleet's platform or other forthcoming innovations are in their infancy.

What might be some of the noblest uses of this transformational technology? Here is one example: Human-Centric Computing (HCC).[148] We are fast becoming slaves to our technologies. We are hamstrung by their limitations, but they are already essential to most of our lives. Unfortunately, it is either their way or the highway. But what if the roles can be reversed? What if there are no more wires, no mouse pads, no monitors, indeed no more conventional computers? We know that today's computers will soon shrink to micro-sizes and morph into far more human-friendly (concentric) forms. Already, virtually unlimited computing power is now available to you whenever you want to learn something new, or think, or have some creative idea. What if you could simply talk to your computer and your story is instantly understood and acted on or translated into any language you wish? What if the modality adapts perfectly to your own personal and idiosyncratic way of learning? ICT is already the foundation of a multi-billion-dollar industry which is likely to reach $ trillions in the 2020s. It is a precursor of Human Centric Computing, which will be the platform within the next five years of your Personal Explorer's Wheel and of the Explorer's Network as whole.

Human Connectome Project

The mission of the Human Connectome Project (HCP) is to navigate the brain in a way that was never before possible: to fly through major brain pathways, compare essential circuits, and zoom into a region to explore the cells that comprise it and the functions that depend on it. The HCP aims to provide an unparalleled compilation of neural data, an interface to navigate this data graphically, and the opportunity to achieve never before realized conclusions about the living human brain.[149]

Numenta

Numenta is the brainchild of inventor-engineer Jeff Hawkins. Its first product, a software program, will enable smart, brain-inspired machines that learn from experience and make novel predictions about the world.[150]

Varieties of Explorer's Wheels

I conceive of a large number of special-purpose Explorer's Wheels which incorporate the basic framework. They will be linked in various ways and will become bridges among groups of people who are not yet connected.

- Special Interest Wheels (SIW)—Imagine a wide number of SIWs focused on specific activities or interests. High on my list is a Women's Explorer's Wheel which will honor the contributions of women pioneers.[151] The list of women explorers is extensive. We may know about the explorer-scientist, Madame Curie, the aviator Emilia Earhart, the authors Isak Dinesen or Beryl Marham (also a pilot), the explorer/humanitarian/anthropologist Jane Goodall, or Sylvia Earle, one of the great explorers of the oceans (whose friends refer to her as "Her Deepness"). But how many of us have heard of Sabriye Tenberken, a young blind girl who traveled by horseback within Tibet to found a Braille School Without Borders?[152] What might happen if millions and millions of other courageous women around the world suddenly dare to venture into new horizons? The virtuous multiplier effects would be profound. According to the UN Educational, Scientific and Cultural Organization (UNESCO), providing girls with an education is "the key to health and nutrition; to overall improvement in the standard of living;

to better agricultural and environmental practices; to higher gross national product; and to greater involvement and gender balance in decision making at all levels of society."[153] A Women's Explorer's Wheel provides an immediate means for self-learning among women on a global scale, without huge investments of public funds, bureaucracy, or fanfare. It can simply begin.

- Eradicating Global Blindness—This is another marvelous candidate. One important precedent is Surgical Eye Expeditions (SEE) International, founded by pioneering opthalmologist and inventor, Dr. Harry Brown. [154] During the past thirty years SEE International has restored sight to over one hundred thousand cataract patients at a cost of less than one hundred dollars per person. SEE International now has taken aim at diabetic retinopathy which is blinding millions not only in poor countries but in the industrialized world as well. According to Dr. Brown there is no medical reason why any person on this earth should go blind from diabetic retinopathy, the leading cause of blindness today.

- Change Agents and Collaborative Entrepreneurship— "Everyone is a change agent, not just a tiny elite. Our mission is to not to give people fish, or even teach them how to fish, but rather to build a fishing industry." This is how my friend and college classmate, Bill Drayton, describes the mission of Ashoka, which he founded in 1981.[155] There are now over 3,000 Ashoka Fellows in 80 countries, which constitute a formidable cadre of battle-tested change agents who are ready to take on the world's tough challenges. Bill Drayton's new direction for Ashoka is Collaborative Entrepreneurship designed on the premise of forging strategic alliances in hybrid value chains (HVCs) between for-profit businesses and a great number of citizen sector organizations (CSOs), especially in the Third World. Drayton points out that the markets in clean air and water, energy, healthy food, medical care, housing, and education are vast and the demand is growing. What entrepreneur worth her or his salt, he asks, wouldn't be interested in a trillion-dollar market opportunity? By bundling the comparative talents, knowledge, and resources of companies and CSOs in HVCs, Ashoka has been able to build successful businesses that return "triple bottom line" commercial, social, and environmental returns to their investors.

Please scan

- Scientific Inquiry Special Wheels—As discussed in the previous chapter, a top priority for California is to organize a Discovery Expedition, as described in Book II, Chapter II, to generate breakthroughs in the science of earthquake prediction. An Explorer's Wheel will provide a means to transform a complex scientific and technical issue into an opportunity for society-wide education and learning. The Explorer's Wheel will provide the vessel and the connections, and mobilize the creative energy to democratize the search for solutions. I envision many other Special Scientific Wheels. One excellent candidate would be an Explorer's Wheel linked to the Human Connectome Project.[156] Another might be a Longevity Explorer's Wheel. An important area of research will be to explore whether a life spent in curiosity, inquiry, and self-learning produces not only a more interesting journey, but whether it will also extend human lifespan.[157] I hope this book will stimulate fellow explorers to conceive and to launch many Discovery Expeditions of their own and that their Expeditions will attract patrons— wealthy individuals, foundations, and corporations—who will endow specific discoveries, attaching their names to these intellectual territories, much as early explorers like Columbus enjoyed the patronage of kings and queens.

- Global Disaster Wheels—Some friends and I have tried for some time to establish a Global Center for Emergency Management (C-GEM) based in Los Angeles. At present there is no effective coordinating body for global emergencies, which include natural disasters, terrorist attacks, and infrastructural (financial) breakdowns, and no center to study comprehensively the inter-relationships of emergencies such as Fukushima or their cascading repercussions. Also lacking is a repository of global best practices, an international standard setting authority, and a place where EMA professionals can learn and train together. Even before someone recognizes the importance of establishing C-GEM in physical form, C-GEM can be rapidly organized virtually as an Explorer's Wheel, and its good work can begin.

- Philanthropic Wheels—Philanthropic Wheels will be the financial engine of the Explorer's Network. One source of potential funding is the Gates Foundation and its affiliated Microsoft Alumni Network which represent the gold standard of leveraged philanthropy.[158] An excellent candidate for financing is See Your Impact, a wonderful organization established by Scott Oki, one of the early VPs for Marketing at Microsoft. Many other alumni of Microsoft are now actively engaged in social entrepreneurship and philanthropy, and they and their organizations collaborate on projects around the world. In November 2011, a company I helped to found, Smartcode FX Solutions, was a lead sponsor at the Gates Gala Opening Event. All of the other lead sponsors are deeply committed to social entrepreneurship. One, Growums, must be specially noted. Growums teaches kids to become gardeners with special kits introduced by Growum's proliferating menagerie of animated creatures. Kids have an opportunity to hang out with their families and friends and together watch the seeds they plant grow into fruits and vegetables they learn to harvest. Growums has a strong policy of giving back to the world through creative philanthropy.[159]

- For–Profit and Non-Profit Corporate Wheels—For–profit companies and non-profit organizations seeking to stay on the leading edge of innovation will want to consider designing their own Explorer's Wheels, customized to their specific missions and unique cultures.

- Hybrid Wheels—Some Explorer's Wheels will closely overlap. For example, a Longevity Wheel and the HCP Wheel are natural allies. As suggested, innovation often occurs in the intertidal zone between fields. It is virtually certain that new discoveries will emerge from the coupling of frontier research on the brain, brain mapping, longevity, and new models of continuing lifelong education.

- The Power of Communities—"Change happens through the power of communities," writes Richard Branson. The photo journalist David Brancaccio traces this principle in a recent video, "Sustainable Connection" which describes how communities across the U.S. are rediscovering and recreating themselves, producing new jobs, and contributing to a healthy sustainable environment. He calls this movement, The Sustainable Connection,[160] and it has already engendered some important social innovations, which are described in the PBS series. These include: a network of manufacturing cooperatives in Bellingham, Washington, St. Paul, Minnesota, and Detroit, Michigan; an Hour Exchange in Portland, Maine, based on a barter trade in hourly contributions; and the Bremer Bank in South Dakota which is owned by its employees and the community and founded on social entrepreneurial principles. Communities are ideal candidates for Explorer's Wheels dedicated to their special needs and interests.[161]

- International Explorer's Wheels—I am just becoming involved in a fascinating project. It is dedicated to the rebirth of the Tohoku region in Japan, which was the epicenter of the 2011 Fukushima earthquake. Many young people in Japan—social entrepreneurs, innovators, community-minded companies—and a wide array of international organizations are involved in helping Tohoku revive—not just to recover, but more interestingly, to stimulate a national course correction toward the birth of a New Japan.[162] An equally interesting project is GII-China, the establishment of a program to cultivate China's one hundred global innovative champions. The project is being coordinated through my colleague Professor Jie Li at Beijing University. Forging new and innovative relationships with China is one of the other great bridges I hope to build through the Explorers' World project.

Some Intriguing Questions: Areas for Further Research

Before proceeding, let us step back and reflect for a moment on some interesting questions presented by a Global Network of Explorer's Wheels.

- What is the relationship of an Explorer's Wheel to energy?— The English word "energy" derives from the Greek *energos*, "the power within."[163] While writing this final chapter, the idea suddenly struck me that an Explorer's Wheel is a concentrator of energy, and in its liquid and most dynamic form, it is a spiral, a vortex of energy. I was stunned by the potential creative energy that might be produced by thousands, if not millions, of networked spirals, spinning virtually forever. Inspired to research the spiral, I learned that:

○ In Nature—Spirals in nature display a dazzling beauty. Spirals are everywhere.[164] On a cosmic level, the spiral galaxy is a system of billions of stars with a central bulge of older stars surrounded by a flat disk with spiral arms of gas and dust nebulae and young stars. The Milky Way is a spiral galaxy.[165] Wormholes, as conceived by artists, are also essentially spirals.[166]

○ In Society—Since ancient times virtually every society in the world has recognized in its art, legends, or ceremonies the numinous power of the spiral.[167]

○ In Industry—Wheels and spirals play a central role in most industrial processes. My own personal experience with the subject is through a several year Discovery Expedition on energy storage sponsored by the Electricity Power Research Institute (EPRI). We surveyed flywheels, capacitors, and other energy storage modalities, including a remarkable, as yet unexploited technology, the Ring Power Multiplier—itself a spiraling coil.[168]

○ In Living Systems—Spirals are also fundamental to all living systems. The DNA of all living systems is based on the helix or spiral. Various *qigong* energy/healing systems, in particular "silk reeling or energy twinning" from the Chen style of *tai chi chuan*, are used to generate spirit and concentration. The spiral is fundamental to the Chinese hard martial arts.[169]

• What could be the relationship between the Explorer's Network and enhanced intelligence?—I can report a curious discovery. As a child I attained the status of a chess expert with a fairly strong national ranking, but I haven't played chess since college. Recently, I purchased two chess programs, Shredder and Real Chess, which I run on my iPad. They are both weak grandmasters and they provide "hints" to their users. When I play against these two programs without assistance, I **always** lose. Sometimes, however, I ask them for a little help—not a whole lot, mind you, but an occasional tip—and when I do, I often draw with these grandmasters, and on occasion I beat them. What can we make of this? Is there a general principle? What are the implications for the Explorer's Network? Perhaps if you pair an expert with an intelligent database, it need not take more than a minor boost to enhance the expert's skill significantly. I call this the "Intelligence Booster Effect." What may be in play is a tipping point: once players achieve an advanced level of skill, it may not take too much assistance to accelerate to a significantly higher aptitude.[170]

- There may also be something special about coupling closed and open systems. Chess is an example of a closed system, which, although deeply complex, is why programmers at IBM were able to construct Big Blue's brain and beat the current World Champion Gary Kasparov over twenty years ago. The Explorer's Wheel is an example of a closed system, but far more complex than chess. In other words, there is a framework (Explorer's Wheel) and an algorithm (Trust the Connection). But the proposed system is also different from chess because the domain with which you are connecting is not known, nor even knowable. It is infinite. I am suggesting that this coupling of closed and open systems may have profound implications in the design of more intelligent systems.

- How might we harness the potential energy of spiraling Explorer's Wheels?—Most discussions of the Internet are concerned with accelerating the search, compilation, and storage of information and knowledge. The relationship to energy seems less studied. In fact, there is much evidence that the Internet is scattering energy, *i.e.,* increasing entropy and noise. For example, ten years ago email was heralded as a wondrous new communications technology, but today most people are overwhelmed and can't wait to escape from an avalanche of emails, mostly from people or companies they don't care to know. Suppose, however, that there is a way to concentrate the vast pools of human energy currently being invested each day but dissipated over the Internet? This might well be one of the anticipated contributions of the Explorers' Network.

- Might there be a relationship between continuous life-learning and longevity? Is it possible that by participating in the Explorers' Networks we might enhance not only our personal creativity and intelligence, but also conceivably empower life force, longevity, and well-being? We cannot yet scientifically prove such a claim. But we intend to test it thoughtfully and systematically. It seems to me that we are dealing with a phenomenon of "compounding intelligence" in which individual action, group dynamics, network dynamics, intelligent data bases, the technologies themselves, and the overall design and structure of the enterprise are synergistic: the "system" simultaneously becomes smarter, both individually and collectively. Why might this conceivably be so?

- What are the implications of the convergence of optoelectronic computing and the neuroplastic brain?—According to the neuroscientists, electronic media and our brains are already rapidly merging. In some sense our brains cannot distinguish electronic media from natural phenomena. How will this process be further accelerated by the arrival of optoelectronic computing? What is the bright potential of this convergence? With adequate funding, our Discovery Team can deliver the first commercial prototypes of Human Centric Computing in three to five years. As noted earlier, the relationship of humans and computers will be reversed. We will no longer be slaves to our technology. The processing of information and knowledge by light seems a close metaphor for human consciousness. What remarkable discoveries and inventions will explorers make within our generation, as they themselves and their tools become more conscious? As our industrial infrastructure becomes increasingly supported by convergent light-processing industries, what new opportunities will be created for global economic prosperity? Today we have data processing, information processing, even knowledge processing industries. But within our lifetimes it may be possible for us to have the benefit of wisdom (consciousness) processing industries as well.[171] And then to what brave new horizons will we reach, beyond the eclipse of our present imaginations? As Hamlet soliloquizes: "What a piece of work is a man, How noble in Reason, how infinite in faculties, in form and moving, how express and admirable! In action how like an angel...." (Shakespeare, *Hamlet*, Act 2, Scene 2)

- What about the shadow of disruptive technologies?—I have no delusion about the shadow side of optoelectronic computing and other disruptive (transformational) technologies. The technologies in themselves are arguably neutral. They can be deployed by their users for good or ill. The question is into whose hands will they fall? Some readers may challenge the benefits of having humanity's collective knowledge available to anyone, anywhere, in an instant.

Some may urge that these advances will place the tools and power in the hands of the privileged and increase class division.[172] Or worse, they may fall into the hands of despotic regimes or terrorist groups. For example, with all the early promise of computers, how many people anticipated that computers would become the fiendish instrument of the Nazi Holocaust?[173] Given the possibility that such things might occur as these new technologies enter the stream of commerce, an important legal question arises: should the law hold developers of these technologies to a higher than ordinary standard of care, even a fiduciary duty to invest significant corporate resources in guiding such innovations toward their highest and best uses for humanity?[174]

- How might a network of exploring minds (brains) and culture reciprocally change each other? Although the conventional position has been that human culture is an artifact of the human brain, the new discoveries in neuroplasticity suggest that the reverse is equally true. Culture modifies the physical structure of our brains and the relationship is dynamic and synergistic. One writer, Merzenich, expresses it this way:

  > Our brains are vastly different, in fine detail, from the brains of our ancestors.... In each stage of cultural development ... the average human brain had to learn new skills and abilities that all involve massive brain change.... Each one of us can learn an incredibly elaborate set of ancestrally developed skills and abilities in our lifetimes, in a sense generating a re-creation of this history of cultural evolution via brain plasticity.[175]

- In his book, *The Brain That Changes Itself*, Dr. Norman Doidge[176] provides numerous examples of this fundamental proposition. One is Burmese divers, called Sea Gypsies, who have acquired an ability to see under water by learning to control the shape of the lenses and the size of the pupils in their eyes, shrinking them by 22 percent, thereby influencing the refraction of light. This is a remarkable achievement because pupil adjustment has been customarily thought to be a fixed, innate reflex, controlled by the brain and nervous system. Other prominent examples cited by Dr. Doidge, are the neurological changes in the brains of musicians and artists (he cites Michelangelo's ordeal in painting the Sistine Chapel) and changes in the hippocampus of London taxi drivers.

Dr. Doidge goes on to make several other important observations relating neuroplasticity to culture:

- The brain's ability to adapt with culture, or "cognitive fluidity," is a primary factor that enabled *Homo sapiens* to emerge both physiologically and culturally from the Pleistocene.

- The fundamental rule of brain plasticity is that when brain centers interact they influence each other and form a new whole. This provides insight into how our brains can absorb daily assaults of violence, vulgarity, and noise and the sublimity and tranquility of nature within an integrated and coherent gestalt. Our brains are being massively remodeled by constant exposure and "practice" on the Internet, television, video games, contemporary music, and modern electronics. What is keeping us "sane" is the time off, the recourse to nature, as Dr. Andrew Weil is prescribing in his book, *Spontaneous Happiness*.[177]

- At times, culturally induced neurological perceptions play a critical role in survival. Dr. Doidge mentions that not one Sea Gypsy was killed in the tsunami of December 26, 2004. Apparently the Sea Gypsies sensed that "The Wave That Eats People" was coming and, using an exceptional wide angled lens of perception, they pieced together the unusual events and signs—the "patterns" in Jim Schrager's terminology. When asked how it was that they survived but the Burmese boat people (who also knew the sea) all perished, the Sea Gypsies replied: "They [the Burmese] were looking at the squid. They were not looking at anything. They saw nothing, they looked at nothing. They don't know how to look."[178]

- Will future Explorers Wheels consciously create themselves?—As the Explorers' Wheels spin their magic spirals, the Explorer's Intelligent Data Base will become exponentially smarter. Within the next few years optoelectronic computing will be an integral part of the Human Connectome Project, vastly enhancing our capacity to map the human brain and explore mind and consciousness. We will begin to see patterns and potentialities we scarcely imagine today. What if the system begins to do so on its own, unbidden and uninstructed? Surely it will have this capacity. If our brains can change themselves, in which directions will they take us? How can we influence both our individual brains and the Collective Networked Brain to evolve in ways that will enhance the quotient of human kindness and generosity?[179] Perhaps we can use this awesome power to find an answer to our most basic quest: to find a way, within the next few years, for every person on this anguished planet to realize a happier, more peaceful and bountiful life. What if we find an answer?

Improvisational Theatre and Jazz Models

The creative power of the Explorer's Network will flow from the exuberance of its members. But who will guide it? What models will be most congenial? One is improvisational theatre which was developed by the Commedia dell'Arte on the streets of Italy between the sixteenth and eighteenth centuries. It would be wonderful if the Explorer's Network and its Personal Learning Networks can inspire a kind of improvisational theatre conducted around the world and distributed through the New Media. Participants have all the tools they require, online and off, to connect and combine realms of knowledge, hitherto only remotely linked, following their own artistic and entrepreneurial instincts.

A second model is jamming, a jazz form which became the regular after-hours pastime at Minton's Playhouse in New York during the 1940s and early 1950s. Jam sessions may be based upon existing songs or forms, or may be loosely based upon an agreed chord progression or chart, suggested by one participant; or they may be wholly improvisational.[180]

A third model is the Orpheus Chamber Orchestra, established by cellist Julian Fifer in 1972. The distinctive personality of Orpheus is its unique practice of sharing and rotating leadership roles. For every work, the members of the orchestra select the concertmaster and the principal players for each section. These players constitute the core group, whose role is to form the initial concept of the piece and to shape the rehearsal process. In the final rehearsals, all members of the orchestra participate in refining the interpretation and execution, with members taking turns listening from the hall for balance, blend, articulation, dynamic range and clarity of expression.

Spinning Wheels, Storytelling, and the Fates

Although the Explorer's Network will rely on the most advanced modern technologies, the primary means of transmission will likely be an ancient form: storytelling. From earliest times, spinning wheels, storytelling, myths, and the Fates have been closely tied. Storytelling builds and releases the spiraling energies by which societies weave their destinies. In ancient Greece, the Moirai, or the Fates, were portrayed as three women. Clotho spun the thread of life from her distaff onto a spindle. Lachesis, the "allotter," measured out the thread of life which is allotted to each person. Atropos, the "inexorable," cut the thread of life.[181]

There is some speculation on how spinning came to be linked with storytelling in the English language. Some suggest the comparison with a spider spinning its web. Others opine that in the old days women used to spin yarn on spinning wheels. As they frequently did this in groups, they told each other stories to pass the time. Eventually the words came to mean the production of the stories themselves. The common theme is continuous connecting. A story is a story because it is connected; it is not just a collection of random incidents, characters, sentences. In fact, in the absence of a storytelling we will fill in the blanks for ourselves. We yearn for coherence. Even when we sleep, the brain weaves together a narrative that brings sense and meaning to our random neural firings.[182]

Some writers observe that storytelling is the primary means by which we process "reality" and, therefore, is closely related to intelligence. Roger Schank, a leading narratologist, notes that the human brain stores life experience as distinct patterns which are woven into larger narratives. These stories are then indexed as "gists'" in what he calls "Memory Organization Packages."[183] Other writers claim that shared stories are what constitute a culture.[184] Cultural ideas, or memes, are compared to biological viruses and, it is conjectured, replicate and proliferate in analogous ways.

Not all stories are written or even orally narrated. Some are expressed in photographs, paintings, and lithographs, as described in the footnote.[185] In this living, adaptive, multi-media book (LAMB™), I envision storytelling in what the theoretical physicist David Bohm imagined as its purest form, a dialogue, or what I call, "A Conversation Among Friends." It is the means by which participants can connect with and discover their shared humanity.[186]

A Parable—Beginning the Journey

As I write this concluding section, an idea arrives. It comes as a parable I discover in the movie, *Blindsight*. It is about an expedition of six blind Tibetan teenagers who set off to climb the twenty-three thousand foot Lhaka Ri on the north side of Mount Everest.[187] At first I don't see the connection. But then the fragments come together. The voice of the Narrator: "Imagine climbing the highest peak on earth. Imagine climbing it blind." The expedition's leader, Erik Weinhenmayer, himself the first blind person to climb Everest, expresses the basic existential question, "The fear of climbing comes when I am reaching out in the darkness, when I don't know what I will find." He defines the mission as they set off, "The kids are doing their own expedition. If they can find their *own* Everest, what a statement that will make to the world!" One of the expedition's guides, an extraordinary German girl, Sabriye Tenberken, herself completely blind, has ventured on her own by horseback to Tibet and helped to found its Braille School Without Borders.[188] Sabriye tells us, "In Tibet blind people have a big, big problem. These children are believed to be possessed by the devil. They are completely outcast. But one child, a blind little girl, comments, 'The sighted see with their eyes. But we blind children see with our hearts'."

Please scan

They begin the journey and it is very hard. Everyone must proceed with extreme caution and agility. With each step they could stumble to their deaths. Avalanches are a constant threat. Some of the kids get sick from the altitude. Now they are at about two thousand feet from the crest. Three of the kids must be sent down the mountain for their own protection. One little girl breaks into tears; the others are desolate. As viewers we sense their profound loneliness and isolation. A debate takes place within the team. There is an increasing sense of urgency. Erik wants to press on; he is a warrior and a visionary. Sabriye counters: "Is it really the right thing, this goal, to get every child to the summit?" In the end Erik and the other expedition leaders relent. They will all go down. They do not need to get to the top. Their accomplishment is already extraordinary. These kids have climbed twenty-three thousand feet of the second highest mountain in the world. Erik summarizes, "When you suffer together, that is when you make the closest connections with those around you. That is when you make friends. Getting to the summit was less important than that in the end."

For me the lesson of *Blindsight* is that we needn't reach the summit. Obsession with the summit is the hubris of Icarus. The journey is what matters, to be sure-footed, stay aware, and as Sabriye and Erik note, to have fun and make new friends. You simply let go, step aside and enjoy the moment—and things appear just as they are. Smiling is important. When you relax control, the world approaches. It is essentially friendly.

AUTHOR'S GIFT
TO THE READER

Once again, let us invoke Daikoku, the Japanese god of Abundance and the Harvest. He provides lightness, bounce, and play when times are tough. May he bring you good fortune and much cheer on your journey.

Appendix 1

TWENTY-FIRST CENTURY HUMANISM AND A SECOND RENAISSANCE

RENAISSANCE HUMANISM— THE BEGINNING OF THE LINEAGE

Who is the bright symbol of his times, bringing the light on a chariot of fire out of the darkness of the late Middle Ages?[189] Giovanni Pico della Mirandola. The prodigy of the Renaissance, at twenty-three he was already a master of twenty-two languages and much more. He expresses the resurgent spirit of his age:

> We have made thee neither of heaven nor of earth,
> Neither mortal or immortal,
> So that with freedom of choice and with honor,
> As thought the maker and molder of thyself,
> Thou mayest fashion thyself in whatever shape thou shalt
>   prefer.
> Thou shalt have the power out of thy soul's judgment,
> To be reborn into the higher forms, which are divine.[190]

Renaissance Humanism was an activity primarily of cultural and educational reform, centered principally in Florence and Naples in the fourteenth and fifteenth centuries. It was a response by scholars, writers, and civics to a mediæval scholastic education, which stressed practical, pre-professional, and scientific studies to prepare men to be doctors, lawyers, or professional theologians. It was taught from approved textbooks in logic, natural philosophy, medicine, law, and theology.

Renaissance humanists rebelled against the rigidities of the pre-scribed learning of the mother church. Rather they sought to create a citizenry (sometimes including women) able to speak and write with eloquence and clarity, who they believed would be more capable of engaging in the civic life of their communities and persuading others to virtuous and prudent actions. The New Humanism focused on the study (*studia humanitatis*) of grammar, rhetoric, history, poetry, and moral philosophy.

People in the Renaissance lived in a dynamic struggle between two worlds: the world of faith in the medieval Christian matrix, in which the significance of every phenomenon was ultimately determined through uniform points of view, and a larger awakening world of reason and providence.

Beauty was believed to afford a glimpse into a transcendental existence. The ideal life was no longer a monastic escape from society, but a full participation, rich and varied, in human relationships. Humanism, as many commentators point out, was fundamentally an aesthetic movement.

But the humanist mind did not free itself entirely from subservience to another authority. As one writer notes:

> If the humanists revered Aristotle less than the schoolmen did, they worshipped Neoplatonism, the Cabala, and Cicero more. They shifted authorities rather than dismissed them. Even Aristotle, the greatest of scholastic authorities, did not lack humanist admirers. The great libraries assembled by wealthy patrons of literature, like Cosimo de' Medici, Pope Nicholas V, and the Duke of Urbino, devoted much space to the Church Fathers and the scholastic philosophers. The humanists did, however, read their authorities for aesthetic pleasure as well as moral uplift.
>
> The intellectuals of antiquity, in contrast to the Christians, were relatively unconcerned about the supernatural world and the eternal destiny of the soul. They were primarily interested in a happy, adequate, and efficient life here on earth. Hellenic philosophy was designed to teach man how to live successfully rather than how to die with the assurance of ultimate salvation. This pagan attitude had been lost for about one thousand years when Europe followed the warning of Augustine against becoming too engrossed in earthly affairs lest assurance of successful entry into the New Jerusalem be jeopardized. Humanism directly and indirectly revived the pagan scale of virtues.[191a]

THE AGE OF EXPLORATION
AND THE ENLIGHTENMENT

Twenty-first century Humanism also has some of the spirit of the Age of Exploration, also known as the Age of Discovery, and also of the Enlightenment. The Age of Exploration began in the early fifteenth century and continued into the early seventeenth century, and chartered most of the unknown world. Europeans dominated, although a great Chinese explorer/sea captain, Zheng He, is also credited with important discoveries throughout Asia, Australia, and even in North, Central, and South America.[191] Accounts from distant lands and maps spread with the help of the new printing press fed the humanist curiosity, ushering in a new age of scientific and intellectual inquiry.

The Age of Enlightenment (or simply, the Enlightenment or the Age of Reason) was a cultural movement of intellectuals in eighteenth century France which sought to mobilize the power of reason in order to reform society and advance knowledge. It promoted science and intellectual interchange and opposed superstition, intolerance, and abuses in church and state. Originating about 1650-1700, it was sparked by philosophers Baruch Spinoza (1632-77), John Locke (1632-1704), and Pierre Bayle (1647-1706); mathematician Isaac Newton (1643-1727); and Voltaire (1694-1778). The wide distribution of the printing press, invented in Europe in 1440, made possible the rapid spread of knowledge and ideas which precipitated the Enlightenment. Ruling princes often endorsed and fostered figures and even attempted to apply their ideas of government in what was known as Enlightened Despotism. The Enlightenment flourished until about 1790–1800, after which the emphasis on reason gave way to Romanticism's emphasis on emotion and a Counter-Enlightenment gained force.

The centre of the Enlightenment was France, where it was based in the salons and culminated in the great *Encyclopédie* (1751-72) edited by Denis Diderot (1713-84) with contributions by hundreds of leading philosophers (intellectuals) such as Voltaire (1694-1778), Rousseau (1712-78), and Montesquieu (1689-1755). Some twenty-five thousand copies of the thirty-five volume set were sold, half of them outside France. The new intellectual forces spread to urban centres across Europe, notably England, Scotland, the German states, the Netherlands, Russia, Italy, Austria, and Spain, then jumped the Atlantic into the European colonies, where it influenced Benjamin Franklin and Thomas Jefferson, among many others, and played a major role in the American

Revolution. The political ideals influenced the American Declaration of Independence, the United States Bill of Rights, the French Declaration of the Rights of Man and of the Citizen, and the Polish–Lithuanian Constitution of May 3, 1791.

Gregory Bateson's Ecology of Mind[192]

Another direct ancestor of twenty-first century Humanism is Gregory Bateson (May 9, 1904–July 4, 1980), an English anthropologist, social scientist, linguist, visual anthropologist, semiotician, and cyberneticist whose work intersected that of many other fields. He had a natural ability to recognize order and pattern in the universe. In the 1940s he helped extend systems theory/cybernetics to the social/behavioral sciences, and spent the last decade of his life developing a "meta-science" of epistemology to bring together the early forms of systems theory developing in various fields of science. Some of his most noted writings are to be found in his books, *Steps to an Ecology of Mind* (1972) and *Mind and Nature* (1979) and *Angels Fear*, which was published posthumously in 1987 and co-authored by his daughter Mary Catherine Bateson.

Twenty-first Century Humanism and a Second Renaissance

Implicit in the optimism of *Abundance* is a flowering in the twenty-first century of a New Humanism and a Second Renaissance. As the new economic prosperity was the garden of the Italian Renaissance, so also the benevolent forces which Peter Diamandis and Steven Kotler describe will be reflected in, and themselves transformed by, culture. This seems especially likely if thousands of Explorer's Wheels begin to spin and millions of people become excited about entering a second Age of Exploration. As this is a prediction based on history, it may be useful to understand how the emergent patterns of today resemble those of the past and why they may also be fundamentally different.

Although twenty-first century Humanism and a Second Renaissance it may inspire will draw unmistakably upon its historical precursors, the times we live in and the shape of the arc are significantly different. For starters, the challenges are global and deeply involve the natural world which is in perplexed rebellion. Nor did people living during the Renaissance possess weapons that could blow the world apart. Second, twenty-first century Humanism is neither religious nor anti-religious, as some forms of Humanism are. It is open and exploratory. Third, science and technology, especially new discoveries relating to the brain and human consciousness, will transform fundamentally who we are. Fourth, the Age of the Internet and New Media will alter how knowledge is compiled and transmitted. There are over 900 million smart phone users in China alone. Fifth, our time sense is also altered. If Renaissance Humanism looked primarily to the **Past**, twenty-first century Humanism will embody **Past, Present,** and **Future** in new and creative ways. Lastly, twenty-first century Humanism will not be confined to the West or even the industrialized world. The vast potential of the BRIC countries (Brazil, Russia, India, and China) and beyond, the Arabian Peninsula, South America, and Africa lies largely untapped. These gigantic regions with billions of people have yet to make their unique contributions.[193]

Appendix 2

ADDITIONAL STORIES FOR DISCUSSION

Case # 1—Yagyu's Apprenticeship

Paul Reps tells another story of how Matajuro Yagyu, son of a famous swordsman, mastered the uncertainty principle. It illustrates the empirical, learning-by-constant-practice dimension of cultivating the Explorer's Mind.

Apparently, the father was so disgusted by his son's mediocre work, he disowned him, and so Matajuro went to Mount Futara and there found the swordsman Banzo. But Banzo confirmed his father's assessment. "You wish to learn swordsmanship under my guidance?" asked Banzo. "You cannot fulfill the requirements."

"But if I work hard, how many years will it take me?" inquired Matajuro.

"The rest of your life," replied Banzo.

"I cannot wait that long," explained Matajuro. "My father is old, and I must hurry. If I devote myself heart and mind, how long will it take? I implore you."

"Oh, seventy years, I don't know. A man who is such a hurry as you are to get results seldom learns quickly," said Banzon.

Realizing at last that he was being rebuked for impatience, the youth yielded, "I agree."

Matajuro was told never to speak of fencing and never to touch a sword. He cooked for his master, washed the dishes, made his bed, cleaned the yard, cared for the garden, all without a word of swordsmanship. Three years passed. Thinking of his future he was disconsolate. He had not even begun to learn the art to which he had now devoted his life.

Then one day Banzo crept up behind him and gave him a terrific blow with a wooden sword. The following day when Matajuro was cooking rice Banzo sprang upon him unexpectedly. After that, day and night, Matajuro had to defend himself from unexpected thrusts. Not a moment passed when he did not have to be aware of the taste of Banzo's sword.

He learned so rapidly that Banzo smiled in disbelief. Matajuro became the greatest swordsman in the land.[194]

In the past, many fighters in Japan were killed by wooden swords. And now this story has become part of our own popular culture, depicted in both old and recent versions of *The Karate Kid*. Managing the mind under uncertainty enters the story in two ways. Matajuro does not know that he will ever amount to anything as a swordsman. He must learn to accept the uncertainty of failure. Then, after his mind is stabilized, he is confronted by another form of uncertainty: at any moment chaos erupts and he must respond precisely or die.

You do not have to be a martial artist to learn the basic skill of managing the mind in uncertainty. Any serious negotiator can learn and refine the art.

Case # 2—A Personal Encounter

Not every sense of the connection comes in a thunderstorm. You get hints along the way. At times you find traces by odd experiences that appear like slight tears in the fabric of ordinary reality. Such experiences give us glimpses into a different order of things. I remember a singular experience during a hot sultry July summer in Kamakura during the 1980s when I had been struggling with the *koan Mu* (無; Japanese: emptiness, nothingness).The *shoji* in the *zendo* was slightly ajar, and there was only the faintest breeze. I decided to escape for a few moments. The more serious students were fastened on their practice. Nothing moved. I stepped out of the *zendo*, and there coiled at the *genkan* was a large and beautiful spotted yellow snake. Fascinated, I froze. Why a snake? Why here and just now? Why doesn't someone turn around to see what I am seeing? No one did. I rushed into the kitchen and called the maid and other attendants. "Quick, there is a large snake coiled in front of the *zendo*." They hurried out. The snake had vanished. Though snakes were uncommon around the *zendo,* and though no one else saw what I saw, my rational mind insists it was simply a snake. My intuitive mind, however, tells me otherwise.*

Case # 3—Finding Land in the Mists

Explorers are well acquainted with the adversity's creative wave. Wade Davis in *Wayfinders, Why Ancient Wisdom Matters in the Modern World*, describes the voyage of the Hokule'a, the great seafaring canoe in which he set out with its legendary captain, Nainoa Thompson. Their mission was "to pull" the tiny island of Rapa Nui "out of the sea," with no instruments save the knowledge of his forefathers, the moon and the stars, the waves and currents, birds, and the creatures of the deep.

> At one point close to their goal, Nainoa snapped awake in a daze and realized that with the overcast skies and the sea fog, he had no idea where they were. He had lost the continuity of mind and memory essential to survival at sea. He masked his fear from the crew and in his despair remembered Mau's [his teacher's] words. *Can you see the image of the island in your mind?* He became calm and realized that he had already found the island. It was the Hokule'a, and he had everything he needed on board the sacred canoe. Suddenly, the sky brightened and a beam of warm light appeared on his shoulder. The clouds cleared and he followed that beam of light directly to the island of Rapa Nui.

---

* Note: As noted elsewhere in this book, snakes have an important symbolic significance. They are the form in which dragons, or dragon consciousness, are thought to manifest on our ordinary plane of consciousness. In the yogic traditions a snake can represent the coiling energy of the *kundalini*. Generally, the Zen tradition warns against these phenomena, which are referred to as demons (*makyo*) that can impede the explorer on the path. At the same time, they are also seen as harbingers of discovery. Adepts are strongly encouraged to take them as interesting signs and to press on. In my case this particular *makyo* arrived the evening before Yamada Roshi formally acknowledged my first taste of the Zen world (*kensho*).

NOTES

Author's Preface (Second Edition)

1   Alan Moorehead, *The White Nile* 1960; *The Blue Nile* (1983); http://en.wikipedia.org/wiki/Alan_Moorehead.
2   Tim Jeal, *Stanley* (2007).
3   http://www.ted.com/talks/peter_diamandis_abundance_is_our_future.html.
4   Indeed, in their mentor, colleague, and co-founder of Singularity University, Ray Kurzweil's book, *The Singularity is Near*, a powerful exploration of the future, wisdom is not even mentioned.
5   In the first, the German baritone, Dietrich Fischer Dieskau was singing the solo from Cantata 158 (Der Freide sei mit dir) "...World, adieu, I am weary of you." The aria begins with his solo; but then, rising like the white cliffs of Dover, an extraordinary chorus answers him, "World, adieu, I am weary of you." "I wish to enter heaven, where there shall be true peace and everlasting calm of spirit." You might also enjoy another glorious work, Cantata 140, Wachet auf, ruft unds die Stimme (Sleeper's Awake!)

Please scan

6 The Explorer's Wheel™ is a registered trademark of the author.

7 Holography may be an essential element of integrity. On an audio tape of her life, Isak Denisen provides an account of a magnificent lion she had just shot and had skinned for the King of Denmark. 'He was magnificent in his lionhood, every part of him a lion, through and through.'

8 http://www.squidoo.com/femaleexplorers.

9 There is also a venerable journal published by MIT, *Leonardo*, which is tracking their contributions, and there are new educational programs such as the Arts and Technology Program headed by my friend, astrophysicist and editor of *Leonardo*, Roger Malina, at the University of Texas in Dallas.

10 I cannot resist recommending a new biography, the first complete portrait of the great explorer in half a century, *Columbus: The Four Voyages* by Laurence Bergreen (2011).

Book II

11 Peter H. Diamandis and Steven Kotler, *Abundance* (2012). http://www.youtube.com/watch?v=BltRufe5kkI;http://www.youtube.com/watch?v=IyXik42ASAg. http://www.youtube.com/watch?v=FWsMofsOxLs.

12 *The World of Renaissance Florence*, trans. Walter Darwell (1999).

Book II Chapter I

13 John Tarrant, *Bring Me the Rhinoceros* (2004).

14 Jerry Thompson, *Cascadia's Fault* (2011). See, also, "Nature's Extremes-Inside the Great Natural Disasters That Shape Life on Earth," *Time Magazine* (2006).

15 Jasan Makansi, *Lights Out: The Electricity Crisis, the Global Economy, and What it Means to You* (2007). It is interesting to note that more government regulatory attention is devoted to the location of a small sewage plant than protecting the vulnerable nodes to the electricity grid.

16 Charles Perrow, *Normal Accidents* (1984). Joshua Cooper Ramo, *The Age of the Unthinkable* (2009).

17 Private communication from Kenneth S. Cohen.

18 See Book II, Chapter II.

19 See Pico Iyer, "The Joy of Quiet" Sunday Review, *New York Times*, January 1, 2012.

20 Diamandis and Kotler, *Abundance*, 32, Prescript, n1 (2004).

21 http://www.ted.com/talks/jared_diamond_on_why_societies_collapse.html.

22 My definition is closer to the Japanese and Chinese concept of *shin* (心), or *kokoro,* which can be approximated as heart/mind or consciousness.

23 Shakespeare, *Henry V,* 2.iii.

24 We are not alone in this respect. The will to survive may be basic for all life. An English friend recalls a memory when he was a boy during the World War II of his father preparing to drown a litter of unneeded puppies, and how these frail little creatures fought like tigers to survive.

25 Laurence Gonzales, *Deep Survival* (2009).

26 Gonzales, *Survival,* 239.

27 Laura Hillenbrand, *Unbroken* (2010). The reader may enjoy the following smart links:
http://www.youtube.com/watch?v=BltRufe5kkI.
http://www.youtube.com/watch?v=IyXik42ASAg.
http://www.youtube.com/watch?v=FWsMofsOxLs.
http://www.youtube.com/watch?v=I9O5yVzc0vQ.
http://www.youtube.com/watch?v=R9Hlu0yHb9Q.
http://www.youtube.com/watch?v=8PETjKuk7Rw.
http://www.youtube.com/watch?v=iHeJpFHl0uY.
http://www.youtube.com/watch?v=uKuJ2LI2gOs.
http://www.youtube.com/watch?v=4oJ9_cR8ymA.
www.keynotespeakers.com/zamperini/video.php.
bolstablog.wordpress.com/2011/01/19/zamperini/.

28 Mu Soeng Sunim, *Heart Sutra* (1991). Vast emptiness can sometimes suddenly take form, like a mirage. In the movie, *Elizabeth, the Golden Age,* there is a scene where Sir Walter Raleigh, portrayed by Clive Owen, describes the "immensity" of sea and sky, just at the break of dawn, as land emerges and with it a New World. This gives the flavor of it.

28a One of my teachers, the great Japanese Zen master Koun Yamada gave many Dharma talks (teisho) where he mentioned his understanding of the relationship of the phenomenal world to the world of abundance and connectedness. He even developed a mathematical formula, which puzzles my mathematician friends but nonetheless works for me as a non-mathematician. Here is an excerpt to Yamada-sensei's own words.

"As many of you know, I often make use of a fraction (a/∞) when attempting to explain the true state of the universe. Because describing this fraction another time would be redundant, I simply wish to emphasize again that the fraction's denominator, which is essential nature, cannot help but reveal itself in the numerator, which is our world itself or all phenomena. Whether this occurs as a result of a particular instinct or will, I do not know. Nevertheless, there is a certain very strong force at work here, a force which nevertheless remains constant regardless of the time or place in history. But if you were to ask me where this force comes from, I would be at a loss for an answer, even though I cannot deny the existence of the force.

The denominator in my fraction is both zero and absolute oneness. Thus, seen in this light, the world of phenomena, since it is essentially zero, is also one. And, as I have said above, the denominator or essential world apparently possesses this irresistible, instinctive power to reveal its own essence in the numerator or phenomenal world." (*Kyosho*, April 3, 1988)

29 Excerpted from John Tarrant, *Bring Me the Rhinoceros* (2004).

30 Indigenous peoples approach the Connection indirectly, perhaps with greater sophistication, through myths, stories, parables, riddles, songs, and chants. Curiously, a great part of Buddhist written and oral teachings is devoted to pointing out what the Connection is not. I am indebted to my friend and colleague, Noelle Oxenhandler, for pointing out the Vedic practice of "not this!" and "not that!"

31 Takuan Soho, *The Unfettered Mind* (1986).

32 Trevor Leggett, *Zen and the Ways* (1978).

33 The term in Japanese is akirameru (諦める), or acceptance. It is not a passive act. It is an act of humility, recognizing that there are larger forces at work which we accept, and we dedicate ourselves to work within our limitations as human beings.

34 http://search.aol.com/aol/image?q=Scylla+and+Charybdis&v_t=comsearch51.

35 The classic Judeo-Christian example of Adversity's Spiraling Creative Wave Form is the conclusion of the Book of Job, where it states (42:12):

"So the Lord blessed the latter end of Job more than the beginning: For he had fourteen thousand sheep, and six thousand camels, and a thousand yoke of oxen, and a thousand she asses .... And it is written that Job lived until the age of 140, and saw his sons and his sons' sons, even four generations" (42:16), and new sons and daughters were born to him, and in "all the land were no women found so fair as the daughters of Job. (42:15)

36 Kenneth S. Cohen's recent article on tea, healing, and martial arts is a wonderful introduction to the next chapter subsection on life force.

http://www.kungfumagazine.com/ezine/article.php?article=1046. Blossoming teas are themselves a meditation.

Please scan

http://search.aol.com/aol/image?q=blossoming+tea&v_t=comsearch51.

37 Many such biofeedback devices are easily obtainable over the Internet. For example, http://bio-medical.com/products/stress-thermometer-sc911.html?gclid=CJX51qHV860CFYhgTA odrFjBsA.

38 John Tarrant private communication to Julian Gresser, December, 2011.

Book II Chapter II

39 See also, the Net of Indra, a similar concept in the Mahayana Buddhist canon.

40 The Explorer's Wheel is a variation of the Wheel of Life or the Compass. The Wheel, especially the spiral, in many cultures combines the symbol of the circle of life with the idea movement, of becoming and passing away. In his treatise on Native American healing practices, *Honoring the Medicine* (2003), Kenneth S. Cohen describes a Medicine Wheel in which different teachings are placed on different quadrants of a circle and used as a device for teaching and contemplation. The mandala in Buddhism is considered a metaphysical space occupied by the Five Wisdom Kings. The Wheel of Life is estimated to be 2,500 years old and is claimed to be a gift from Buddha. When the Tibetan Lama, Losang Samten, brought this gift to the United States he was the first to create this Mandala in sand. No two mandalas look the same, yet each is exactly the same in concept. The Mandala reflects back to us the nature of the human mind, which has a strong tendency toward the illusion of permanence. The medium of sand reminds the viewer of the ultimate impermanence of this existence as well as of all things. The author's intention behind calling his image, "Explorer's Wheel," is to highlight its secular, non-denominational character, while keeping the process inclusive and inviting to possibility. Boris Mathews, trans., *The Herder Symbol Dictionary* 1986. http://www.losangsamten.com/wheel_of_life_2.html#introduction.

41 Audrey Yoshiko Seo, *Enso* (2007). Kazuaki Tanahashi, *Brush Mind* (1990). An extraordinary demonstration of an *enso* in nature is rendered in the smart illustration by a master bird artist and architect. (http://www.techkings.org/pet-central/35417-bird-nest-structural-engineers-action.html) http://search.aol.com/aol/image?q=enso+images&v_t=com search51. http://www.youtube.com/watch?v=VPGIUk-24dk. (master works)

42 Book I f.n.3.

43 Synchronicities also occur frequently. We usually think of synchronicities—the term Carl Gustav Jung employed for sudden, coincident, meaningful events—as happening in the external world. But synchronicities can also arise inside as well, memories rising precisely at the moment they are most meaningfully connected to other thoughts or some external occurrence.

44 Dickens had a marvelous appreciation of the throttling grip of facts on the creative spirit. See his first two chapters in *Hard Times*, in particular the humorous dialogue between Sissy Jupe, a student, and her teacher, Mr. Gradgrind, "a man of realities."

45 Al Seckel, *The Art of Optical Illusions* (2000). http://www.ted.com/talks/al_seckel_says_our_brains_are_mis_wired.html Also, Phillpe L. Gross and S. I Shapiro, *Tao of Photography, Seeing Beyond Seeing* (2001).

46 Michael Shermer, *The Believing Brain*, 272. http://www.youtube.com/watch?v=vJG698U2Mvo. Akira Kurosawa's movie classic, *Rashomon*, illustrates the same point in the accounts by multiple witnesses to a murder.

47 John Tarrant, *Bring Me the Rhinoceros and other Zen Koans to Bring You Joy* (2004).

48 Charles Dickens, *A Christmas Carol*.

49 It may be possible to uncover a repository of all the scattered images of our **Past**—in fact, the collective images of all of humankind since the beginning of Time. In the theosophical literature this is referred to as the Akashic Records (akasha is a Sanskrit word meaning "sky", "space" or "aether"), which is roughly described as the "library of the cosmos." One might say that in contemporary computer terminology the Akashic Records are the "cloud," although at a different level of consciousness. How does one connect to and enter this vast library? It may already be a part of us. The key to the library is again the **practice of presence, or not-knowing** (section I, p. 138); the more our minds are

free, the more we become *akarmic*, the more we will find ourselves within the library, the more readily the information will
present itself, often fully formed, and projected onto the screen
of our minds. We see it, face to face. Compare St. Paul's passage
in second address in Corithinthians.

50 In the Book of Proverbs it is written, "Wisdom is more precious
than rubies, and all things that may be desired are not to be compared with it." King James Bible, Proverbs, 8.11. For a review of
the interesting academic work on wisdom, see Stephen S. Hall,
"Can Science Tell Us Who Grows Wiser?" *New York Times Magazine*, May 6, 2007. The reader may want to review the many
parts of Book II which address different aspects of **Wisdom**, at
least as defined under the integrity model.

51 Earlier chapters have proposed that **Wisdom** is a dynamic consciousness in which the hand of action, the eye of intelligence,
and heart of compassion work coherently together. Further, we
have suggested that integrity or **Wisdom** is a learned skill that
can be measurably strengthened and deepened through practice. The Artful Navigator is a useful tool which enables us to
encode the oral and written **Wisdom** traditions, but it does not
capture the living, embodied quality of wisdom. You can now
download part of The Artful Navigator directly as apps. The
data base of quotations is encoded into the integrity system,
which enables you more effectively to apply the insights of past
great masters. Following the format I have used for my own
insights, you can encode and harvest your own **Wisdom** as it
develops.

52 http://www.youtube.com/watch?v=1fcvj5w0eBw.

53 http://www.youtube.com/watch?v=45SxIYk7eTM.

54 Paul Reps, op.cit. fn.60.

55 See Byron Katie: http://thework.com/thework.php; http://
www.youtube.com/watch?v=K_k6sfCJtwY

56 Kenneth S. Cohen raises an important point about resorting to
inquiry at the wrong time, at a moment of immediate peril. He
asks "How do you move all those legs? The centipede falls over
in confusion." He continues, "Demanding proof, etc. may, for
some people, be a useful stage in dealing with chaos. When the
brain produces some outrageous claim, I believe it is far more
important to learn to trust that which underlies both intellect and emotion, 'the peace that passeth understanding'." A
martial artist who pauses with thoughts or emotions or who
weighs evidence is immediately hit. D. T. Suzuki suggests that

intelligent action does not involve choice. It is im-mediate: without mediation of any kind. My reply is the situations are basically different. Here we are speaking of situations where we give in, without questioning to a propensity toward panic. This is very different from acting decisively when confronting true danger. Further, the vast majority of people are not martial artists. Not giving up on reason and logic, especially when we are contending with a propensity to panic, is certainly useful. In my own experience, the data summoned up by our internal Propaganda Department is almost invariably inaccurate, exaggerated, or just plain wrong. In his recent book, *Thinking Fast and Slow* (2011), Nobel Laureate, Daniel Kahneman, provides numerous examples where statistical facts trump the decisions of experts. The ordinary person facing the complex problems of today not only often lacks expertise, he or she is cut off by panic from the direct knowing Kenneth S. Cohen and Dr. Suzuki are describing. This seems a fascinating subject for one thread in the Conversation Among Friends developed on: www.explorerswheel.com

For a critique of *Thinking Fast and Slow* see: Freeman Dyson (http://www.nybooks.com/articles/archives/2011/dec/22/how-dispel-your-illusions/)

57 Shakespeare expresses this same idea in Lorenzo's courtship of Jessica in the *Merchant of Venice*:

Look how the floor of heaven
Is thick inlaid with patens of bright gold
There's not the smallest orb which thou behold'st
But in his motion like an angel sings.
Still quiring to the young-eyed cherubins
Such harmony is in immortal souls.

58 For a discussion of Einstein's conviction of the relation of nature to science through elegant simplicity see: http://consumedblog.blogspot.com/2007/07/albert-einstein-on-beauty-science-and.html.

59 http://www.native-american-market.com/navajo_beauty_way.html.

60 http://www.quotationspage.com/quote/2737.html

61 My friend, Noelle, asks, "How does 'mad frenzy' relate to **Beauty**?" This is far too interesting a question to proffer an easy answer. Let's turn her inquiry into a *koan*, muse upon it, and see what we can discover.

62 For a similar idea about siphoning creative energies, see Elizabeth Gilbert's TED presentation. http://www.youtube.com/

watch?v=86x-u-tz0MA. There is, of course, a very developed field of music and creativity and music therapy. One of the seminal works is Don Cambell's *The Mozart Effect* (1997), itself based on the work of Dr. Alfred Tomatis. See also, Don Cambell, *Music and Miracles* (1992). Important here is the connection of music, **Beauty,** and in the next section, healing or life force, all mediated through a process of awakening which we are calling the Explorer's Mind. See the effects of AIS, Auditory Incubator System, even on neo-natal babies. Music Education Therapy, Inc. Also, John M. Oritz, *The TAO of Music* (1997).

63 http://www.youtube.com/watch?v=hGoaQ433wnw. You can also find **Beauty** in food. In the marvelous movie, *Jiro Loves Sushi*, we learn that the secrets of this Japanese *shokuin* master, Jiro, are not only the highest quality fish, which he serves, or even his unrivalled mastery or lifelong dedication to his art. There is something more—a consciousness, an ability to see within this dedicated practice, an art form which Jiro embodies and transmits through his two sons, his staff (disciples), the ambiance of his *sushi-ya*, and all along the supply chain. Everyone is engaged in the pursuit of an elusive perfection. And all of this expresses itself, quintessentially, in the most refined, yet humble, simplicity. http://www.youtube.com/watch?v=M-aGPniFvS0.

64 http://www.sciencedaily.com/releases/2011/07/110706195 800.htm.

65 Candace Pert, *Molecules of Emotion* (1997). See also, Paul J. Zak, *The Moral Molecule* (2012).

66 Is it possible that our DNA itself contains "heavenly harmonies?" The late UCLA geneticist, Susumu Ohno, assigned a different note to each of the four chemical bases in DNA (*do* for cytosine, *re* and *mi* for adenine, *fa* and *sol* for guanine, and *la* and *ti* for thymine.) In a paper in *Immunogenics* (1986) he noted: "The all pervasive principle of repetitious recurrence governs not only coding sequence construction but also human endeavor in musical composition." For a discussion of Einstein's conviction of the relation of nature to science through elegant simplicity see: http://consumedblog.blogspot.com/2007/07/albert-ein stein-on-beauty-science-and.html.

67 http://www.youtube.com/watch?v=sNlwh8vT2NU.

68 "I visited and returned; it was nothing special. Mount Ro veiled in misty rain, the Sekko River at high tide." The *Zenrinkushu*. I am indebted to Kenneth S. Cohen for bringing this quote to my attention. For a history of the transition of **Beauty** from its

Platonic ideal to its modern expression and interpretation, see Umberto Eco (editor) *History of Beauty* (2002), and also his interesting companion, *On Ugliness* (2007).

69 The insight of the relationship of *qi* and indigenous people's similar traditions I owe to Kenneth S. Cohen, as well as many other valuable insights on *qigong* practice. See Ken S. Cohen, author, *The Way of Qigong (1997); also, Kenneth S. Cohen, Honoring the Medicine, op. cit, p. 146*. In many indigenous traditions death is conceived as a transformation of different forms of *qi* energy.

70 Kenneth S. Cohen observes, "In fact, facets or correlates of *qi* can easily be measured and with a great deal of accuracy; for example, endorphin levels, SOD levels, DHEA/cortisol levels, EEG, bioelectric fields." (From personal correspondence with author).

71 For a more careful exposition see linked video by Ken S. Cohen, *The Way of Qigong* (1997).

72 See, generally, Kenneth S. Cohen, *The Way of Qigong*, n35. http://www.youtube.com/watch?v=7qZanIByNhE; http://www.youtube.com/watch?v=I3GuK1OVbCc.

73 http://www.healingtaousa.com/pdf/emb1a_ch01.pdf. See also Hotei (Budai), smiling monk. Credit must be paid to Mantak Chia who developed the technique; See: Mantak Chia, *The Inner Smile: Increasing Chi Through the Cultivation of Joy* (2005). http://www.healingtaousa.com/pdf/emb1a_ch01.pdf. There is a fascinating statement in Mantak Chia's *Inner Smile*: "Smile to the senses and let them all open and feel light and happy to learn. Let them all be involved in learning." There is thus a direct connection between continuous personalized lifelong learning as described in section 6.4 and the development of life force. http://www.youtube.com/watch?v=P7jXd6Qt1DM; http://www.youtube.com/watch?v=eDwESq1ZGcs; http://www.youtube.com/watch?v=dZT__DOuT_8.

Please scan

74 Elizabeth Gilbert, *Eat, Pray, Love* (2006).

75 The practice of downloading energy from nature through *qigong* is actually one of the classical forms. See Yang, Jwing-Ming, *The Root of Chinese Qigong* (1989); My system of "tree-gong" is a modest innovation. (Note: Each member in the Personal Learning Network can have a Personal Survival Page with a Battery Status Report based on IBUs—full, half-full, or alert, needing recharge.)

76 Longevity—Throughout human history people have searched for an elixir, a Fountain of Youth. Could Life Force be the elixir?

The United States is reputed to have the highest absolute number of centenarians, although other countries, in particular "longevity clusters," have a greater percentage in comparison with the population.

One such "longevity village" is Bama, China, a hamlet located in Kangxi Provence, near the Vietnam border. By last account Bama has several centenarians at least one villager over 110. (http://www.chinahighlights.com/community/video/bama-longevity-village.asp) Bama is located by a gentle, peaceful river, cloistered by mountains. The villagers lead simple, peaceful lives. It is farming community. They earn their livings mainly from physical labor. The diet is mainly vegetables. The air and water are pure. Scientists who have studied Bama report that the river water contains high levels of calcium biocarbonate $(Ca(HCO_3)_2)$, with a high alkaline PH between 7.2 and 8.5, and the negative oxygen content by the river is 3,000 per cubic cm. The gauss reading of the magnetic field around the village is .58 which some maintain is salubrious to health. The centenarians express a strong will to live. One old lady, now over 100, informed the interviewer, "I plan to live another hundred years!" Most of the centenarians are still active helping in household chores. One in her late nineties even has her own small business. The centenarians are accepted, appreciated, and honored as teachers and role models for this small community.

Much of the longevity literature is anecdotal, but anecdotes are data points, and suggest patterns when they continually repeat themselves. One colorful anecdote is Lucille Thompson, an eighty-eight-year-old great-grandmother who decided to take up taekwando Korean karate, and earned a black belt within twenty months of her first kick. "People (including her youngest daughter with whom she was living at the time) thought I was nuts. I told 'em, 'You're gonna get older while I get younger'."

One of my teachers is Dr. Elmer Green, physicist, pioneering psychologist, and the "father" of biofeedback. Elmer lives alone in Ozawkie, Kansas, now ninety-six, sharp as a tack, productive, and still exploring. I asked him if he might be willing to reflect on what keeps him going.

Elmer: "Attitude. It's all about attitude. I treat every hour of the day, beginning with the first minute, with cheer the whole time."

77 Mark Twain, "On the Joy of Discovery," *Innocents Abroad.*

78 "Wicked problem" is a phrase originally used in social planning to describe a problem that is difficult or impossible to solve because of incomplete, contradictory, and changing requirements that are often difficult to recognize. Moreover, because of complex interdependencies, the effort to solve one aspect of a wicked problem may reveal or create other problems. Many of the tightly coupled problems noted in the beginning of this chapter can be classified as wicked problems.

79 The reader may want to refer to Charles Perrow's work discussed in Book II, Chapter I, f.n.16.

80 This section is based on an earlier article, *"Inventing for Humanity—A Collaborative Strategy for Global Survival,"* which itself was based on a conference by this name organized by the author at the Smithsonian Institution in 2002; published in VIA, vol. 1, no. 4, 2003.

81 See Book I Chapter II on the central role of individual creativity as opposed to teams in the discovery/invention process. See, also, the discussion on small groups in *Abundance*, Prescript, fn1.

82 The Explorer's Mind, observing multi-dimensionally, can hold the paradox of not-knowing, simultaneously with the realization that the discovery may exist already on different plane(s) of consciousness. The paradox recalls Albert Einstein's sense of the "mystery."

83 C.K Ogden & I.A. Richards, *The Meaning of Meaning* (1923); Glanville Williams "Language and the Law" 61 Law Quarterly Review (1945), 71-86, 293-303,384-406; 62 Law Quarterly Review, 387-406 (1946).

84 See Alfred Korzypski's work on general semantics. C.K.Ogden & I.A Richards, *The Meaning of Meaning (1923).* Also Glanville Williams, *The Language of the Law,* (op.cit.fn. 83). Professor Glanville Williams while setting out to analyze linguistic fallacy in a legal context may not have been fully aware that he brilliantly developed a general method to expose fallacy in any line of inquiry. See, also, Nassim Nicholas Taleb, *The Black Swan: The Impact of the Highly Improbable* (2007). A startling recent illustration of the power of dropping assumptions is the "discovery" that the free standing heads of the statuary

at Easter Island actually have bodies. However, in October 2011, when the Easter Island Statue Project began its Season V Expedition, scientists developed remarkable photos showing that the bodies of the statues go far deeper underground than just about anyone had imagined. Is it possible that not one scientist over all these years of study did not investigate why the detached heads might not be accompanied by bodies? http://www.messagetoeagle.com/easterislandbodies.php.

Please scan

85　The seminal article is Amos Tversky and Daniel Kahneman, "A Judgment Under Uncertainty, Heuristics and Biases," appearing as an Appendix in Daniel Kahneman, *Thinking Fast and Slow* (2011). Smart links: http://www.youtube.com/watch?v=i_UVDD7ErJ4. For a critique of Kahneman see, Freeman Dyson—http://www.nybooks.com/articles/archives/2011/dec/22/how-dispel-your-illusions/?pagination=false.

Please scan

It may be useful to review the discourse so far in the light of Daniel Kahneman's *Thinking Fast and Slow*.

* I agree with Dr. Kahneman that the psyche has both a lightening intuitive (Kahneman's "System One") capability and a slower, more analytic ("System Two") functionality. The Logos as previously noted is a continuous process of toggling between intuition and reason (both of Dr. Kahneman's systems).
* Dr. Kahneman is asking us to pause and to find the data. This (System Two) is a scientific parallel with the virtue of "negative capability." The earlier chapters of this book are an

attempt to provide an analytic, if not quantitative, methodology, in a largely behavioral field, *i.e.* negotiation.

- I agree with Dr. Kahneman's skepticism about expertise, especially to the extent it depends on "expert intuition." The data on creative amateurs is interesting and needs to be studied more quantitatively, lest it also suffer from an availability illusion. However, if in fact many significant inventions are being generated today (and perhaps have been throughout history) by creative amateurs with little or no formal schooling in the areas of their discoveries or inventions, it is possible that these talented people are working from a broader data base, which seems also consistent with Kahneman's framework.

- Book II, Chapter IV offers the reader a way of expanding the resource (data) base for both Systems One and Two, by exploring the connections through horizontal thinking among many fields which are largely presumed to be unrelated. However, some caution is advised about the reliability of "facts" and the interpretations based upon them, which themselves are often as vulnerable as intuitive biases.

- Book II invites a secular pathway for explorers into a terrain which the author has found to be profound and beautiful.

86 For a fascinating discussion of hunches see Steven Johnson, *Where Good Ideas Come From* (2010);

87 See generally, Robert Root Bernstein, *Discovering* (1989). Many of the most important discoveries in astronomy are attributed to creative amateurs. For example, William Herschel-English, oboist and composer, discovered several moons and a planet. See Timothy Ferris, *Seeing in the Dark: How Amateur Astronomers are Discovering the Wonders of the Universe* (2002). The active participation of amateurs in science has now blossomed into a global "movement." See discussion of "Do-It-Yourself" entrepreneurs and innovators in *Abundance* (Diamandis and Kotler, op.cit. f.n. 11.)

88 Kekule's famous statement, "As if by the flash of lighting I awoke. . . Let us learn to dream gentlemen," quoted in Willis Harman and Howard Rheingold, *Higher Creativity* (1984). For a comprehensive study of hypnagogia, see, Andreas Mavromatis, *Hypnagogia* (1987). A related important methodology is explained in Win Wenger and Richard Poe, *The Einstein Factor* (1996). An Ouroboros is an example of an "archetype" which Carl Jung believed expresses the "collective unconscious" of all of humankind. In more advanced discovery engineering explorers learn to "dialogue" with their own unconscious. This is not dissimilar to the creative dialogue inventors have with

the problems they are seeking to solve. One client of mine (a true genius) who has invented a revolutionary new motor regularly dialogues with the materials, components, and parts, as if they were living beings, asking them what they need to help them solve their concerns or make them happier.

89 I have found in my own explorations my "best" ideas come unbidden when I completely let go. This is when I am re-connected to my own creative powers. Biofeedback training provides a systematic, and if the explorer is interested, quantitative basis to explore the subject. For example, in the early days of DEI we coupled the DEI machines to a Fast Fournier Transform which indicated the brain wave patterns of the Discovery Teams and showed the precise areas in the brain wave record of their epiphanies.

90 For some examples of lead user applications see http://www.anis samoeini.com/images/LeadUserInnovationSlides.pdf; http://lltoolbox.eu/methods-and-tools/methodologies/ lead-user-method. smart links: http://www.youtube.com/ watch?v=kbQ5mAEE1lk.

91 See, also, Steven Johnson, *Where Good Ideas Come From* (2012).

92 The reader may want to review some of the case studies provided by Triz Master, Zinovy Royzen, and his web site generally. http://www.trizconsulting.com/contactus.htm.

93 For an interesting discussion of the virtues of chaos in creativity see Johnson op.cit. f.n. 91.

94 This discussion is particularly interesting to me in light of my present work in establishing a Global Innovation Integration Network based in China. China has initiated a major drive toward innovation, but there is considerable concern over the extent to which this might unleash "disruptive" innovation. Triz may offer a more comfortable, orderly approach, which can be associated with "incremental" innovation. However, ultimately if China wants to be recognized as a global innovation leader, which is what the government's new policies state, then the Chinese government will need to encourage all forms. The integration of these various techniques, methodologies, and technologies in a Discovery/Innovation Engine will ultimately prove as important for China as the rest of the world.

95 The following references may be most useful:

a. The Brain software—http://www.thebrain.com/.
b. Other mind-mapping software—http://www.mindgenius. com/mind-mapping-software.aspx?_kk=mindmapping%20 software&_kt=4177e8e2-10b4-4473-a251-c8b3cd2d9e80. http://www.ithoughts.co.uk/iThoughts/Welcome.html.

c. Triz software—http://www.pretiumllc.com/soft/.
d. Invention Machine software—http://inventionmachine.com/.
e. Contact mapping—http://news.muckety.com/.
   Data linking and smart data bases—http://www.devon-tech nologies.com/products/devonthink/.

96 See discussion of Lightfleet Corporation Book II, Chapter IV on optoelectronic computing which will vastly increase computer power and with it the possibility of developing more reliable search engines.

97 http://www.amazon.com/Swarm-Creativity-Competitive-Collaborative-Innovation/dp/0195304128.

98 See Johnson, *Where Good Ideas Come From* fn. 91.

99 For a discussion of strategic alliance mediation, Julian Gresser, "Strategic Alliance Mediation: Creating Value from Differences and Discord in Global Business" *European journal of Law Review vol. 2 issue 4 (2000).*

100 Diamandis and Kotler, *Abundance*, 221-222, Prescript, fn. 11. The reader may also want to reconsider the Butterfly Effect in light of Humanitarian Explorer's Wheels financed by smart platforms.

101 Also, F. David Peat, *Synchronicity, The Bridge Between Matter and Mind* (1987). For a discussion of serendipity, see, also, Johnson, *Where Good Ideas Come From*, fn. 93.

102 There is a large literature on heart/mind which can easily be researched on the Internet. The concept of the Explorer's Mind draws on this literature and incorporates the third element of "hand" based on the integrity model. In fact, the non-dualistic conception of heart/mind/hand is recognized in most of the wisdom traditions, not only Eastern philosophy. The *lōgōs* in classical Greek philosophy, as discussed in Book I, is just one prominent example among many. Despite the general recognition of these principles in the world's wisdom traditions, it is interesting to note that the widespread belief in all "modern" industrial societies is that these are really separate concepts and "physical" phenomena.

103 Malcolm Cowley, ed., *The Portable Emerson* (1946).

104 Swami Vivekananda, *Karma Yoga* (1970).

105 Burton Watson, ed., *The Complete Works of Chuang Tzu* (1968).

106 http://www.ncbi.nlm.nih.gov/pmc/articles/PMC1088908/.

107 http://www.huffingtonpost.com/2011/07/12/berry-family-car-crash_n_896403.html.

108 Smart Butterfly Effect.

109 www.SeeYourImpact.org/.

110 A particularly poignant case is *The Devil's Miner* about kids working in Bolivia's silver mines http://www.amazon.com/Devils-Miner-Basilio-Vargas/dp/B000EULK14. Another moving cause is described in the documentary movie, *A Small Act*, the story of Hilde Back, an Auschwitz survivor, now living in Sweden. When she decided to sponsor the education of a young rural Kenyan student by sending in a modest contribution she thought nothing of it. She certainly never expected to hear from him, but years later she does. Now a Harvard Law School graduate and a human rights observer/advocate for the United Nations, Chris Mburu decided to find the stranger who changed his life. Inspired by her generosity, he starts a scholarship program of his own and names it for his former benefactor, The Hilde Back Educational Fund (http://asmallact.com/). The opportunities for engaged creative philanthropy are limitless.

111 Paul Hawken, *Blessed Unrest* (2007). See Humanity Wheel discussion in section 6.4. smart links: http://www.youtube.com/watch?v=N1fiubmOqH4. http://www.youtube.com/watch?v=NzMPUKAXM7U http://www.youtube.com/watch?v=Xkz2OjMOg88.

112 The next chapter discusses the brain; Chapter IV will explore the implications of a convergence between brain, mind, consciousness and optoelectronic computing.

113 The following summary is based principally on Norman Doidge's (M.D.) excellent synthesis, *The Brain That Changes Itself* (2007) and V.S. Ramachandran, *The Tell-Tale Brain* (2011). Smart links (Doidge): http://www.youtube.com/watch?v=t3TQopnNXBU. http://www.youtube.com/watch?v=LvEZfnlYX0U. http://www.youtube.com/watch?v=gI1BT7E58WU. Smart links V.S. Ramachandran: http://www.youtube.com/watch?v=Rl2LwnaUA-k. http://www.ted.com/talks/vs_ramachandran_the_neurons_that_shaped_civilization.html.

Please scan

114 Pascual-Leone taught two groups of subjects who had never studied piano a sequence of notes, showing them which

fingers to move and letting them hear the notes when played. One group practiced two hours a day. The other sat in front of the piano and only imagined themselves playing. Both groups learned to play equally well and produced the same results in the motor system as if they actually played the piece.

115   Daniel Kahneman seems slightly ambivalent when he arrives at the Bias of Optimism (Kahneman, *Thinking Fast and Slow*, 2). While he points out that optimism cannot often be supported by hard data, he recognizes that optimism is closely tied to resilience, and resilience, he concedes, is a core survival skill. Herein is an interesting question: Do not the recent discoveries of brain neuroplasticity suggest that the brain has the power to manifest its own realities and the data to go along with it? The implication is although optimism might begin as an illusion, the brain, especially the collective brain, can so creatively transform itself, that optimism becomes a self-fulfilling empirical (statistical) reality.

116   See Johnson, *Where Good Ideas Come*, fn. 93 *The Age of Spiritual Machines: When Computers Exceed Human Intelligence* (1999). See also, Lewis Hyde, *Trickster Makes This World* (1998).

117   Ray Kurzweil, *The Age of Spiritual Machines: When Computers Exceed Human Intelligence*, New York: Viking Adult (1999).

Book II, Chapter III

118   See, Charles Freeman, *The Closing of the Western Mind* (2002); also Roger Shattuck, *Forbidden Knowledge* (1996).

119   See Book II, Chapter II.

120   Peter L. Bernstein, *Against the Gods* (1996); among the best introductions to scenario planning see, Clayton M. Christensen, Scott D. Anthony, and Erik A. Roth, *Seeing What's Next* (2004). On a mundane level, the arthritis in my ankle which dislocated over one hundred times was highly predictable to any competent orthopedist.

121   Many journals such as *Future* and specialized research institutes are dedicated to the study of the **Future**. For example, the Institute for the Future in Palo Alto, California; http://www.iftf.org/about. A recently published book makes a significant contribution to this important field: Nate Silver, *the Signal and the Noise—Why so many predictions fail—but some don't* (2012).

122   James E. Schrager, and Albert Madansky, "Individual Decision Processes as a Foundation of Behavioral Strategy" January 3, 2012—a paper presented to a faculty seminar at the Booth School of Business, University of Chicago. My friend,

Dr. Elmer Green, once made the following interesting observation: both Churchill and Hitler were brilliant in their own ways; Hitler of course in a demonic way. A critical difference in Churchill's and Hitler's war strategies was that Churchill was able to see farther, broader, and more deeply than Hitler. He had access to a richer base of human experience. In Dr. Shrager's terms, he saw and acted on the patterns. This in the end proved decisive.

123 See previous note.

124 See Book II, Chapter II.

125 If we look to the Latin derivation of the English word "**Future**," we find the root "*sum*," meaning, "I am." **Future** is the irregular participle of esse, "to be." Similarly, and as noted earlier, the Latin meanings of "discover" and "invent," both of which have the connotation in English of actions pointing to something which is "out there," imply that that which is out there exists already in the present. It is only a matter of seeing it.

126 See Appendix 2 for a discussion of a strange personal encounter.

127 Fitjof Capra, *The Tao of Physics* (1975).

128 In East Asia and the West, the idea of reading the "character" of a person has a double meaning, in that character also refers to the ideograph as well as a person's deeper drives, emotions, intellect, etc. Accomplished martial artists in Japan and China have claimed that they can read an opponent's weaknesses or strengths simply by looking at their character (writing), as popularized in the scene when Michelle Yeoh recognizes her formidable opponent by observing her calligraphy in the movie, *Crouching Tiger, Hidden Dragon,* directed by Ang Lee.

129 Book I, Chapter III.

130 See discussion on discovery engineering in Book II, Chapter II.

131 Dr. McAdam's dreaming process is very close, if not identical to, creative reverie, as described in the section on discovery engineering, enhanced by AI which itself closely resembles the Art of the Question in Book I Chapter III. Dr. McAdam's work with communities grows directly out of her family therapy work with sexually abused children for which she has become prominent. http://www.nordicbaltic.org/the-2012-lecturers/; http://www.taosinstitute.net/elspeth-mcadam; Based on a large data base on therapeutic cases spanning over thirty years, she has extrapolated her findings to applying creative dreaming, AI, and enhanced performance to communities around the world. She has lectured widely on this subject both in Europe and the U.S. She has also applied her methods

to the design of new educational learning models working with schools in Denmark and Sweden. My colleague, George Lindamood, points out that Dr. McAdam's insights relating to **Present/Future** time recall Alfred North Whitehead's seminal treatise, *Process and Reality: An Essay in Cosmology* (1929); corrected edition, edited by David Ray Griffin and Donald W. Sherburne, Free Press (1979).

132   Although apparently none of her subjects has undergone brain scans, it would not be surprising to find neurological correlates to this dreaming process in the critical parts of their brains. See, Peter Lang and Elspeth McAdam, "*Narrative-ating: Future Dreams in Present Living*"; "*Drugs, Hopes, and Dreams: Appreciative Inquiry with Marginalized Young People Using Drugs and Alcohol.*" In the present case Dr. McAdam reports that many of the kids went on to realize their dreams of becoming entrepreneurs. For example, one group developed a tourist business; another launched a street theatre business; the King of Thieves became a successful entrepreneur and started a number of businesses with his chums.

133   For an interesting critique of precognition and parapsychology generally, see Michael Shermer, *The Believing Brain* (2011).

134   See also, David Allen Moorehouse, *Psychic Warrior: The True Story of America's Foremost Psychic Spy and the Cover-up of the Top Secret Stargate Program* (1966).

135   http://www.farsight.org/. See, also, Joseph McMoneagle, *Remote Viewing Secrets* (2000). Also by the same author, The Stargate Chronicles (for the Army's view); also, Commander L.R. Bremseth, "*Unconventional Human Intelligence Support-Transcendent and Asymmetric Warfare Implications of Remote Viewing*"; also the controversial research of Courtney Brown; http://en.wikipedia.org/wiki/Courtney_Brown_(researcher).

136   This is a huge subject with many aspects: (1.) Government Resistance—Governments have displayed throughout history a resistance to acting effectively on signs and signals, even when the prediction of a **Future** catastrophe is very plausible. See, *The Devil Came on Horseback* (2007), the book and movie of the same name. There is at least some data to suggest that other public events like 9/11 could have been anticipated and addressed more effectively. One prominent remote viewer actually recorded the attack in a remote viewing session and was later interrogated by FBI agents who presumed that she could not possibly have forseen the attacks and thus must have somehow been implicated in them. For a fascinating discussion see, David

Ray Griffin, *The New Pearl Harbor—Disturbing Questions About the Bush Administration and 9/11* (2004). It is unlikely we will ever know the truth about 9/11, just as it is improbable we will know the full circumstances of President Kennedy's Assassination, or for that matter, who really was Shakespeare. (Mark Anderson, *"Shakespeare" By Another Name* (2005)). In the end, we will see what we want to see, or what others in power decide we are supposed to See also, Herman Kahn, *Thinking About the Unthinkable in the 1980s* Simon and Schuster, New York, 1984. (2.) Official Release of Responsibility—There are even court decisions which explicitly relieve government agencies from seeing and planning effectively. http://earthquakepredictors.com/About_ The_Book.html; http://earthquakepredictors.com/About_ The_Author.php; http://www.huffingtonpost.com/2012/03/30/ earthquake-warning-systems_n_1392960.html?ref= science&icid=maing-grid7%7Cmain5%7Cdl3%; 7Csec1_lnk3% 26pLid%3D148838. http://blog.sfgate.com/green/2011/03/14/ are-californias-nuclear-plants-vulnerable-to-big-earthquakes/; http://www.commondreams.org/view/2011/04/28-10, http://www.energy.ca.gov/nuclear/california.html. http://www. bakersfieldnow.com/news/local/118132414.html. (3) Experts' Duty of Care—At the same time some legal systems are actually advancing the proposition that experts have a duty to see. The best example is the recent criminal prosecution of seismologists in Italy for failing to predict the L'Aquila earthquake. http:// articles.cnn.com/2011-09-20/world/world_europe_italy- quake-trial_1_geophysics-and-vulcanology-l-aquila-seismic- activity?_s=PM:EUROPE. (4) Penchant for Folly—Finally, there seems to be a human penchant for folly. See Desiderius Erasmus, *The Praise of Folly and Other Writings*, trans. and ed. by Robert M. Adams, 1989; also Sarah Bakewell, *How to Live or A Life of Montaigne* (2010). A very deep and related question is why do we forget? When we discover the true glory, generosity, and abundance of life—even if it is a fleeting epiphanal moment, why is it so difficult for us to recall these triumphs during the moments when we doubt and despair? What can rescue these lovely moments from oblivion? I would conjecture that it is steadiness of character that holds the vessel of memory. "Why Do We Forget?" is itself wonderful material for a *koan*. I hope it becomes the subject of a deep and ongoing theme in the Explorer's Network.

136a See Julian Gresser, "March 2011 Great East Japan Earthquake: Fukushima and Forseeability" New Concepts in Global Tectonics Newsletter, no. 64 September, 2012. www.

ncgt.org; also, Nate Silver, *the signal in the noise—why so many predictions fail but some don't* (2012); See also decision of L'Aquilla court convicting seven seismologists and sentencing them to six years each in prison. http://www.kentucky.com/2012/10/22/2380205/decision-near-on-scientists-in.html; and author's blog, "Natural Disasters & Public Innovation" at: www.explorerswheel.com.

136b The reader may want to refer to footnote 28a, which quotes Koun Yamada Roshi on the dynamic relationship of phenomena and the essential nature of reality.

137 Erwin Griswold (1904-1994), the eminent Dean of the Harvard Law School and former United States Solicitor General, has been quoted by a colleague on the faculty at that time, "At the Harvard Law School we train the mind by narrowing it."

Book II, Chapter IV

138 See Book II, Chapter II.

139 I first heard the phrase "a more abundant life" from my friend, Jacqueline Hoeffer, who wrote a beautiful book by this name. It was about the artists in her beloved New Mexico, who had benefited from the encouragement and support of FDR's New Deal. It was also a phrase used by FDR with scriptural reference in his address to the Inter-American Congress for the Maintenance of Peace, Buenos Aires, Argentina, December 1, 1936. I only later learned of the scriptural reference.

140 This theory recalls David Bohm's and Karl Prigram's earlier work on the holonomic brain, where they also observed the brain's similarities to the hologram.

141 Susan Cain, *Quiet: The Power of Introverts in a World That Can't Stop Talking* (2012).

142 Perhaps the best example is Srinivasa Ramanujan.

143 As noted in Book II, Chapter II, the Butterfly Effect refers to the phenomenon where a small change at one place in a non-linear system can result in large differences in a later state. An illustration is a hurricane formation being contingent on whether a butterfly flapped its wings several weeks before. The premise here is that hundreds of Networked Explorer's Wheels, dedicated to noble causes and guided by the principle of **paying forward** will accelerate Butterfly Effects. This would seem especially so if informational feedback loops can be created so that all participants can instantly see the Butterfly Effect manifesting in real time, and also sense their personal contribution to it. www.SeeYourImpact.org/

143a Gordon Dryden and Jeanette Vos, *The Learning Revolution: How Britain can lead the world in learning, education, and schooling* (Stafford, United Kingdom: Network Educational Press, 2005).

144 Link to open source license.

145 http://www.khanacademy.org/.

146 See Prescript, pp. 99-100.

147 The author has designed such a game.

148 I am indebted to my colleague, Howard Lieberman, a pioneer of HCC and my esteemed partner in Global Innovation Integrators (GII) which is establishing a network of global innovation centers, one of the first of which will be GII-Hong Kong dedicated to accelerating HCC.

149 http://www.humanconnectomeproject.org/; http://www. gatesfoundation.org/Pages/home.aspx.

150 See "The Brain" *Discovery Magazine Special*, Spring 2012, 46-49.

151 http://www.nationalgeographic.com/explorers/women-of-national-geographic/England's Elizabeth I was perhaps the greatest patron of explorers, although she was one only vicariously. http://www.elizabethan-era.org.uk/elizabethan-explorers.htm.

152 See Book II, Chapter IV.

153 Diamandis, *Abundance* (2012).

154 http://www.seeintl.org/.

155 http://www.ashoka.org/; http://www.amazon.com/Collabor ative-Entrepreneurship-Communities-Continuous-Innova tion/dp/0804748012. http://hbr.org/2010/09/a-new-alliance-for-global-change/ar/1. Smart video: http://vimeo.com/29873324.

156 There will be many opportunities for creatively combining Discovery Expeditions with philanthropy and entrepreneurship. For example, in 2012 I met the president and CEO of a company which has developed a screening using ultrasound for pre-malignant crystalline structures in breast tissue. The technology may offer a way to prevent breast cancer in hundreds of millions of women. In China alone this technology by my estimates could save the lives of 150 million Chinese women who have dense breast tissue. I envision this being a project supported by the Women's Explorer's Wheel. It would also seem a good idea to produce a "smart" version of the present breast cancer stamp, link it to the Butterfly/Philanthropy Wheel and tithe a part of the proceeds to support research on preventing and curing breast cancer, while sharing some of the other proceeds with the hardworking men and women of the U.S. Post Office.

157 See Book II, Chapter IV, contemplating a "Longevity Wheel."

158 http://www.microsoftalumni.org/Home.aspx.

159 http://www.growums.com/. Another presenter at the Gala Event was Dr. Robert Abel, a pioneering ophthalmologist who has created a software program, "Lumi." Lumi teaches kids about their own bodies so they can have fun, discover, innovate, and make sensible decisions.

160 The inspirations of Sustainable Connection are the writings of Nobel Laureates Joseph Stiglitz and Amartya Sen who advocate an alternative calculation of Gross National Product. Their method which accounts for happiness, health, well being, education, and other social indicators, which are not currently reflected in present GNP statistics. The prototype country which has based its national accounting on happiness, is Bhutan. Most recently the Japanese government has announced its serious consideration of a National Happiness Index. On the new Japanese plan see: http://www.gnhc.gov.bt/2011/12/japan-unveils-plan-to-develop-happiness-index/.

161 See wonderful video, *Fixing the Future*, by David Brancaccio. http://www.pbs.org/now/fixing-the-future/index.html. http://www.youtube.com/watch?v=CXJwNSkdTH0).   The same theme is covered in Arthur C. Brooke's 2008 book, *Gross National Happiness: Why Happiness Matters for America—and How We Can Get More of It*. In his important book, *Agenda for a New Economy: From Phantom Wealth to Real Wealth* (2010), David C. Korten advances the simple premise that the only legitimate purposes of an economy are to support people in: a. meeting their needs for basic goods and services and b. realizing a healthy, dignified, and fulfilling spiritual life. If these basic conditions are not met, he argues, citizens have a right to change the conditions of how goods and services are produced and distributed.

162 http://www.resilientjapan.org/www.resilientcommunities.org.

163 "Enthusiasm," en-theos, the god within.

164 http://www.google.com/search?q=spiral+images+in+nature&hl=en&rlz=1R2GPCK_enUS332&prmd=imvns&tbm=isch&tbo=u&source=univ&sa=X&ei=SCsYT_KdEbCGsAKB9IXcCw&sqi=2&ved=0CC8QsAQ&biw=946&bih=560.

165 http://www.pbs.org/wgbh/nova/gamma/cosm_nf.html#spir.   http://www.pbs.org/wgbh/nova/universe/spiral.html.

166 http://www.google.com/search?q=wormholes+images&hl=en&rlz=1W1GPCK_en&prmd=imvns&tbm=isch&tbo=u&so

urce=univ&sa=X&ei=XQQbT-zrNsitsQLHqsngCw&sqi=2&v
ed=0CCEQsAQ&biw=946&bih=560.

167 What would prompt them to do such a thing? In an interesting video Kiesha Crowther introduces a short history of the
spiral as it appears as the most sacred of symbols, in all cultures from pre-history to the present day. She narrates, "We
have the Celts from the North, the meaning of their spiral is
eternity or god; the Greeks and Romans believed the spiral
represented oneness with the gods, the soul; the aborigines
in Australia use the spiral; to them it means all things that
are growing; the Islamic peoples use the spiral for holy things
which cannot be written; the African cultures see the spiral as
the womb of the Great Mother; in the Orient the spiral rep-
resents the origin of all life, the place where the deities come
from; in India the spiral is the female generative sexuality; the
Native Americans used the spiral, signifying the Consciousness of the Great Spirit; for the Hopi it is the journey of everything living; the Mayans used the spiral, for them the seasons,
the solstice, the circle of life; for the Polynesians, it is immor-
tality. So why did all these indigenous peoples create the spiral? No one taught them. Every one of these ancient cultures
saw exactly the same thing. They did not teach each other,
they knew it themselves, they witnessed. . . We had a meeting
before it happened. [She refers to the appearance of a series of
heavenly blue spirals culminating in the largest of all at the end
of 2009] Grandfather told us it was on its way. And with it comes
new energy and new life to this planet, an energy which has not
been here for a very long time. In that meeting Grandfather told
us science will seek to provide a solution. The scientists will tell
the people what to believe, but the scientists will not find the
solution, they will be without an answer. Scientists cannot tell us
what it is, but our ancestors can. The great energies will return to
our planet to help us remember who we are, to help us change
from living in our minds only to living in our hearts as well."
http://www.youtube.com/watch?v=C5qpW2MLhZQ. (somewhat paraphrased for literary purposes.)

168 http://www.youtube.com/watch?v=3q3fdwaVIfE.   http://
www.youtube.com/watch?v=3q3fdwaVIfE.   Serendipity
again—Just as I begin writing this chapter I receive a call
from a remarkable young woman entrepreneur, Marcia
Heronemous-Pate, daughter of the later William Heronemous,
one of the pioneers of the American wind industry and alternative energy systems. Marcia is the CEO of the company her
father founded, Ocean Wind Energy Systems (OWES), and is

carrying out his legacy of introducing an entirely new economic paradigm for wind energy production, based on an array of "wind wheels." The core technology involves arrays of smaller wheels that can adapt to various wind currents and direct the power closer to the earth ("down power") which stabilizes the system. The OWES eliminates the gear box, massive blades and generator problems of current tower designs and captures power efficiently at three to four cents/kw/hr. The Heronemous wind wheels significantly reduce noise and are more protective of birds and other wildlife than its competitors. The Reader can explore the vision of William Heronemous and Marcia Heronemous-Pate at: http://www.oceanwin denergysystems.com/about.asp.

169 http://www.youtube.com/watch?v=4UOsk8nlq-g. http://www.youtube.com/watch?v=hq8WpytRJWs. The Reader may enjoy pausing to learn this basic silk reeling practice, as taught by *qigong* teacher, Kenneth S. Cohen.

170 This finding may be a special case and consistent with Metcaffe's Law, which states that the value of a telecommunications network is proportional to the square of the number of connected users of the system.

171 Even in the 1990s, Japanese government planners had drafted special legislation (Zunō Senta Ritchi Hō) for the establishment of creativity (brain) centers across the country.

172 I am indebted to Kenneth S. Cohen for urging this line of inquiry.

173 An important reference is Edwin Black, *IBM and the Holocaust: The Strategic Alliance Between Nazi Germany and America's Most Powerful Corporation* (2001).

174 If we acknowledge the great benefits to society of such innovations, it may produce a strong disincentive if corporations are made guarantors of the technologies they unleash. The wisest policy, in the author's view, is to recognize the "public good" benefits and reward these strategic applications by intelligently directing private and public resources toward these applications.

175 Norman Doige, *Brain That Changes Itself* (2007).

176 Norman Doidge, *Brain That Changes Itself* (2007).

177 Andrew Weil, *Spontaneous Happiness* (2011) emphasizes the importance for basic sanity of finding sanctuary and refuge in nature.

178 Norman Doidge, *The Brain that Changes Itself*, Book II, Chapter II.

179 Although this may sound like science fiction—a Frankenstein Effect—it is not at all improbable that a closed/open system as described will tend in this direction, unless some controls are set in place. However, in the author's view this is less likely than the opposite, *i.e.* that the system which is based on consciousness and building toward a higher consciousness will evolve beneficently and in harmony with the minds of its human creators.

180 For an exploration of the jamming model in business, see John Kao (1996), http://www.youtube.com/watch?NR=1&v=oFRbZJXjWIA.

181 The exploration of myths was an important dimension in the work of Carl Jung. Whereas Freud saw the Unconscious as being entirely personal, the product of a lifetime's repressed sexual urges, Jung identified a layer of consciousness below this—the Collective Unconscious. To Jung, Collective Unconscious was a vast psychic pool of energized symbols, embodied in myths, and shared by humanity as a whole.

182 http://www.livingmyths.com/What.htm.

183 Roger C. Shank, *Tell Me a Story* (1990). The mark of an "expert" is an ability felicitously to draw upon and to utilize the most appropriate story to match the challenges and conditions in any situation.

184 J.M. Balkin, *Cultural Software* (1998). The art of storytelling is closely related to competitive advantage in business. Jim Schrager scrutinizes the stories which companies, their competitors, and customers tell themselves when helping his clients formulate corporate strategies. Ideas Orlando, a professional storytelling advisory company, has found that stories are the bedrock for corporate branding, which emerges from the story, innovation, effective marketing, and dispute resolution. Ideas Orlando has even developed a proprietary product, "Story Jam," which has proven useful in a broad range of such applications. Stories dominate in politics. Demagogues like Hitler or Mussolini succeeded in captivating minds and emotions by telling dark stories that their audiences could identify with. Demagogues are often the best storytellers.

185 See: famous photo by Eugene Smith of the pieta of the mother holding her child in Minamata, Japan; or Picasso's *Guernica*, or Gustav Dore's the *Creation of Birds and Fishes*.

186 The word, dialogue, in Greek (dia—"moving across" *lōgōs*—the "word,") as noted earlier in this book is linked with the *logos*,

which corresponds closely with the concept of "Tao" ("way" or a universal connecting energy) in Chinese.

187   http://www.youtube.com/watch?v=QznxOy5Ms-E.

188   http://www.disaboom.com/blind-and-visual-impairment/ braille-without-borders-creating-hope-where-darkness-once-dominated.

Appendix 1

189   http://www.progressiveliving.org/william_blake_poetry_jerusalem.htm

190   http://how-to-learn-any-language.com/e/polyglots/pico-della-mirandola.html.

191   Gavin Mendes, *1421: The Year China Discovered America* (2002).

191a http://intranet.tdmu.edu.ua/data/kafedra/internal/i_nurse/classes_stud/en/BSN-(4y)/2%20year/Foreign%20culture/8%20Culture%20of%20the%20Renaissance%20and%20the%20Enlightnment.htm

192   In formulating the idea of a Second Renaissance the author pays tribute to his colleague, Roger Malina, Chairman of *Leonardo*, a journal which is at the frontier of science and the arts. He has recently also learned of the visionary work in proposing the Renaissance Project of Dr. Wen Wenger, author of *The Einstein Factor*.

193   An extraordinary example of the blending of old and new, East and West, craft and advanced technology and science, is the video, *Independent Lens—Between the Folds*—http://www.youtube.com/watch?v=8gynsE184d0; http://www.youtube.com/watch?v=KsvSt3GNTDQ; http://www.amazon.com/Independent-Lens-Dr-Erik-Demaine/dp/B002NWRMO0

Appendix 2

194   Wade Davis, *The Wayfinders* (2009).

GLOSSARY OF KEY TERMS AND CONCEPTS

Act with Integrity To embody integrity by action. Goethe writes: "It says: 'In the beginning was the word; already I am stopped. It seems absurd. The word does not deserve the highest prize.... The spirit helps me. Now it is exact. I write: 'In the beginning was the Act.'" Without using words or thoughts, see if you can express your integrity to someone else, right now!

Agenda A technique used to address real problems, our and another player's concerns (baggage), what we want, and what happens next. Agenda always "floats" in **The Five Rings** system meaning that you can use the technique at any stage in a negotiation.

Agent An agent is a person who acts on behalf of, or in lieu of, a principal.

Ask Your Integrity To seek guidance from your innermost core. Timing is important and so is auspices: we pay respect to the source. In Japanese the word for "god," *kami*, is written with the Chinese character "to speak" beside "platform" or "dais." To ask your integrity is to initiate a dialogue with your True Self, face-to-face.

Assessor   An assessor is a person with superior analytical abilities.

Assumptions   The word "ass-u-me" tells it all. Assumptions invariably make an ass of you and me. The goal is to test all important assumptions.

Attack Integrity To assault another's integrity with the intention of severing the connection.

Blocker   A blocker is a player who guards the interests of the key decision makers.

Brush   Interrogatory questions—'who', 'when', 'where', 'why', 'how',—are powerful techniques to open our and another player's discovery processes.

Budget   Negotiating **budget** includes time with a value of 1, effort with a value of 2, money (meaning percentage of resources actually committed) with a value of 3, and creative emotion (vitality) with a value of 4. The Artful Navigator manages all four elements of budget efficiently, paying special attention to safeguarding creative vitality (emotion), the most precious asset.

Catalyst   A catalyst is a player who brings energy and sparkle to his/her comrades and inspires change.

Catastrophe   An act of panic resulting from the perception (usually invalid) of extreme need.

Checkpoint   Whenever you reach an "understanding" in a negotiation or discover something important, you can anchor this perception with the **checkpoint**. The **checkpoint** simply repeats and reflects back (usually three times or more) the perception. Most people wear 'masks.' (The word 'person' originally meant 'mask.') They have become so accustomed to the mask they can no longer see the face. The **Checkpoint** helps you see the face behind the mask.

Compromise Integrity To prostitute or to give up integrity for some thing of lesser value

Containment	The ability to hold thoughts and emotions coherently together, especially under duress.
Contaminate Integrity	Refers to how one person's lapse of integrity can infect and undermine another's.
Critical Parent	A move designed to make you feel like an angry, helpless and accommodating child. A recent example of Critical Parent is the Japanese government's blaming American consumers for their "dirty habits" as an explanation of why seatbelts provided by Japanese companies were defective in the United States. The best antidote to Critical Parent is simply to stay present and light, and to keep your sense of fun and play.
Cultivate Integrity	Refers to the process by which we gradually build the vessel of character that allows us to navigate productively in the world.
Decision Makers	Key people who are in a position to make what you want happen.
Dragon	"Dragon" comes from the Greek word "dukein" meaning "to see." "There is a famous Buddhist saying, "When the universe roars, only the heavenly dragon watches calmly and with pure delight." The world can be topsy-turvey, but your dragon energy observes, seeing all, understanding all, content in its power. The dragon is the child of the four elements: air, water, earth, fire. She lives in pools, in the bowels of the earth, in the shadows of caves, in the mists. She is your reticulated power. When you connect to your integrity, the power uncoils and then the dragon, in all its glory, steps forth.
Dumping	To divulge information impulsively.
Expectations	An assumption with an ego complex (see Assumptions). Unruly expectations get us into even more trouble than assumptions. The rule is the same: drop all expectations and become alive!
Fall Out of Integrity	To lose your line (connection) to the universe.

"Field Effect"	A change in one person's consciousness as the result of changes in another's consciousness or in the physical environment.
Follow Your Integrity	The specific act of being guided by integrity as well as the pursuit of its life-path.
Gather Integrity	To collect one's scattered consciousness by becoming aware and present.
Goal	An action or quality of behavior or character that advances your mission. You must focus on goals you can manage well—*i.e.,* your own action/behavior—not illusory goals such as results or other people's actions or behavior that you cannot manage.
Gravitas	The condition of wakefulness, steadiness, and equanimity derived from disciplined practice of presence.
Hold Integrity	To maintain integrity—connectedness, coherence, whole ness, and vitality—under stress or in the face of pain.
IBUs	A measure of your complete budget consisting of time, energy, financial reserves and creative vitality (emotion).
Integrity	Sense of connectedness, coherence, wholeness, and vitality.
Kaizen	Japanese term for continuous improvement. Originally used in engineering systems, and adapted and broadened here as a fundamental principle of effective action.
Know Your Integrity	To feel whole and alive, connected and coherent, and willing to let your spirit go forth into the world and be of use.
Listen to Integrity	We listen to our integrity not only with our ears, but also with our eyes, our stomachs—with our whole body and mind. It is different from ordinary listening—quieter, more profound. And what we listen for is also different. Our integrity may express itself not only in words or thoughts, but also in images, dreams, or events in the external world. When we listen to our integrity in

this way we open ourselves to the signal wherever it appears.

Lōgōs

In Greek, *Lōgōs* meant both the spoken word and the pervading principle of reason. The Stoics saw *lōgōs* as the ordering principle of the universe. Like the Chinese *Tao*, the wise person, they believed, would aim to live in harmony with it. In the prologue of the Gospel according to John, the *lōgōs* is the Divine Word, a self-communicating divine presence that exists with God and is uniquely manifest in Jesus Christ.

Loss

Any move away from integrity.

'Maybe'

An equivocal limbo-state between 'yes' and 'no'. A 'maybe' moves an untrained negotiator into precarious waters because it defers an effective decision.

Mission and Purpose

The negotiator's navigational compass, the basic discovery tool and means to allocate scarce resources of time, effort, money, and creative emotion. "Mission" is the overall direction; "purpose" captures in a single word or phrase the intention of an enterprise.

Muses

In Greek mythology the Muses were daughters of Mnemosyne (Memory) and Zeus—the fruits, it is said, of nine nights of love-making. They presided over thought in all its forms: eloquence, persuasion, knowledge, history, mathematics, and astronomy. Hesiod claimed that they accompanied kings and inspired them with the persuasive words necessary to settle quarrels and re-establish peace, and gave to kings the gentleness that made them dear to their subjects.

Navigate

To move your cause forward by intelligent and wise decision making, character, and effective negotiation. "Navigation" is the process of doing so.

Need

Field dependence. Need says, "If I don't have it, I will surely die." Examples of what we really need: O_2, water, food, sleep, shelter—not much else.

Negative Multiplier
This principle refers to a falling out of integrity in one place that impairs integrity in another place, and with compound interest. In the history of kings such as Achilles, King Lear, Macbeth, and Othello, the single flaw of hubris—overweening pride—could so eat away at character that the whole person was destroyed. It is the same with organizations, communities, even nations. When integrity is torn, troubles come not singly but in troops.

Negotiate
"To succeed in getting over or across, or up and down (as a hill), or through (as an obstacle)."—*Webster's 3-D International Dictionary*

'No'
A signalling device. The trained negotiator welcomes a **'no'** because he/she understands it enables an effective decision.

Pain
The first noble truth in Buddhism, the universal condition. Everyone alive has pain in one form or another.

Pain/Need Ratio
The relationship between pain and need. The most effective negotiators are able to become present to their pain or "hold integrity" in the face of pain and thereby find their power.

Pay Forward
To celebrate a win and then pass its joy and other benefits onward to another person without seeking any monetary compensation or other recompense.

Pendulum
A technique and indicator of where to position one's self emotionally in a negotiation. When another player is very positive, the **Pendulum** suggests we stand positive, but slightly less positive; when another player is negative, the **Pendulum** counsels that we place ourselves in a slightly more negative position to allow the other player space to exercise his/her right to say 'no'.

PIPs
Player Integrity Profiles—a key tool in assessing the "source code" of character from the perspective of integrity.

Positive Multiplier	As the number of beneficial deeds increases and their rate accelerates, much like bombarded neutrons in a nuclear chain reaction, a critical mass is reached. Then an explosion can occur of such human warmth, kindness, generosity and cheer that the world might never recover from it.
Practice Integrity	The conscious and disciplined process of cultivating integrity, particularly by the accumulation of "cases" from the field of action. **The Five Rings** and the Weekly, Action, and Discovery Logs in combination with the tutorial on "How to Practice" constitute a complete system for the cultivation and practice of integrity.
Presentation	The act of helping another player discover how his/her pain can be relieved and principal problems can be addressed. In **The Five Rings** the most effective presentations are made to the key decision maker(s).
Rebuild Integrity	Conscious work to strengthen the container or foundation, *i.e.,* character.
Reclaim (Restore) Integrity	Refers to the process of returning to the path of integrity.
Reverse	The act of turning the tables on an opponent or situation. For example, the move of pausing, struggling, and then responding to a question with a countervailing question, usually an interrogatory question. As you practice integrity, you learn the art of reversing "reversals" of fortune.
Scalpel	Verb-led questions such as 'are', 'do', 'should', 'can', 'will', 'may'. The Scalpel is a risky way for an untrained negotiator to initiate a dialogue.
Scouts	Scouts are players with a superior ability to gather information and to perform reconnaissance.
Spilling	Impulsively breaking the container and leaking the emotions.
Surrender Integrity	A general reference to relinquishing integrity.

Trainability	The ability to adjust instantly in any situation resulting from an openness and curiosity to learn from error and failure.
Trolls	Trolls (*Trollensis Horribilis*) are unpleasant, smelly creatures usually found living under bridges (concrete and spiritual) in troops. As creatures of the shadow world, **trolls** will attack and seek to undermine your integrity. Advanced players learn how to tap **troll** energy for constructive purposes.
Undermine Integrity	An assault upon integrity either by direct or surreptitious means with the intention of disturbing the very foundation.
The Will	The **Will** is the capacity of complex living things to choose freely, often in unprogrammed and unpredictable ways, and to take responsibility for their actions. If you are the Captain, the **Will** is the means by which you direct your ship. It is the way you pilot your course and set the sails to take advantage of the winds and currents. The **Will** is a "meta-force" to be distinguished from "will power," which implies simply brute force.
Win	Any step, however modest, that advances a valid mission.

BIBLIOGRAPHY

The following books have been helpful to me and may be useful to readers who wish to explore further some of the themes in this book.

Peter Ackroyd, *Dickens* (New York: Harper Collins, 1990)

Robert Aitken, *Taking the Path of Zen* (San Francisco: New Point Press, 1982)

Mark Anderson, *"Shakespeare" By Another Name* (New York: Penguin Group, 2005)

Marcus Aurelius, *Meditations* (translated by Maxwell Stanforth) (New York: Penguin Classics, 1964)

Sarah Bakewell, *How to Live or A Life of Montaigne* (New York: Other Press, 2010)

J.M. Balkin, *Cultural Software* (New Haven: Yale University Press 1998)

John Beebe, *Integrity in Depth* (College Station: Texas A&M University, 1992)

Peter L. Bernstein, *Against the Gods* (New York: John Wiley & Sons, 1996)

Robert Root Bernstein, *Discovering* (Cambridge: Harvard University Press, 1989)

The Bible, Old and New Testaments

Edwin Black, *IBM and the Holocaust: The Strategic Alliance Between Nazi Germany and America's Most Powerful Corporation* (Washington: Dialog Press, 2001)

Susan Cain, *Quiet: The Power of Introverts in a World That Can't Stop Talking* (New York: Crown Publishing, Random House 2012)

Don Cambell, *Music and Miracles* (Wheaton, Ill. The Theosophical Publishing House,1992)

Don Cambell, *The Mozart Effect* (New York: Avon Books, 1997)

Fitjof Capra, *The Tao of Physics* (Boston: Shambhala Publications,1975)

Lewis Carroll, *Alice in Wonderland 1865*

Richard Carson, *Taming Your Gremlin* (New York: Harper Perennial, 1983)

Deepak Chopra, *Ageless Body, Timeless Mind—The Quantum Alternative to Growing Old* (New York: Three Rivers Press, 1993; 1998)

Mantak Chia, *The Inner Smile: Increasing Chi Through the Cultivation of Joy* (Rochester, Vt; Destiny Books, 2005)

Thomas Cleary, *The Japanese Art of War* (Boston: Shambhala Publications, 1991)

Kenneth S. Cohen, *Honoring the Medicine* (New York: Ballantine Books, 2003)

Kenneth S. Cohen, *The Way of Qigong* (New York: Ballantine Books, 1997)

Steven R. Covey, *The 7 Habits of Highly Effective People* (New York: Simon & Schuster 1990)

Malcolm Cowley, ed., *The Portable Emerson* (New York: Penguin Books, 1946)

The World of Renaissance Florence, trans. Walter Darwell (Florence: Giunti Grupo Editoriale, 1999)

Wade Davis, *The Wayfinders* (Toronto, ON: House of Anansi Press, 2009

Peter H. Diamandis and Steven Kotler, *Abundance (New York: Free Press,* 2012)

Charles Dickens, *A Christmas Carol* (Simon and Schuster, 1939)

Charles Dickens, *Hard Times* (New York: Penguin Books, original copyright 1854)

Takeo Doi. *The Anatomy of Independent* (Amae no Kōzō) (Tokyo: Kobundo Ltd., 1971)

Norman Doidge, *The Brain That Changes Itself* (New York: Penguin Books, 2007)

Gordon Dryden and Jeanette Vos, *The Learning Revolution: How Britain can lead the world in learning, education, and schooling* (Stafford, United Kingdom: Network Educational Press, 2005)

J. W. Dunne, *An Experiment With Time* (London: Macmillan Publishers Ltd. 1927)

J.W. Dunne, *The Serial Universe* (New York, The Macmillan Company, 1938)

Umberto Eco, *History of Beauty* (New York: Rizzoli International Publishing, 2007)

Umberto Eco, *On Ugliness* (New York: Rizzoli International Publishing, 2007)

Ralph Waldo Emerson, *Essay on Compensation* in *The Portable Emerson* (New York: Viking paperback, 1946)

Desiderius Erasmus, *The Praise of Folly and Other Writings*, trans. and ed. by Robert M. Adams (New York: W.W. Norton, 1989)

Timothy Ferris, *Seeing in the Dark: How Amateur Astronomers are Discovering the Wonders of the Universe* (New York: Simon & Schuster, 2002)

Roger Fisher/William Ury, Bruce Patton, *Getting to Yes* (New York: Penguin Books 1981)

Victor Frankl, *Man's Search for Meaning* (New York: Touchstone Books, Simon & Schuster,1984)

Charles Freeman, *The Closing of the Western Mind* (New York: Vintage Books, 2002)

Howard Gardner, *Creating Minds* (New York: Basic Books, 1993)

Laurie Garrett, *The Coming Plague* (London: Macmillan, 1994)

Elizabeth Gilbert, *Eat, Pray, Love* (New York: Penguin 2006)

Peter Gloor, *Swarm Creativity* (Oxford: Oxford University Press, 2006)

Goethe, *Faust* (translated by Walter Kaufmann) (New York: Random House Digital, 1961)

Elmer and Alyce Green, *Beyond Biofeedback* (Ft.Wayne, IN., Knoll Publishing Company, 1977)

Steven Greenblatt, *The Swerve: How the World Became Modern* (New York/London: W.W. Norton, 2011)

Julian Gresser, *Breaking the Japanese Negotiating Code: What European and American Managers Must Do to Win* (European Management Journal Vol. 10 No. 3 September 1992)

Julian Gresser, *Partners in Prosperity: Strategic Industries for the United States and Japan* (New York: McGraw Hill, 1985)

Julian Gresser, *Understanding the Japanese Negotiating Code: The Virtual Dojo and Other Critical Capabilities for the Late 1990s* (Presented at the Southwestern Legal Foundation Symposium on Private Investments Abroad June 20-21, 1995)

Laurence Gonzales, *Deep Survival* (New York: W.W. Norton & Co. 2009)

David Ray Griffin, *The New Pearl Harbor—Disturbing Questions About the Bush Administration and 9/11* (Northampton, Mass: Interlink Publishing Group, 2004)

Phillpe L. Gross and S. I Shapiro, *Tao of Photography, Seeing Beyond Seeing* (Berkeley/Toronto: Ten Speed Press, 2001)

Willis Harman and Howard Rheingold, *Higher Creativity, Liberating the Unconscious for Breakthrough Insights* (Los Angeles: Jeremey P. Tarcher, Inc. 1984)

Paul Hawken, *Blessed Unrest* (New York: The Penguin Group, 2007)

Hekiganroku, *Blue Cliff Record* (translated by Koun Yamada and Robert Aitken; unpublished manuscript)

Herakleitos, *Herakleitos and Diogones* (translated by Guy Davenport) (Bolinas, CA: Grey Fox Press,1983)

Laura Hillenbrand, *Unbroken* (New York: Random House Publishing, 2010)

I Ching, *Book of Changes* (translated by Hellmut Wilhelm)(Princeton, New Jersey: Princeton University Press, 1950)

Homer *Iliad* (New York: New York: Anchor Books Doubleday 1974)

Homer, *Odyssey* (translated by Robert Fitzgerald)(New York: Anchor Books Doubleday 1963)

Victor Hugo, *Les Miserables* (translated by Norman Denney)(New York: Penguin Books, 1976)

Lewis Hyde, *Trickster Makes This World* (New York: Farrar, Strauss and Giroux, 1998)

Tim Jeal, *Stanley* (New Haven: Yale University Press, 2007)

Steven Johnson, *Where Good Ideas Come From* (New York: Riverhead Books, Penguin, 2010)

Herman Kahn, *Thinking About the Unthinkable in the 1980s* (Simon and Schuster New York, 1984)

Daniel Kahneman, *Thinking Fast and Slow* (New York: Farrar, Strauss, and Giroux, 2011)

Nikos Kazantzikas, *Zorba the Greek* (translated by Carl Wildman) (E. Housman, London: Longmans, Green & Co.1952)

Andrew Kilpatrick, *Of Permanent Value—The Story of Warren Buffett* (Birmingham, Alabama: AKPE Publishers (1994)

Arthur Koestler, *The Act of Creation* (London: The Macmillan Company 1964)

David C. Korten, *Agenda for a New Economy: From Phantom Wealth to Real Wealth* (San Francisco: Berrett-Koehler, 2010)

Ray Kurzweil, *The Singularity is Near* (New York: Penguin Books, 2005)

Ray Kurzweil, *The Age of Spiritual Machines: When Computers Exceed Human Intelligence* (New York: Viking Adult, 1999)

Takie Sugiyama Lebra, *Japanese Patterns of Behavior* (Honolulu: University of Hawaii Press, 1976)

Trevor Leggett, *Zen in the Ways* (Tokyo: Charles E. Tuttle & Company, 1978)

Jacques Lusseyran, *And There Was Light* (New York: Parabola Books, 1991)

Jasan Makansi, *Lights Out: The Electricity Crisis, the Global Economy, and What it Means to You* (New York: John Wiley & Sons, 2007)

Masters of Huainan, *The Art of Politics* (Translated by Thomas Cleary (Boston: Shambhala, 1961)

Boris Mathews, trans., *The Herder Symbol Dictionary* (Wilmette, Ill. Chiron Publications, 1986)

Michihiro Matsumoto, The Unspoken Way (Tokyo: Kodansha International, 1988)

Andreas Mavromatis, *Hypnagogia: the Unique State of Consciousness Between Wakefulness and Sleep.* (London: Routledge and Kegan Paul, 1987)

Joseph McMoneagle, *Remote Viewing Secrets* (Charlottesville, VA: Hampton Roads Publishing Company, 2000)

Lynne McTaggart, The Intention Experiment (Free Press, Simon & Schuster, New York 2007)

Gavin Mendes, *1421: The Year China Discovered America* (New York: William Morrow, 2002)

Alan Moorehead, *The Fatal Impact* (New York: Harper and Row, 1966)

Alan Moorehead, *The White Nile* (New York: Harper & Bros, 1960)

Alan Moorehead, *The Blue Nile* (New York: Harper and Row 1983);

David Allen Moorehouse, *Psychic Warrior: The True Story of America's Foremost Psychic Spy and the Cover-up of the Top Secret Stargate Program* (New York: St Martin's Paperbacks,1966)

Mumonkan, *Gateless Gate* (translated by Kōun Yamada) (Los Angeles: Center Publications, 1979)

Musashi Miyamoto, The *Book of Five Rings* (trnaslated by Victor Harris)(Overlook Press, 1974)

Alfred North Whitehead, Process and Reality: An Essay in Cosmology (1929); corrected edition, edited by David Ray Greiffin and Donald W. Sherburne, Free Press (1979).

C.K.Ogden & I.A Richards, *The Meaning of Meaning* (New York: Harcourt, Brace & World, Inc. 1923)

F. David Peat, *Synchronicity, The Bridge Between Matter and Mind* (Toronto, New York: Bantam Books, 1987)

Charles Perrow, *Normal Accidents*-Living with High Risk Technologies (New York: Basic Books, 1984)

Candace Pert, *Molecules of Emotion* (New York, Scribner, 1997)

Donald T. Phillips, *Lincoln on Leadership* (New York: Grand Central Publishing, *1992*)

Plato, *The Phaedrus* (translated by Walter Hamilton (New York: Penguin Books, 1973))

V.S. Ramachandran, *The Tell-Tale Brain* (New York: W.W.Norton, 2011)

Joshua Cooper Ramo, *The Age of the Unthinkable* (New York: Back Bay Books-Little Brown and Company, 2009)

Michael Ray and Rochelle Meyers, *Creativity in Business* (New York: Random House, 1986)

Paul Reps, *Zen Flesh Zen Bones* (New York, Anchor Books, Double day & Co., 1961)

Howard Rheingold, *The Virtual Community* (Cambridge: MIT Press, 1993)

Rainer Maria Rilke, *Selected Poetry* (Edited and Translated by Steven Mitchell, 1980)

Erik A. Roth, *Seeing What's Next* (Boston: Harvard Business School Press, 2004)

Al Seckel, *The Art of Optical Illusions* (London: Carlton Books Ltd., 2000)

Audrey Yoshiko Seo, *Enso* (Boston: Weatherhill, 2007)

Shakespeare, *Henry V, MacBeth, King Lear, Othello, Richard III, Julius Caesar, The Merchant of Venice, Hamlet*

Roger C. Shank, *Tell Me a Story* (Evanston, Ill. Northwestern University Press, 1990)

Roger Shattuck, *Forbidden Knowledge* (New York: St. Martin's Press, 1996)

Michael Shermer, *The Believing Brain* (New York: Times Books, Henry Holt and Company, 2011)

Bernie Siegel, M.D. *Love, Miracles, and Medicine* (New York: Harper & Row Publishers, Inc., 1986)

Nate Silver, *the signal and the noise—why so many predictions fail—but some don't* (New York: The Penguin Press, 2012)

Shōyorōku, *Book of Serenity* (translated by Koun Yamada and Robert Aitken)(Hudson, NY. Lindisfarne Press, 1990)

Mu Soeng Sunim, *Heart Sutra* (Cumberland, Rhode Island: Primary Point Press, 1991)

Lawrence Susskind/Jeffrey Cruikshank, *Breaking the Impasse* (New York: Basic Books 1987)

Kazuaki Tanahashi, *Brush Mind* (Berkeley, CA: Parallel Press, 1990)

John Tarrant, *The Light Inside The Dark* (New York: Harper Collins, 1996)

John Tarrant, *Bring Me the Rhinoceros* (New York: Harmony Books, 2004)

Tao Te Ching, *The Way of Subtle Virtues* (translated by John C. H. Wu, 1961)

Jerry Thompson, *Cascadia's Fault* (Berkeley, CA: Counterpoint Press, 2011)

Mark Twain, *The Unabridged Mark Twain* (Philadelphia: Running Press, 1976)

Sun Tzu, *The Art of War* (translated by Lionel Giles (Boston: Shambhala Press, 1988)

Swami Vivekananda, *Karma Yoga* (Calcutta, India: Published by Swami Budhananda) 1970

Sam Walton, *Sam Walton Made In America* (New York: Penguin Books, 1992)

Burton Watson, ed., *The Complete Works of Chuang Tzu* (New York: Columbia University Press, 1968)

Andrew Weil, *Spontaneous Happiness* (New York: Ballantine, 2011)

Win Wenger and Richard Poe, *The Einstein Factor* (Roseville, CA: Prima Publishing, 1996)

Alfred North Whitehead, Process and Reality: An Essay in Cosmology 1929; edited by David Ray Griffin and Donald W. Sherburne (New York, Free Press, 1979.)

Yang, Jwing-Ming, *The Root of Chinese Qigong* (Roslindale, Mass: Quality Books, Inc. 1989)

Paul J. Zak, *The Moral Molecule* (New York: Dutton, 2012)

CONTINUING YOUR PRACTICE

The secret of enhanced performance in the arts of negotiation and exploration is continuous focused practice supported by effective coaching. The smart SCFX platform, supported by my websites on Facebook, Linked-in, and other social media, include coaching tips, blogs, commentary from masters (living and dead!), podcast and webinars, all designed to enable you to hone your skills and to realize your dreams. There is no better dojo than life itself. Please visit: www.explorerswheel.com

INDEX

Julian Gresser

Julian Gresser is an international attorney, negotiator, inventor, and recognized expert on Japan. As a negotiator his most dramatic success involved helping a San Francisco-based trading company transform its $8 million after-tax branch into a $1 billion Japanese company in seven years. From 1976-  1983 he was twice Visiting Mitsubishi Professor at the Harvard Law School and also taught courses as a Visiting Professor at MIT on the legal issues of strategic industries.

He has served as legal advisor to numerous U.S., Japanese, and European companies on a wide array of business issues, including joint ventures, limited (venture capital) partnerships, technology licensing, export controls and customs fraud, antitrust, and intellectual property protection, particularly patent infringement disputes. He has been a senior consultant to the U.S. State Department, The World Bank, The Prime Minister's Office of Japan, The People's Republic of China, and the European Commission (where he trained the Commission's Japanese negotiating teams).

In addition to the present work, Julian Gresser is the author of *Environmental Law in Japan* (MIT Press, 1981), *Partners in Prosperity: Strategic Industries for the U.S. and Japan* (McGraw Hill, 1984; in Japanese, *Cho Hanei Sengen*), and *Piloting Through Chaos: Wise Leadership/Effective Negotiation for the 21st Century* (Five Rings Press, 1996), (in Japanese, *Ishi Kettei Isutsu no Hosoku–Koshodo no Gokui*, Tokuma Shoten Publishing Company, Tokyo, 1997). In May 2012 Julian Gresser established a new company, Global Innovation Integrators (GII), based in Silicon Valley and Beijing. GII's mission is to build a Global League of Innovation Champions, beginning with China, and assist its clients in rapidly expanding global brand and market share through an International Innovation-Driven IPO on the Hong Kong and other world exchanges.